Undermining the Kremlin

A volume in the series

CORNELL STUDIES IN SECURITY AFFAIRS

a series edited by Robert J. Art, Robert Jervis, *and* Stephen M. Walt

A full list of titles in the series appears at the end of the book.

Undermining the Kremlin

AMERICA'S STRATEGY TO SUBVERT THE SOVIET BLOC, 1947–1956

GREGORY MITROVICH

Cornell University Press

ITHACA AND LONDON

First published 2000 by Cornell University Press

LIBRARY OF CONGRESS CATALOGING-IN-PUBLICATION DATA

Mitrovich, Gregory, 1964–
Undermining the Kremlin : America's strategy to subvert the Soviet Bloc, 1947–1956 / Gregory Mitrovich.
p. cm. — (Cornell studies in security affairs)
Includes bibliographical references and index.
ISBN 0-8014-3711-3 (cloth)
1. United States—Military policy. 2. National security—United States—History, 20th century. 3. Cold War. 4. United States—Foreign relations—Communist countries. 5. Communist countries—Foreign relations—United States. I. Title. II. Series.
UA23. .M58 2000
327.1273'047'09045—dc21 99-047443

Cornell University Press strives to use environmentally responsible suppliers and materials to the fullest extent possible in the publishing of its books. Such materials include vegetable-based, low-VOC inks and acid-free papers that are recycled, totally chlorine-free, or partly composed of nonwood fibers. Books that bear the logo of the FSC (Forest Stewardship Council) use paper taken from forests that have been inspected and certified as meeting the highest standards for environmental and social responsibility. For further information, visit our website at www.cornellpress.cornell.edu.

Cloth printing 10 9 8 7 6 5 4 3 2 1

For Miki:

Who Made This Possible

Contents

Acknowledgments

Authors frequently write that their books could not have been written without the help of others; however, it is not until one actually writes a book that one realizes such claims are not mere cliché. Indeed, had it not been for the fortuitous intervention of several people over the course of the eight years I have worked on this project, this book would not exist today.

First, and foremost, I thank Robert Jervis for taking the time to teach me how to turn my research into a publishable work. Bob read numerous drafts and provided me with many pages of indispensable comments that enabled me to prepare a manuscript that Cornell University Press could publish.

Melvyn Leffler, Marc Trachtenberg, and Bruce Cumings provided me with significant comments, criticisms, and advice, which gave me the confidence that I had a manuscript that one day would be worth publishing.

Ron Steel not only encouraged me to revise my dissertation but also undertook the onerous task of reviewing the work for a third time as a fully revised book manuscript.

Eduard Mark, David Foglesong, Anders Stephanson, and Jaclyn Stanke provided me with voluminous and highly detailed reviews as well as extensive marginal comments. Their intervention proved enormously important during the latter stages of this project. I am very grateful for their having taken such efforts on my behalf.

No history could be written without the help of the extraordinary archivists who staff the National Archives and Presidential Library system. Dwight Strandberg and David Haight of the Eisenhower Library; Dennis

Bilger and Sam Rushay of the Truman Library; and Bill Walsh and Martin McGann of National Archives II aided my research enormously during my many trips to each location. In addition, they patiently responded to all my numerous telephone requests for information regarding the release of formerly classified material.

It has indeed been a pleasure to work with the people from Cornell University Press. In particular, I thank Roger Haydon for his interest in my proposal and his consistent support of my project from submission to publication. Additionally, I thank Candace Akins, Lois Rankin of G&S Editors, and Megan Hendershott for the careful editing and preparation of my manuscript.

During my years at the School of International Relations at the University of Southern California, I was very fortunate to have befriended two professors: Bill Tow and Jerry Bender. Bill introduced me to security studies on my entry into the school and has provided me with advice and friendship throughout the twelve years I have known him. Likewise, Jerry has been a source of constant encouragement.

This book would have made two people extremely proud: my late mother Myra Mitrovich and my late grandfather Mitchell Medigovich. My mother never stopped stressing the importance of education and learning, while my grandfather piqued my interest in history with his numerous stories about American politics during the first half of the twentieth century.

Finally, I thank the person who made this book possible: my wife, Miki. Not only has she supported me both spiritually and financially during the long process it has taken to complete this book, but she even took the time to help proofread its many drafts. It is to her that this book is dedicated.

GREGORY MITROVICH

New York City

Undermining the Kremlin

Introduction: The Origins of Postwar U.S. National Security Policy

Today, the cold war is a distant memory. The world's attention now focuses on ethnic conflict and economic reform, not East-West diplomatic crises, arms races, and contentious disarmament negotiations. With the Iron Curtain shattered, integration into the NATO alliance and inclusion in the European Union are paramount concerns of the newly independent Eastern European states. From the ruins of the Soviet communist regime fifteen new countries have emerged—led by a new Russia and a new Ukraine—all struggling to reform their centrally organized economies and follow their Eastern European brethren into the free-market system.

Conventional wisdom holds that the decades-long application of containment—the prevention of Soviet communist expansion beyond its post–World War II sphere of influence—led directly to the collapse of the Soviet bloc.[1] By containing Soviet expansion long enough, the United States was able to achieve one of the most significant peaceful restructurings of the international system in history. The emergence of democratic, market-oriented regimes within many of the former Eastern European satellite states and nations of the former Soviet Union seems to have demonstrated the wisdom of America's postwar national security planners.

My contention is that postwar U.S. policymakers in fact did not envision a decades-long commitment to defeat Soviet communism; instead they feared that a long-term division of the world into two hostile blocs would lead inevitably to economic depression and world war and they believed that only an open international economic system absent competing political-economic blocs promised the stability necessary to allow the world to recover from World War II.[2] Therefore, American planners decided that the United States must eliminate the Soviet threat expeditiously and construct a global political-economic order that included the Soviet Union and Eastern Europe. For much of the early cold war, planners from both administrations considered this objective eminently feasible, despite the enormity of the undertaking.

Containment was only the first step in a determined effort to destroy Soviet power. Recently declassified documents confirm that, from 1948 to 1956, U.S. decisionmakers developed a national security doctrine significantly more assertive than generally understood, a policy designed to roll back Soviet power from Eastern Europe and to undermine communist control within the USSR itself—and to do so by "measures short of war."[3] Through the aggressive application of psychological warfare (ranging from regular diplomacy to covert paramilitary actions) American national security elites hoped to influence the minds of the Soviet leadership and population.[4] They believed either they could compel the Soviet Union to abandon its efforts to subvert the nascent postwar international system, and so restore the independence of the Eastern European states, or they could precipitate the collapse of the Soviet communist system itself.[5] This book reveals that these planners were so confident that the United States could subvert communist rule in both Eastern Europe and the Soviet Union that they premised a significant part of the cold war objectives of the United States on achieving this result, objectives that received the support of all the key administration decisionmakers, including both presidents Harry S. Truman and Dwight D. Eisenhower. They were convinced that psychological warfare, given its success during World War II, offered the best method to meet U.S. objectives without the use of armed forces. Furthermore, they believed that by maintaining military superiority, the United States could achieve its goals without necessarily provoking the Soviets into responding militarily to American provocations.

Consequently, American planners determined that the United States, within a matter of years, could create what we have today—a world based upon the principles of open markets and geopolitical cooperation and absent the conflict of two competing political-economic systems. The alternative, as they saw it, was the possibility of economic collapse, a devastating third world war, and the destruction of the American way of life.

This book recounts the history of America's early cold war efforts to undermine the Kremlin. It explores the origins of this policy, the various strategies planned to exploit the Soviet Union's vulnerabilities, and the instruments devised by the United States to subvert communist power behind the Iron Curtain. It examines the bureaucratic squabbling that threatened to hinder implementation of these policies and shows how the shifting nuclear balance of power forced the United States to abandon these efforts altogether.[6] By the mid-1950s, U.S. policymakers had concluded that resolution of the German question in Europe, the containment of Soviet expansion in Asia and Africa, and the cultural infiltration of Soviet society, supported by a stable balance of nuclear power, offered the only effective cold war strategy.[7]

Historian John Lewis Gaddis writes of the new cold war history that is coming out of the recently opened Eastern European and Russian archives.[8] Unquestionably, these new materials give promise of enormous new vistas in our understanding of the origins and conduct of the cold war. But the chapters that follow make clear that in writing the new cold war history (to which, it is hoped, this book makes a contribution), there is still much to be learned from the American side.

America's Postwar Strategic Vision

America's postwar vision was heavily influenced by the chaos of World War II. Policymakers recognized that had Germany successfully consolidated its control over Europe and extended its sphere of influence to include Africa, the United States would have had to respond so vigorously to safeguard the security of the Western Hemisphere that the American system and way of life would have been fundamentally altered.[9] With Germany's co-optation of Europe's productive capacity, U.S. officials feared that they would have had to dramatically alter America's economic and political system to survive, imposing controls on American production and curbs on individual liberties. The Allied victory in World War II would not ease the concerns of U.S. national-security planners unless no postwar power arose that could emulate the Germans.

To avoid the devastation of a third world war and to ensure the survival of the American system, planners favored the creation of a pseudo-Wilsonian model, incorporating some of the elements of President Woodrow Wilson's vision for U.S. foreign policy, including the creation of the United Nations and institutions designed to promote free trade and convertibility of currency, but with less emphasis on ethnic self-determination in Europe.[10] Yet to build such a system required that the United States prevent the global economy from returning to a world of competing economic trade blocs and the imposition of Soviet power throughout Europe and Asia. American strategists believed that an important cause of the instability that plagued the first half of the twentieth century was the development of discriminatory trade restrictions that led to the creation of blocs which tied the imperial possessions of the British, French, German, and Japanese empires to the economy of the core country. This way these countries were able to maintain full control over the economies of their possessions, ensure exclusive access to their raw materials, and provide markets for the finished products of the mother country. Thus, the core country could prevent any of its rivals from benefiting economically from its territories.[11]

American planners believed that these economic practices were inconsistent with the development of a stable international system—particularly when they compared the history of the twentieth century with the period of British supremacy in the nineteenth century—and unnecessarily introduced a combustible zero-sum element to world politics. As one 1944 State Department analysis concluded:

> The development of sound international economic relations is closely related to the problem of security. The establishment of a system of international trade which would make it possible for each country to have greater access to world markets and resources would reduce incentives to military aggression and provide a firm basis for political cooperation. Conversely, if such a system is not established, the international frictions which would result in the economic field would be certain to undermine any international security organization which might be created. Past experience makes it clear that close and enduring cooperation in the political field must rest on a sound foundation of cooperation in economic matters.[12]

Or, as Secretary of State Cordell Hull stated more simply in 1945, "if the goods can't cross borders, soldiers will."[13]

Thus U.S. planners envisioned a postwar world absent such blocs, where currencies were convertible and trade free flowing. Consequently, they created numerous multilateral institutions such as the International Monetary Fund and the World Bank to ensure the success of the liberal internationalist policies as established by the Bretton Woods accords of 1944.

The Soviet rejection of the Bretton Woods system on 31 December 1945 confirmed that the Soviets were unlikely to cooperate in the postwar era and that their occupation of Eastern and Central Europe and the communization of these countries was only the prelude to the creation of an autarkic Soviet bloc. The rise of communist, leftist, and other Soviet-sponsored associations threatened a ravaged Europe, the Middle East, and a post-colonial Asia and Africa. It had begun to seem—as George Kennan argued—that the Soviet decision dashed hopes for "general economic collaboration among nations" and that Kremlin policy would "really be determined by the pursuit of autarky for the Soviet Union and Soviet dominated adjacent areas taken together."[14] With its worst fears confirmed, the question now centered on how the United States would respond.

The top priority of the Truman administration was to respond to the Soviets' geopolitical challenge by stabilizing Western Europe, Japan, and the Middle East and preventing their capture by the Soviets. These strategic regions represented the foundation for the new international order and their loss would devastate the possibility of its creation. Truman administration planners understood that great efforts would be needed to successfully contain Soviet expansion, secure and resurrect Western Europe, rebuild and reshape Germany and Japan, control Middle East oil production, and co-opt the key raw-material–producing regions of the third world.[15] For the rest of its tenure, the administration would struggle to deploy the enormous resources required to develop the crucial structures necessary to maintain the new international economic system.

Yet the Truman administration also realized that a long struggle would itself pose substantial dangers to the American system. A lengthy struggle might accentuate the instability of a world of competing economic blocs or force the United States to adopt harsh domestic controls in order to compete with the strength of the emerging totalitarian bloc. The survivability of the American system in the cold-war struggle was of preeminent concern to U.S. policymakers and in the early going the expectations were grim. George Kennan expressed concerns as early as 1946 when he warned that "we must have courage and self-confidence to cling to our own methods and conceptions of human society. After all, the greatest danger that can befall us in coping with this problem of Soviet communism, is that we shall allow ourselves to become like those with whom we are coping."[16] Shortly after assuming office, President Dwight D. Eisenhower similarly declared that:

> The United States was confronted with a very terrible threat, and the truth of the matter was that we have devised no way of meeting this threat without imposing ever-greater controls on our economy and on the freedom of our people. . . . The real problem was to devise methods of meeting the Soviet threat and of adopting controls, if necessary, that would not result in our transformation into a garrison state.[17]

Therefore, American policy had to incorporate strategies that would not only construct the liberal international economic order but undermine the newly developing communist bloc as well. Containment was not itself the solution; it would only cement the creation of a two-bloc world and therefore represent the first step toward an eventual global conflagration. For that reason, once the administration established the foundation for global economic recovery, it began to search for the strategy that could best achieve it. Kennan seized the occasion and filled the policy vacuum with his famous "long telegram" and legendary *Foreign Affairs* article "The Sources of Soviet Conduct," upon which most scholars base Kennan's reputation as the father of "containment."[18] The ideas he expressed there and in his numerous government studies would determine the parameters for all future analysis of Soviet vulnerabilities.

Kennan believed the key to defeating the Soviet threat was to eliminate the communist regime and restore the Russian problem to "normal dimensions." In both the "long telegram" and "The Sources of Soviet Conduct" Kennan would describe the significant instabilities that plagued the Soviet system and made the regime susceptible to aggressive U.S. action.[19] First, communist control of the USSR lacked popular support and therefore was both precarious and ephemeral, forcing the Kremlin to employ the most brutal of police tactics to retain power. Such tactics included the collectivization of Soviet agriculture, the instigation of a famine that killed an estimated 14.5 million Russian peasants, and the purges of Stalin's opponents that decimated the ranks of both the Communist Party and the Military High Command.[20] This problem was compounded by the devastation of World War II, which cost the lives of over twenty-six million Soviets, destroyed Communist Party control over much of the European Soviet Union, and left the Soviet peoples both "physically and spiritually tired" and "far removed from the doctrines of the Communist Party."[21]

Second, the Communist Party itself was undergoing a dramatic change of generation as new members filled the ranks left by war and purges. As a result, a new leadership would soon be coming to power whose life experiences came after the revolution and who might be less supportive of the Stalinist party line. How this next generation of mid-level leaders would comport themselves would determine the future of the USSR.[22]

Third, Kennan believed that the very structure of Soviet power invited instability, crisis, and possibly collapse. The Soviet system suffered from what Kennan's close friend and colleague Charles Bohlen referred to as the "jealousy and paranoiac suspicion [with]in the ruling groups."[23] Political intrigue was an intrinsic part of everyday Soviet political life, and Stalin, the master political manipulator, encouraged controversy amongst his subordinates at every opportunity. Both Kennan and Bohlen recognized that the highest echelons of Soviet power were consumed with political machinations and that by applying the right techniques the United States could exploit this weakness. The most promising occasion would come with the succession of leadership after Stalin's death. Kennan pointed out that Lenin's death had led to a power struggle that "wracked [the] Soviet state for fifteen years."[24] Should such a struggle reoccur after Stalin's demise it might provide the potential catalyst for the collapse of the regime. The next leadership change, he argued, could "take place quietly and inconspicuously, with no repercussions anywhere," or it might "unleash, to use some of Lenin's words, one of those 'incredibly swift transitions' from 'delicate deceit' to 'wild violence' which characterize Russian history, and may shake Soviet power to its foundations." If anything were to occur to disrupt the party's control, "Soviet Russia might be changed overnight from one of the strongest to one of the weakest and most pitiable of national societies." Consequently, if the United States tailored its policies to exploit Soviet vulnerabilities it was possible that "within five or ten years" Russia would be "overwhelmed by clouds of civil disintegration."[25]

Kennan's analysis established the basic criteria emulated by all other government-sponsored studies of Soviet vulnerability, particularly two of the most important studies of the time: Project TROY and the Soviet Vulnerabilities Project, which were prepared in association with the Center for International Studies at MIT. The teams of scholars who prepared both reports adopted Kennan's judgment regarding the nature of Soviet weaknesses and based their psychological-warfare strategies upon his principles. As the following chapters demonstrate, these strategies all centered on the need to heighten frictions between the various power centers of the Soviet hierarchy and anticipated significant opportunities for action upon Stalin's death. Thus even after Kennan's departure from the administration the government's psychological-warfare planning would continue to depend upon his groundbreaking treatment of the Soviet Union.

Kennan never provided, however, anything more than vague guidance as to how the United States could exploit Soviet vulnerabilities. This led to significant confusion as to what strategy he actually supported. His analytical imprecision was most egregiously apparent in "The Sources of Soviet Conduct," where he called for the application of "counterforce" to resist Soviet encroachment for ten to fifteen years so that the internal weaknesses of the Soviet system might manifest themselves and lead to the collapse of the Soviet state. Kennan's use of the term "counterforce" led to the mistaken belief that he supported the unrestricted use of American military forces in a series of limited engagements designed to prevent Soviet aggression along the Eurasian periphery.[26] While Kennan recognized that military power was an important element of U.S. foreign policy, as will be examined in the following chapters, he did not support a policy of indiscriminate use of military forces to "contain" Soviet expansion.

The ensuing debate only confused the essence of his argument: that Soviet power was unstable and that with direct American action it could be eliminated. While most public attention centered on the various interpretations of counterforce, a crucial aspect went largely unnoticed: the belief that a struggle for power within the highest levels of the Kremlin could engulf the entire Soviet administrative apparatus and destabilize the Soviet regime.

Kennan made sure that the U.S. government did not misconstrue his ideas. He quickly entrenched himself as the State Department's chief strategist and prepared two top-secret studies that led directly to NSC 20/4, the basic statement of the administration's cold war objectives that would remain the cold war goals of the United States even into the Eisenhower administration. The United States would use all methods short of war:

> To reduce the power and influence of the USSR to limits where it will no longer constitute a threat to the peace, national independence and stability of the world family of nations.
>
> To create a basic change in the conduct of international relations by the government in power, to conform with the purposes and principles set forth in the UN charter.

Containment was not, however, the strategy to achieve these objectives. Nor would the rollback of communist power from Eastern Europe alone end the Soviet Union's threat to the United States. Instead, Kennan argued that the United States must "compel" the Soviet government to fundamentally alter its national security policy, abandon its expansionist aims, and accept the principles of the liberal international order. The Soviet government itself was the primary target of American policy, and its reform or removal the ultimate objective. With President Truman's approval of NSC 20/4, American policy had shifted from solely a defense of the free world to the elimination of the Soviet communist bloc altogether. The question remained: How would the United States accomplish this feat? Could the Soviet leadership be made to abandon its international ambitions, or would the United States have to develop the means to overthrow the Soviet regime itself? Most important, how would the United States do either without inciting global war? The answer lay in the development and employment of psychological warfare.

The Instruments of Exploitation

Definitions of psychological warfare (alternatively known as political warfare) varied greatly depending upon how much support officials accorded these activities. While its detractors hoped to limit its implementation to radio-based propaganda only, advocates sought to define the responsibilities and instruments of psychological warfare as widely as possible. For example, one U.S. government study dating from 1948 declared that:

> Psychological warfare employs any weapon to influence the mind of the enemy. The weapons are psychological only in the effect they produce and not because of the nature of the weapons themselves. In this light, overt (white), covert (black), and gray propaganda; subversion; sabotage; special operations; guerrilla warfare; espionage; political, cultural, economic, and racial pressures are all effective weapons. They are effective because they produce dissension, distrust, fear and hopelessness in the minds of the enemy, not because they originate in the psyche of propaganda or psychological-warfare agencies.[27]

Other explanations were equally nebulous. A study prepared by the Center for International Studies at MIT defined psychological warfare as the "coordinated exploitation by conflicting states of all possible techniques (diplomacy as well as subversion, propaganda as well as sabotage, military force as well as infiltration) in pursuit of their interests," suggesting that any governmental activity short of actual military hostilities fell under the rubric of psychological warfare.[28] With the approval of NSC 10/2, the Truman administration's principal directive regarding psychological warfare, the expansive definition took hold throughout the government.[29] In adopting such an expansive mandate, the administration declared that whoever controlled the psychological-warfare apparatus could significantly influence the entire foreign policy of the U.S. government. Consequently, much of the psychological-warfare effort would suffer due to the struggle to control that apparatus.

American planners determined the instruments of psychological warfare according to the level of responsibility they wished to accord the United States. White operations were those activities publicly associated with the U.S. government, such as the Voice of America, which broadcast news, entertainment, and cultural programs worldwide. U.S. involvement in gray operations, which entailed spreading disinformation about an opponent, was never publicly announced but was implied. Because black—or covert—operations included support for paramilitary resistance forces, counterinsurgency, sabotage, and other warlike acts, the U.S. government planned them in such a way as to "plausibly deny" any responsibility. The most famous covert operations were Radio Free Europe and Radio Liberty (also known as Radio Liberation) broadcasts and the efforts to overthrow the communist regime of Albania's Enver Hoxha. Both campaigns will be discussed in a later chapter. What is important to note about each is that the U.S. government was determined to avoid any association with either activity and spent decades trying to maintain the fiction that they were organized by émigré organizations alone.[30]

With the approval of NSC 10/2 the administration acknowledged the central importance of psychological warfare and covert action to America's cold war objectives. Immediately thereafter, President Truman authorized the creation of a new interdepartmental organization known as the Office of Policy Coordination to assist in covert planning and to coordinate the efforts of the State Department, Defense Department, and CIA.

Covert guerrilla operations aimed at toppling unfavorable satellite regimes have long attracted the most scholarly attention. Recently declassified documents demonstrate that American psychological warfare was far more nuanced. Analysts quickly recognized that efforts to subvert communist states were inordinately difficult given the authoritarian power structure of the satellite nations. Only in exposed countries like Albania did the United States have the opportunity to infiltrate insurgent groups with any hope of fomenting a popular uprising. For the rest of Eastern Europe, not to mention the Soviet Union, other techniques were needed. The principal strategy that emerged was to exploit the "paranoid nature" of the Soviet power structure in an effort to incite conflict within the ruling circles, between the party and the military, and between the security services and the army.[31] Such operations might so weaken the Soviet regime that it would be forced to abandon its cold war objectives or be prevented from crushing internal opposition altogether.

One of the most striking aspects of this period was the high degree of expectation surrounding the use of psychological warfare and—contravening accepted history—how much more support for the use of these instruments existed within the Truman administration than within the Eisenhower administration. From 1948 to 1956 both administrations maintained an almost unflagging faith that psychological warfare offered the most propitious method to achieve U.S. objectives. In fact, nearly all the key national-security strategists of the Truman administration and many within the Eisenhower administration actively supported psychological warfare and took a leading role in incorporating these techniques into America's policy.[32] George Kennan not only established the basic objectives of American cold war policy but also heavily influenced the drafting of U.S. covert policy in NSC 10/2 and demanded significant oversight responsibilities for the covert operations planned by the OPC. In addition to his central role in the preparation of NSC 68, Paul Nitze also chaired a special committee that designed NSC 10/5, which escalated the covert program established in NSC 10/2. Charles Bohlen not only revised the administration's Soviet strategy in NSC 135 but also the covert programs as delineated in the Strategic Concept for Cold War Operations. Of course, Eisenhower's support of the use of covert operations as general and as president is well documented.[33]

The question remains as to what made psychological warfare so appealing to these policymakers and why that attraction would continue despite the apparent lack of success in achieving U.S. objectives during the 1940s and 1950s. The key reason seems to be the nature of the enemy: Soviet vulnerabilities—particularly the power struggles within the party leadership—were of such a nature that they seemed particularly susceptible to psychological warfare and if properly exploited had the potential to cause the collapse of the Soviet system. The apparent success of psychological warfare in World War II and in stabilizing Western Europe in the face of the Soviet propaganda onslaught during 1947 and 1948 added to the aura of the effectiveness of these instruments. With the advent of a Soviet atomic capability, psychological warfare became even more important as a peaceful method to eliminate—given sufficient support and time—an ever growing threat to U.S. security. When the strategy first came into effect time was not an issue; the shifting nature of the strategic balance of power, however, forced significant reevaluations of the U.S. effort.

The Strategic Balance of Power

American national-security planners consistently stressed that efforts to foment unrest and revolution behind the Iron Curtain "must be carried out with the full acceptance of the risk of war."[34] Kennan in particular warned that the Soviet Union will not "sit by and allow the dissipation of its bloc and might seek to restore control either by military reoccupation or outright escalation to global war."[35] Since the very objective of American policy was to avoid systemic instability and world war, American planners were unwilling to fight a global war to achieve the objectives of NSC 20/4. Consequently, all U.S. actions had to be weighed against the risk that they might inspire a Soviet military response, and the prime barometer of that risk was the perception of the balance of power between the two nations. Ironically, the period of greatest danger would arise if and when U.S. psychological-warfare activities began to weaken the Soviet power structure. What would prevent the Kremlin from lashing out militarily if American actions were successfully undermining its power base? Truman administration strategists believed that only indisputable military superiority, which Paul Nitze defined as "more power than to win military victory in the event of war," would deter Stalin from taking military counteraction[36] Yet did America ever have such capabilities?

The United States emerged from World War II the world's most powerful nation. It suffered no material damage, possessed nearly fifty percent of the world's productive capacity, maintained an industrial base that outproduced the Soviet Union, Great Britain, and Germany combined, ruled the skies and the seas with its Air Force and Navy, and alone possessed the most intimidating weapon ever made: the atomic bomb. Compared with the rest of the war-ravaged world, the United States, to quote historian Melvyn Leffler, had preponderant power.[37]

With the rapid demobilization of its World War II armies, that preponderance quickly became latent. By 1948, U.S. forces-in-being had been reduced to comparatively insignificant numbers. While Air Force and Navy capabilities significantly outstripped those of the Soviet Union, the U.S. army had shrunk to a mere ten understrength divisions while the nation's nuclear arsenal fielded only fifty nuclear devices, insufficient to defeat the Soviet Union in a nuclear strike.[38] Similarly, military analysts did not question whether the Soviet Union could overrun Western Europe and the Middle East at the outset of war. Nevertheless, the war mobilization capacity of the United States remained vastly superior to that of the USSR and immune to Soviet attack. If the Soviet Union sought to exploit its ground-force advantage by attacking Western Europe and the Middle East, it would only embroil itself in a long and devastating war of attrition with victory at best uncertain. As George Kennan observed:

> In particular, they [the Soviets] are not attracted by the prospect . . . of occupying all of Western Europe before they are able to crush U.S. industrial and military power; for they would thereby only place themselves in a position analogous to that of the Germans in 1942, and incur heavy responsibili-

ties to which there would be no calculable satisfactory termination at any early date.[39]

Thus, even with substantially reduced military capabilities, the recognized superiority of America's war potential and its immunity from serious attack made American planners confident that the level of provocation would have to be very high before the Soviet Union might respond to the administration's risk-taking efforts with military aggression.[40] As Secretary of Defense James Forrestal argued in 1948, "as long as we can out-produce the world, can control the sea and can strike inland with the atomic bomb, we can assume certain risks otherwise unacceptable."[41] Consequently, the United States had the time to achieve its objectives.

The Soviet Union's development of atomic capabilities shook the confidence of these planners, who came to recognize that in the nuclear age war potential was no longer as important as readily available military capabilities. While the end of nuclear monopoly had an important psychological effect on the U.S. leaders, the threat to America's mobilization potential vastly outweighed its significance. Intelligence estimates warned that by 1954 a Soviet nuclear first strike might be able to destroy U.S. mobilization capabilities and preempt its retaliatory atomic forces. Coupled with the Soviet Union's conventional military advantages on the European continent, the United States faced the possibility of total defeat in war. The balance of power had now swung from American preponderance to Soviet advantage, making American risk-taking that much more dangerous. Finally, it transformed the Soviet threat from primarily an ideological menace to the liberal international order into a combined military and ideological threat. The administration needed to fundamentally reassess its national security policy.

The Truman administration's response came in NSC 68 and its plan to rebuild preponderant power by mobilizing American industry and deploying sufficient forces-in-being either to deter a Soviet strike or to survive its initial impact and proceed to victory, while accelerating American efforts to subvert the Soviet bloc and achieve the objectives of policy established in NSC 20/4. NSC 68 reaffirmed Kennan's policy objectives and offered no new policy as is so often argued. Yet the Soviet Union's growing nuclear threat forced the administration to analyze what preponderance meant in the nuclear age. Strategists concluded that the key strategic relationship in the nuclear age was the number of deliverable warheads versus the number of exposed enemy targets, not the size of the two opponents' stockpiles. Therefore, one country did not need military equality to possess a war-winning advantage. This conclusion fueled fears that the Soviet Union might maintain a first-strike advantage against the United States despite the latter's overwhelming strategic superiority. The explosion of the hydrogen bomb by both the United States and the Soviet Union only exacerbated these trends in strategic thought. Could the United States deploy sufficient military power to support aggressive psychological warfare directed against the most vital of Soviet interests? By 1955 the United States had come to the conclusion that it could not, and consequently began to curtail its efforts to subvert the Soviet empire in lieu of containing Soviet expansion and hoping that American cultural infiltration would one day sap the strength from the foundations of Soviet power. By the same token, these planners began to recognize that the developing nuclear stalemate would eventually provide the global stability that formerly only a world absent competing economic blocs promised.

A Note on Sources

American efforts to exploit Soviet vulnerabilities remain among the most sensitive materials in the National Archives system. While this study has benefited from the declassification of thousands of documents, the vast majority of which were released only in the last few years, no more than a fraction of total government materials relating to this topic have been opened. The CIA archives alone are estimated to hold 150 million pages of classified materials, of which only forty to sixty million pages are subject to declassification. Yet despite these enormous numbers it is feared that some important records may no longer exist. As the State Department historians who compiled the *Foreign Relations of the United States* series wrote:

> The documentation on this subject is fragmentary and episodic, and it appears that many early records no longer exist. Very little policy documentation on projects and operations under psychological and political warfare programs has been found, and the documents that have been retrieved tend to be random and scattered in their subject matter. In addition to the paucity of early documents on this subject, it is possible that in many instances the written record was deliberately kept to a minimum.[42]

While the State Department historians referred to U.S. policy from 1945 to 1950, the same problem exists for the entire period discussed in this book. While I believe that I have been able to collect enough material to present a fair and accurate portrayal of the strategy debates within both the Truman and Eisenhower administrations, important details remain unknown regarding operational aspects of America's covert efforts. It is now highly unlikely that these details will be released in the near future. While Executive Order 12958, issued by President Clinton on 17 April 1995, committed the U.S. government to declassify documents dated earlier than 1970 by 2000, little progress has in fact been achieved.[43] While the CIA has released some files regarding covert operations, for the most part it has delayed full implementation of Executive Order 12958 and on 15 July 1998 its director, George Tenet, announced that aside from materials regarding the 1954 Guatemala and 1961 Bay of Pigs operations the agency was postponing indefinitely further declassification of covert operations from the 1940s to the 1960s.[44] Recently, with the support of Congress, the Department of Energy included a provision in the 1999 Defense appropriations bill that would require a thorough review of "all" record collections to prevent the declassification of any material that might contain information relating to the development of nuclear weapons. The parameters of this review cover approximately 495 million pages of classified materials. The passage of this rider by Congress demonstrates an ever increasing effort to limit the release of classified government materials. Consequently, it is most unlikely that new and significant materials regarding U.S. covert operations in Eastern Europe and the Soviet Union will be released in the near future.[45] This is highly unfortunate since, as recent scholarship demonstrates, much documentation critical to our understanding of U.S. cold war policy remains locked in these files.[46]

Nevertheless, while the declassification of covert operations has been delayed indefinitely, significant numbers of documents have been released detailing the broader strategic issues of U.S. national security policy. Furthermore, I have been able to gather information that indicates the type of covert activities engaged in by both administrations. Large swaths of material still lay beyond the access of researchers, but enough is available to provide significant information about the policies analyzed in this study.

[1]

Defining an Offensive Strategy, 1948–1949

By 1948, the United States had completed its shift from trying to maintain the grand alliance that won World War II to engaging the Soviet Union in the new cold war. The administration of President Harry S. Truman recognized the grave threat the Soviet Union posed to the devastated countries of Western Europe and was determined to prevent the Kremlin from undermining the region's non-communist governments and incorporating them into the communist bloc.

Financial and military support for the beleaguered Greek and Turkish governments represented only the beginning of America's efforts. The National Security Act of 1947 created a new bureaucracy to oversee the implementation of U.S. security programs. Marshall Plan aid began to rebuild a shattered Germany, restore hope in France, and bolster an exhausted Britain. Responding to the growing Soviet menace, the United States moved ever closer to restoring its wartime alliance with France and Britain. By preventing the communist takeover of Italy in the 18 April 1948 elections, the CIA demonstrated that psychological warfare would be an effective instrument in defeating the communist threat.

Despite these successes, crisis conditions still prevailed on the European continent. Germany remained under occupation, the United States and its Western allies battled the Soviets over the status of Berlin, communist forces seized power in Czechoslovakia, and riots and work stoppages threatened the stability of the French government. Moreover, despite its massive conventional superiority in Europe, the Soviet Union began a substantial military buildup that further threatened the West's already precarious military position.[1]

Nevertheless, American strategists believed 1948 to be the turning point of the early cold war as the United States could finally switch from a reactive, defensive policy to an aggressive, dynamic effort to subvert the Soviet empire.[2] Despite its outward strength, American planners believed that the Soviet Union's internal vulnerabilities made it susceptible to American psychological-warfare pressures. Therefore, on 24 November 1948, President Truman approved a new national security statement—NSC 20/4—that established a set of objectives that guided American policy toward the Soviet bloc for the next seven years. The new policy aimed to use these instruments to reduce Soviet power to a non-threatening level, restore the independence of the Eastern European states, and force the Soviet regime to change fundamentally its international conduct and accept a legitimate role in the world community. Once this national security strategy had received presidential approval, the CIA, State Department, and Department of Defense initiated a campaign to weaken Soviet control over Eastern Europe and undermine communist control within the USSR. The Soviet break with Yugoslavia and the perceived weakness of the communist regime in Albania represented prime opportunities for action.

While the increasingly hostile postwar environment and aggressive American response heightened the risk of war, Truman administration officials discounted the likelihood of Soviet military retaliation. Underlying America's postwar ambitions was a basic proposition: that the United States possessed substantially greater power than the USSR—what would soon be termed "preponderant power"—and could aggressively exploit the Kremlin's vulnerabilities without significant fear of a Soviet military counterstroke. Assuming the continuity of American superiority, many considered time an asset for the United States, allowing for a slow and methodical prosecution of American efforts to coerce the Soviet Union into changing its international behavior and to win the cold war.[3]

Part One: Holding the Line

Psychological Warfare and the Defense of Western Europe

The consolidation of Soviet control in Eastern Europe, its clandestine inroads into Greece, Turkey, and Iran, and the growing strength and militancy of the French and Italian communist parties placed the United States on the defensive. This demonstration of the Kremlin's tactical flexibility, however, provided Truman administration officials with an important lesson in the value of non-military methods of influencing the behavior of foreign states.

The growing Soviet propaganda offensive demonstrated as early as 1947 that the United States had either to respond in kind to this challenge or lose Europe without firing a shot. Immediately following the announcement of the Soviet-imposed satellite rejection of the Marshall Plan, the Kremlin finalized its plans to create the Communist Information Bureau (Cominform), which the Soviets hoped would undermine the recovery program.[4] Cominform operations extended well beyond the dissemination of information to include rioting and work stoppages throughout France and Italy. Concern grew that the Soviet attempt to portray the Marshall Plan as an example of American imperialism would succeed, as only the most naive would fail to question what the United States gained from its multi-billion-dollar expenditures.[5] With the Marshall Plan at stake and the important 1948 elections in France and Italy drawing near, it became clear that the United States would have to respond to the Cominform's activities in a like manner.[6]

NSC 4, entitled "Coordination of Foreign Information Measures," was the first high-level policy statement responding to the Soviet offensive in Europe.[7] The document, approved on 9 December 1947, warned that the Soviets stood ready to exploit any discrepancies in the U.S. information program and that proper coordination of U.S. information activities was essential for a successful psychological-warfare effort. The document charged the secretary of state—as the principal spokesman for U.S. foreign policy—with the responsibility of formulating and coordinating American information activities through his department.[8] The NSC also approved a top-secret version of this document—NSC 4a—that formally authorized the use of covert operations in Western Europe should the need arise.[9] NSC 4a established a new organization entitled the Special Procedures Group responsible for organizing and conducting these new operations. Unlike its successor, the Office of Policy Coordination (OPC), the SPG was officially under the direction of the CIA, and was located within the Office of Special Operations (OSO), the department responsible for intelligence collection.[10]

The Italian elections were the first testing ground for these new psychological-warfare tactics. As the elections neared and the fear of a communist victory grew, U.S. actions escalated well beyond the initial commitments described in the NSC 4 series. Due to their growing concern that the Italian Communist Party would either triumph at the April 18 elections or overthrow the government if it lost, the National Security Council invoked NSC 4a and expanded U.S. activities to include the use of covert activities.[11] This act reflected the administration's growing concern that the United States must use all its political, economic, and military power to prevent Italy from falling behind the Iron Curtain. The Czechoslovak Communist Party's successful coup d'état only two months before the Italian elections dramatically highlighted these dangers. The resignation of twelve ministers from three non-communist coalition parties on 20 February allowed the communists to take control of the government legally, crush all democratic opposition, and topple the Czechoslovak's ill-fated President Eduard Benes. By 1 March, the new regime had transformed Czechoslovakia into a totalitarian dictatorship, offering a potent warning to all battleground nations of what might befall them should the communists achieve power.[12]

The administration responded with an intensive campaign designed to ensure a Christian Democrat victory. The United States supplied scarce items to ease the constant food shortages of postwar Italy while Italian-Americans mounted a letter-writing campaign to encourage their families to support the Christian Democrats at the polls. Members of Congress delivered speeches urging the Italian people to oppose the communists while President Truman warned that no economic assistance would be forthcoming if the communists won the election or even were part of a coalition government—a threat that VOA broadcasters constantly repeated.[13]

Led by future spycatcher James Jesus Angleton, the CIA orchestrated a subtle, yet powerful, psychological-warfare campaign using many of the same techniques that would become a hallmark of the agency's later years. The agency distributed anti-communist posters and pamphlets, supplied pro-Western newspapers with scarce newsprint, and launched a large disinformation campaign forging documents and letters detailing the communists' post-election plans for Italy. The horrific accounts of looting and rapes within Soviet-dominated Germany and the brutal nature of the communist takeovers in Poland, Czechoslovakia, and Hungary filled the Italian newspapers.[14] The triumph of the Christian Democrats—who won 48.5 percent of the vote—substantiated the use of covert operations to defeat Soviet political aggression and demonstrated that psychological warfare could be the key to winning the cold war altogether.[15]

NSC 10/2 and the Origins of the OPC

This first success inspired George Kennan to encourage the Truman administration to expand the covert apparatus of the United States. On 3 May, Kennan asked Loy Henderson and Charles Bohlen to join the Policy Planning Staff in studying his new memorandum calling for the "inauguration of organized political warfare" by the United States in its struggle against the Soviets.[16] Kennan envisioned the Policy Planning Staff overseeing a new "directorate"—entitled the Office of Special Projects—headed by a nominee of the secretary of state and appointed by the NSC.[17] Kennan's scheme would authorize the director to coordinate the planning and execution of covert operations with other representatives of the State Department and National Military Establishment and to review all aspects of their implementation. He would also be responsible for developing the training program and cataloging the special supplies and logistical support required for each covert activity.[18]

Control of the OSP became a highly contentious issue. The Joint Chiefs of Staff challenged Kennan by arguing that the Defense Department should possess primary authority over covert operations in time of war and significant oversight over the use of military equipment in any peacetime operations.[19] CIA director Roscoe Hillenkoetter attempted to resolve the issue by separating responsibility between times of peace and war. The CIA would control peacetime covert operations with considerable guidance from the State Department, while in wartime a combined committee of JCS and CIA staff would organize covert planning under the direction of the Joint Chiefs.[20]

Kennan rejected Hillenkoetter's compromise outright, arguing that it neglected the State Department's rightful oversight responsibility.[21] Kennan declared that "it is our view that these things [covert operations], if they are to be done at all, must be done under the intimate direction and control of this Department. If this cannot be arranged . . . I think it would be better to withdraw this paper entirely and to give up at this time the idea of attempting to conduct political warfare."[22]

The NSC Staff revised NSC 10 to accommodate Kennan's views.[23] The new draft provided for an operations advisory committee consisting of representatives of the secretaries of state and defense. These liaison representatives would supply full policy guidance on covert projects and would assist in preparing all plans. The NSC would resolve any disagreements between the director of central intelligence (DCI) and the departmental liaison officers.

The NSC reviewed the staff's work on 17 June and added two additional amendments. First, it authorized the DCI to oversee the planning and conduct of covert operations in collaboration with a policy advisory committee representing the secretaries of state and defense, who would have the power to veto operations they disapproved of. Second, the NSC adopted the Joint Chiefs' position that the proposed directorate should conduct wartime planning and operations in *collaboration* with the JCS.[24] President Truman approved NSC 10/2 on 18 June 1948;[25] it would serve as the foundation for American psychological warfare and covert activities until President Dwight D. Eisenhower approved his own directive six years later.[26]

Kennan did not believe that the compromise language used in NSC 10/2 provided the State Department with sufficient oversight responsibilities. Therefore on 6 August he convened a special meeting including CIA director Hillenkoetter, Colonel Ivan D. Yeaton of the Joint Chiefs of Staff, Robert Blum of the Defense Department, NSC executive secretary Admiral Sidney Souers, and Frank Wisner, then deputy assistant secretary of state for occupied areas.[27] Kennan informed those present that the State Department considered political warfare "essentially an instrument of foreign policy" and therefore the Office of Special Projects must operate as a "direct instrumentality" of the State Department and the National Military Establishment (NME). He stressed that while the NSC placed the organization within the framework of the CIA, "it must nevertheless be recognized that it [the OSP] must take direction and guidance from the Departments of State and the NME." Kennan concluded by demanding that since political warfare was a "major political operation," he, as the State Department's designated representative, "would want to have specific knowledge of the objectives of every operation and also of the procedures and methods employed in all cases where those procedures and methods involve political decisions."[28] Kennan quickly received the support of the other participants, including Admiral Souers, who informed Hillenkoetter "that it had been the intention of NSC . . . that the State Department and the National Military Establishment are responsible for the conduct of the activities of the Office of Special Projects."[29] Facing such opposition, Hillenkoetter felt he had no choice but to accept the "understanding" as an official amendment to NSC 10/2, although it meant that despite being the director of central intelligence he would have no authority over the administration's covert operations.

Consequently, while the Office of Special Projects was officially listed as a department of the CIA and sister organization to the OSO, it functioned autonomously, even to the point of being considered an altogether separate entity from the CIA. This division extended so far that the CIA handled the intelligence requests of the office as if they came from an outside agency. Furthermore, the OSP was reluctant to tell the CIA about its operations. In fact, the departmental policy representatives consulted only with the OSP, leaving the DCI out of covert planning, despite having assured Hillenkoetter that the 6 August "understanding" did not exclude him from knowledge of the department's activity.[30] Consequently, the OSP became an intelligence apparatus for the departments of state and defense, a situation that many longtime covert operators found disturbing. Allen Dulles strongly opposed the new OSP because "there would be a duplication of effort, crossing of wires in the use of clandestine agents, and serious risk for the . . . agents used in the respective operations."[31] This situation would last until 12 October 1950, when the new DCI, Lieutenant General Walter Bedell Smith, repudiated the 6 August "understanding" and brought the organization directly under his authority.[32]

Before the new agency could officially begin operation, one more issue needed to be resolved: its name. Government officials realized that given the importance of political warfare to U.S. foreign policy, the profile of the new agency would inevitably grow to such an extent that its activities would come under scrutiny. Therefore it made little sense to deny the existence of the organization, as such denials would only lead to even greater attention. The administration decided to create a "fable" regarding the purpose of the organization in order to deflect attention away from its covert activities. According to the chosen façade, the new organization "was established to coordinate the activities of CIA with national security policy as adopted by those agencies of government responsible for the formation of such policy": hence the change in name to the Office of Policy Coordination (OPC).[33]

With its mandate established and new name finalized the OPC began operation on 1 September 1948 with Frank Wisner serving as the new assistant director for policy coordination. Wisner would continue to serve as assistant director until 23 August 1951 when Walter Bedell Smith promoted him to deputy director of plans, conferring on him authority over both the OPC and the OSO.[34] On 1 August 1952, on the advice of Wisner and CIA deputy director Allen Dulles, Smith ordered the OPC and OSO merged into a new Directorate of Plans, thus ending the OPC's four-year existence. Yet during the course of those four years the OPC would grow into a global organization capable of conducting covert operations on a significant scale.

The Doctrine of Plausible Deniability

One of the most significant legacies of NSC 10/2 was its introduction of the term "plausible deniability" into the lexicon of U.S. foreign relations. NSC 10/2 stipulated that U.S. covert operations must be designed to be "deniable"; that is, "planned and executed so that any U.S. Government responsibility for them is not evident to unauthorized persons and that if uncovered the U.S. Government can plausibly disclaim any responsibility." The administration deemed plausible deniability crucial to its activities since the operations under discussion—propaganda, economic warfare, sabotage, demolition, "subversion against hostile states," and support for underground resistance forces and guerrilla movements—could be considered acts of war.[35] Its objective was to make any U.S.-sponsored insurrection appear to have been the result of a discontented anti-communist populace supported by their refugee brethren in the West. While plausible deniability applied to all U.S.-sponsored covert activities, it was employed with special rigor in operations within Eastern Europe, where the consequences of disclosure were considered the most grave. By imposing limits on the nature of these operations, however, the administration undermined any chance they might have had for success. Consequently, while the United States would create the necessary forces to overthrow a left-leaning government in Guatemala, it would not make a similar commitment to unseat the communist government of Enver Hoxha in Albania for fear of provoking Stalin.

The Development of Radio Free Europe and Radio Liberty

The most famous examples of U.S. psychological warfare were Radio Free Europe and Radio Liberation (later changed to Radio Liberty).[36] Created to complement the State Department's openly funded Voice of America, scholars now consider these radios the most effective elements of U.S. psychological warfare in the cold war. Radio Free Europe beamed propaganda directly to the East bloc, exclusive of the USSR and East Germany, while Radio Liberty concentrated on the Soviet Union.

The creation of the two radios reflected a new and more aggressive attitude in American radio warfare. The VOA represented the official voice of the United States government and as such needed to be considered a reliable source of news about the foreign policy of the United States. Even as late as 1949 officials fought plans to use the VOA for propaganda broadcasts into the Soviet bloc. Other means were required if the United States was to engage in psychological warfare by radio, prompting the formation of the CIA-backed Radio Free Europe and Radio Liberty.[37]

According to the public account, the idea for Radio Free Europe originated in Kennan's seemingly innocuous concern over the number of Eastern European exiles visiting the State Department seeking support for their groups. Kennan concluded that "the proper place for help and comfort lay not in the official chambers of the United States government but in the hearts of the American people."[38] Early in 1949, Kennan approached Joseph Grew, one of the most respected of the "elder statesmen" of foreign affairs, and asked him to establish a private group capable of finding ways to engage the émigrés. On 1 June 1949 Grew, with the assistance of his former State Department colleague DeWitt Clinton Poole and help from the CIA, organized the Free Europe Committee (later changed to the National Committee for a Free Europe—NCFE), composed of a prominent group of individuals and directed by Allen Dulles.[39] By July, a Radio Committee was established, chaired by New York investment banker and Kennan confidant Frank Altschul and charged with producing taped radio addresses for broadcast into the refugees' native countries.[40]

Over the last decade, it has become clear that the U.S. government participated in the development of RFE/RL to a greater extent than previously known. Accounts provided by Cord Meyer and Sig Mickelson indicate that high-level U.S. government officials not only developed the two radios, but also provided funding and program assistance for well over twenty years.[41]

The crucial breakthrough was the formation of the OPC under Frank Wisner. Wisner's position as deputy assistant secretary of state for occupied areas put him into direct contact with the various émigré organizations throughout Western Europe. Wisner immediately recognized the opportunities these groups offered the United States for its intelligence gathering and paramilitary ambitions behind the Iron Curtain.[42]

Upon his appointment as director of the OPC—and with the encouragement of the State Department—Wisner assumed responsibility for these organizations. Despite the State Department's approval of the use of special operations, Secretary of State George Marshall felt it both inappropriate to engage in propaganda and diplomatically dangerous for the department to negotiate with official government representatives and émigré groups from the same country.[43] Consequently he was quite happy to relieve the department of what he considered an embarrassing problem.[44] Wisner assembled

Radio Free Europe and its sister station Radio Liberation (later Radio Liberty) using the two million dollars he retained from the now disbanded Special Procedures Group. Soon after, he successfully arranged for funding directly from the Department of Defense but funneled through the CIA to make the money difficult to trace. RFE/RL also received support through front organizations, such as the "Crusade for Freedom," which held widely publicized fund-raising events to hide the fact that most of its "donations" came from the U.S. government. In addition, the government used highly respected private institutions such as the Ford Foundation's Russian Research Committee and the Rockefeller Foundation to channel money into the RFE/RL budgets.[45]

With the issue of financing solved, Wisner turned his attention to organizing the effort. Production facilities, radio studios, transmitters, and antennas were all key to any radio operation, but to make the broadcasts possible Wisner needed personnel trained in radio broadcasting and program research and writing. Furthermore, the NCFE decided that to be successful RFE/RL would have to compete with the audiences of local radio stations, and therefore would have to remain on air twenty-four hours a day. Consequently the broadcast staffs required the most up-to-date news available or faced losing potential audiences. All these fronts required close cooperation between RFE/RL and the OPC. The OPC provided the equipment, trained the personnel, and, most importantly, provided the news to be broadcast into the "denied areas."[46] From a wooded region near the village of Lampertheim, West Germany, a seven-and-one-half kilowatt transmitter made the first broadcast into Czechoslovakia on 4 July 1950.[47]

With the creation of the OPC and its successful employment in Europe, psychological warfare had become fully ensconced in the administration's cold war repertoire. What Truman's national security planners now needed was a clear statement of policy that would guide America's new offensive posture throughout the cold war.

Part Two: The Establishment of Policy

Establishing American Policy toward Russia: The NSC 20 Series

On 5 May 1947, Secretary of State Marshall selected George Kennan to be the first director of the State Department's Policy Planning Staff (known within the government as the S/P). Marshall charged the S/P with five functions: to formulate and develop long-term programs for the achievement of American objectives in foreign affairs; to anticipate difficulties for the department; to study and report on large problems in politico-military affairs; to evaluate current policy in the context of developments in world affairs;

and, lastly, to coordinate planning within the State Department.[48] The S/P provided the perfect platform for Kennan to influence the formulation of American foreign policy. So important would the S/P become that from 1947 to 1949 many of the most important NSC studies and presidentially approved policy papers emanated from Kennan's Policy Planning Staff. They were the obvious choice to prepare the new national security statement.

Surprisingly, Kennan and his associates were not the first bureau to formulate a new policy; they were upstaged by the staff members of the year-old National Security Council. Established by the council under the direction of Executive Secretary Sidney Souers, the NSC Staff was responsible for providing analysis to the council's members. Made up largely of military personnel below the rank of general, the staff was not nearly as prestigious as Kennan's Policy Planning Staff; nevertheless, it took an active role in policymaking and remained a source of contention for Kennan until the NSC reformed its staff structure in 1950.[49]

Responding to Secretary of Defense Forrestal's request for political guidance, on 30 March 1948 the NSC Staff disseminated an analysis of the Soviet threat, entitled NSC 7 "The Position of the United States with Respect to Soviet-Directed World Communism." This document stunned Kennan and his State Department colleagues and catalyzed the policymaking debate.

The positions of the NSC Staff differed from those of Kennan in two fundamental respects. First, they believed that Soviet power was growing so rapidly that it would eventually overtake that of the United States, resulting in a position of Russian superiority in Eurasia; second, the report completely ignored the glaring Soviet vulnerabilities so crucial to Kennan's thinking. It was less an analysis than a polemic designed to embolden U.S. policymakers to move beyond a reactionary and defensive policy and to launch a "counter-offensive" to reverse the gains of Soviet expansionism. Nevertheless, because of its challenge to defensive containment, NSC 7 exemplified the growing chorus of support for a more aggressive policy against the Soviet bloc, a policy that put the Kremlin on the defensive. The hyperbolic nature of NSC 7, however, resulted in numerous strong criticisms and the eventual cancellation of the report itself.

According to NSC 7, "Stalin has come closer to achieving what Hitler attempted in vain. . . . Today the Soviet world extends from the Elbe River and the Adriatic Sea on the West to Manchuria on the East."[50] Were the Soviets to consolidate their hold on the entire Eurasian continent they would become so superior in manpower, resources, and territory that "the prospect for the survival of the United States as a free nation would become slight."[51] Soviet power was, however, only part of the danger facing Western nations. The non-communist world faced a great threat from "world wide fifth column[ism]"—indigenous subversive movements loyal to Moscow "capable of fomenting disorders, even armed conflicts, within their victims without directly involving any communist state."[52] In response, the authors of

NSC 7 called for the United States to take the offensive in the cold war, in order to force the Soviet Union to respond to U.S. initiatives, and reverse the Kremlin's gains. Such efforts would enable the United States to concentrate its strengths on vital objectives, keep the Soviets off balance, and provide the best deterrent to potential Soviet aggression.

The NSC Staff made an impassioned argument for an aggressive policy to win the cold war. They did not provide an equally clear set of methods necessary to enact this policy, however. NSC 7 called for an unspecified military buildup, expansion of aid to Western Europe, and an intensification of political warfare—all previously articulated policies. The document did make one suggestion that would play an important and lasting role in U.S. policy toward Russia. It called for the development of "a coordinated program to support underground resistance movements in countries behind the iron curtain, *including the USSR* [emphasis added]."[53] This was one of the earliest calls for a program of covert operations against not only Eastern Europe but also the Soviet Union itself. Such a program commenced only a few months later with the approval of NSC 10/2.

Numerous State Department officials denounced NSC 7 for its overstatement of the communist threat and lack of clear and identifiable policy objectives.[54] Its critique of defensive containment, however, resonated within the administration, indicating widespread support for an offensive policy against the Soviet Union. What the administration needed, however, was a sophisticated analysis of Soviet weaknesses and U.S. opportunities. Again, George Kennan would fill this void.

The debates surrounding NSC 7 forced the issue of an offensive policy to the forefront of U.S. national security deliberations. The strategy would emerge in response to Secretary of Defense Forrestal's continued demands for political guidance. The military, still struggling to cobble together its 1950 defense budget, was particularly disconcerted over the lack of direction from the top echelons of the Truman administration. Forrestal informed the Department of State at a 26 May 1948 meeting of the State-War-Navy Coordinating Committee that the armed services were anxious to have an indication of the type of defense preparations required in response to the Soviet threat. In particular, Forrestal wanted the State Department to evaluate whether the U.S. defense effort should be "geared to meet a given anticipated peak period of danger" or should be established "on a basis we could expect to maintain permanently, on the theory that the degree of danger will be relatively static."[55] A concerned Kennan warned Secretary Marshall that Forrestal's request was a bureaucratic ruse "to get this department to take responsibility for an analysis of the world political situation which will cover the military program, so that if the program turns out to be *not* what was required responsibility will rest not on the service departments or the Joint Chiefs."[56]

Despite these misgivings Kennan reluctantly agreed to assemble the analysis, and on 17 June completed Policy Planning Staff paper 33: "Factors Affecting the Nature of the U.S. Defense Arrangements in the Light of Soviet Policies." After incorporating comments from Charles Bohlen and Francis Stevens, Kennan presented PPS 33 to Robert Lovett, who approved the draft and sent it to Forrestal on 25 June.[57] The determining factor in Kennan's analysis was that:

> The events of the past two wars have demonstrated that unless a European aggressor can be sure of dealing a decisive blow to the North American military industrial potential in the initial phase of his effort to dominate the European continent, he can never be sure of final victory.[58]

Since the Soviet Union lacked the capability to strike the continental United States in 1948, Kennan concluded that it would not plan any deliberate armed action against the West, and instead would continue to achieve its expansionist aims through political means.[59] Consequently, there was no need to base military planning on a "peak period of danger."[60]

Kennan expanded this point into his own theory of geopolitics: that it was unlikely the Soviet Union would seek hegemony over Eurasia through military means if it could not first attack and destroy the North American military-industrial potential. To do otherwise would entangle the USSR in a long and difficult war in which it would be at a significant disadvantage.[61] Additionally, the Soviets would have to contend with the devastating aftermath of an American atomic attack and the threat it posed to Soviet control within the USSR. While the Soviets could overrun Western Europe and the Middle East within the first months of war, they could not avoid a crippling atomic counterattack, nor could they prohibit the massive American industrial machine from mobilizing the military forces to defeat the USSR over the course of a long war. Granted these circumstances, Kennan considered it unlikely that the USSR would deliberately initiate war with the United States to establish its dominion over Eurasia in lieu of its quite successful efforts at psychological warfare and political intimidation.

Many cold war scholars argue that Kennan considered the likelihood of a Soviet attack negligible due to his interpretation of Soviet political intentions rather than his understanding of Soviet military capabilities.[62] His position is often contrasted with that of Paul Nitze (Kennan's successor as director of the Policy Planning Staff), who, it is argued, failed to consider the intent of the Soviet leadership and chose instead to base his analysis of the likelihood of global war primarily upon the military capabilities of the USSR.[63] PPS 33 demonstrated that the global balance of power heavily influenced Kennan's strategic thinking, complementing his understanding of the Kremlin's political designs. It was his confidence that the military balance favored the United States that convinced Kennan that the Soviets would not deliberately initiate global war. Instead, the Soviet leadership would use its well-developed psychological-warfare capabilities to undermine the U.S. position along the Eurasian perimeter. Consequently, little difference of opinion existed between the two strategists, demonstrated by Nitze's support for Kennan's analysis in 1948.[64] The disagreements that did erupt during 1950 arose, not from differing opinions regarding Soviet intentions, but from conflicting views with respect to the long-term impact of Soviet atomic weapons on American national security policy.

Forrestal, much to everyone's surprise, felt that PPS 33 did not offer sufficient guidance for preparation of the 1950 Defense budget. On 10 July he again petitioned the State Department to prepare a study on the level of military preparedness required by the world situation, but expanded this request to include a discussion of U.S. objectives in the cold war, a list of programs necessary to achieve these objectives, and an assessment of possible impediments. The NSC agreed to discuss the memo, which it labeled NSC 20, during its meeting scheduled for July 15.[65]

Forrestal's request created great confusion within the State Department. On 13 July, George Butler, Kennan's deputy on the Policy Planning Staff, informed Robert Lovett that PPS 33 already contained the analysis requested by Forrestal.[66] Lovett concurred and to fulfill Forrestal's request simply resubmitted PPS 33 to the NSC.[67] Surprised at his former mentor's disfavor, Kennan appealed to Secretary of State Marshall to intervene. On 5 August—the day scheduled for the NSC to decide upon Forrestal's request—Kennan warned Marshall that given the fluidity of the world situation and the adaptability of Soviet tactics, predictions of the type Forrestal sought were impossible. He stressed that the NSC must always strive for a policy that offered the greatest amount of flexibility. Yet Forrestal, he cautioned:

> believes that we are faced with choices, but the answer is not 'either/or' but 'both.' We cannot say for certain that we should be prepared for a war either in 1950 or 1952 or any other date; that we intend to achieve our objectives by military means or non-military means etc. Things are hopelessly intertwined. The decisions are only decisions of emphasis and priority which must be determined from day to day in the light of shifting situations.[68]

Nevertheless, Forrestal's petition was approved and the council decided that the State Department would prepare two studies: an analysis of the nature and extent of the Soviet threat, including a judgment as to when U.S. security would be most threatened, followed by a statement of the objectives the United States would pursue in the immediate future. The council further ordered the NSC Staff to prepare a list of recommended measures based on the completed State Department drafts.[69] During the meeting, the council's executive secretary Admiral Sidney Souers informed the body that Kennan was already preparing the State Department's study. That paper was PPS 38 "U.S. Objectives towards Russia."

The Policy Defined: Liberation of Eastern Europe and the Reform of the Soviet Union

According to most historical scholarship Kennan's principal contribution to American policy was his contention that the world contained five key industrial regions (the United States, Great Britain, Germany and Central Europe, the Soviet Union, and Japan), of which only one (the Soviet Union itself) was not under American influence.[70] As long as the Soviet Union was unable to co-opt the industrial capacity of the other regions, it could not directly threaten the security of the United States.

While Kennan certainly influenced American geopolitical thinking, this did not represent his major contribution to American policymaking. In fact, Kennan was one of many who recognized the importance of the industrial capabilities and natural resources of these regions to the United States. As historian Melvyn Leffler has argued, by the late 1930s the foundation of American national security planning—including political, economic, and military affairs—had become the preservation of American influence and control over the essential productive centers of Eurasia.[71] Therefore it is more accurate to say that Kennan's analysis fit into an already well-established theory of national security policy than to claim that he was the sole originator of these ideas.[72]

Kennan's paramount contribution to American policy was his determination that concerted U.S. action could dramatically transform Soviet international behavior. Kennan was one of the first analysts to recognize the inherent instability of the Soviet structure of power and believe that its collapse was possible with positive assistance from the United States. It was now necessary for him to assemble these beliefs and opinions into a clearly defined policy paper.

During his tenure at the National War College, Kennan immersed himself in the writings of the great political theorists and military strategists—such as Niccolo Machiavelli and Karl von Clausewitz—whose works convinced him that the United States needed a comprehensive national security policy. "U.S. Objectives towards Russia," the culmination of Kennan's work, represented the needed breakthrough for U.S. cold war policy. It refocused American strategic thinking from its previously defensive inclination into a dynamic policy designed to defeat Soviet communism and to win the cold war peacefully.

Kennan articulated two broad objectives designed to guide U.S. foreign policy in both peace and war. U.S. policy would seek to:

> (a) Reduce the power and influence of Moscow to limits where they will no longer constitute a threat to the peace and stability of the world family of nations.

(b) Bring about a basic change in the theory and practice of international relations observed by the government in power in Russia.[73]

To attain these objectives U.S. policymakers aimed to accomplish four specific goals. First, the United States had to eliminate communist domination of the satellite area and allow for the "emergence of the respective eastern-European countries as independent factors on the international scene." Second, the United States needed to use "every means possible" to promote a federal status for the Baltic nations that would "permit a revival of their national life." Third, the United States needed to attack the Kremlin's credibility outside of its area of control by psychological warfare and "every other means at our disposal." Lastly—and most significant—Kennan argued that the United States needed to:

> create situations which will *compel* the Soviet Government to recognize the practical undesirability of acting on the basis of its present concepts and the necessity of behaving, at least outwardly, as though it were the converse of those concepts that were true.[74] (Emphasis added)

Unless the Soviet regime fundamentally transformed its national security policy, it would be impossible for the Eastern European satellites to gain their freedom, the Baltic states to recover their identity, and the United States to end the communist threat to the non-Soviet world.

"U.S. Objectives towards Russia" was a seminal moment in the development of American national security policy: it refocused American strategy from solely a policy of containment into a policy of coercion. Kennan resolved that it was necessary not just to stop Soviet expansion, but to force the regime into abandoning its expansionist aims and ending its domination of Eastern Europe. He believed that resolution of the cold war required a basic transformation in the national security beliefs of the Stalinist leadership. By understanding the offensive nature of Kennan's policy in 1948, it is possible to understand better the continuity in American policy through 1950 and the policy retrenchment that took place in 1952. The only restriction was that the United States not place:

> fundamental emphasis of our policies [on] preparation for an armed conflict, to the exclusion of the development of possibilities for achieving our objectives without war . . . [or] to bring about the overthrow of the Soviet Government.[75]

Kennan offered no strategy to achieve these objectives and explicitly rejected the very notion of establishing any specific plan of action.[76] Instead, he created a conceptual framework through which U.S. policymakers could better understand the dangers posed by the Soviet Union, as well as the glaring vulnerabilities the United States could exploit. As he had maintained for several years, the overall problem was to defeat the communist structure of power through which the Kremlin had been able to control both Soviet and Eastern European nationalities.[77] How the United States could undermine this power structure without using military force or triggering World War III was the question.

The Reduction of Soviet Power and Influence

To reduce Soviet power and influence the United States would have to break Soviet domination of the satellite region and its control over groups and parties throughout the non-Soviet world. Kennan, in an argument similar to that made in NSC 7, warned that:

> In Soviet power, Western statesmen are now facing something more than just another problem of foreign affairs. They are also facing an internal enemy in their own countries—an enemy committed to the undermining and eventual destruction of their respective national societies.[78]

Unlike NSC 7, Kennan considered indigenous factors, as well as external Soviet interference, a crucial reason for the success of international communism. By restoring the economic well-being of these societies the United States and its allies would eliminate the principal *raison d'être* of these forces. Kennan was confident that programs for economic rehabilitation, coupled with concerted action to destroy the ideological myths spawned by communist propaganda, would break down Soviet influence outside its immediate orbit. Since most of the links between Moscow and these foreign groups were clandestine and "strenuously denied by all parties," the West could eradicate Soviet influence in the third world without compromising Soviet prestige and without much risk of war.

Reducing Soviet influence behind the Iron Curtain was a much more delicate matter. Nevertheless, Kennan was confident that the United States could diminish Soviet power without either threatening the USSR's international prestige or significantly risking war. The Soviets, he reasoned, maintained control of their Eastern European satellites through clandestine links denied by both parties. By creating conditions where Eastern European nations could sever those ties while maintaining stable state-to-state relations with the Soviets, the Eastern European nations could free themselves of Soviet domination without trampling on Soviet prestige. This option would later be termed "Finlandization," after the 1948 Soviet-Finnish treaty that granted the Finns domestic autonomy at the cost of aligning their foreign policy with that of the USSR. This was the model the United States originally hoped the

Soviets would adopt in their relations with Eastern Europe. Soviet security and military forces quickly dashed these expectations when they established domination over most of Eastern Europe shortly after World War II.[79]

Unfortunately, besides these broad generalizations, Kennan never explained how the United States could expel Soviet power from Eastern Europe. The closest example he provided comes from this vague paragraph:

> This can be done by skillful use of our economic power, by direct or indirect informational activity, by placing the greatest possible strain on the maintenance of the iron curtain, and by building up the hope and vigor of Western Europe to a point where it comes to exercise the maximum attraction to the peoples of the East, and by other means too numerous to mention.[80]

Economic power was an important first step in creating strains between the satellite regimes of Eastern Europe and the Soviet Union, as demonstrated by the difficulties arising from Stalin's decision to forbid Eastern European participation in the Marshall Plan. Kennan believed that by exposing "the crude and ugly outlines of their hold over the governments of the satellite countries," the Marshall Plan undermined the USSR's control over the region.[81]

Economic power was only one weapon at the disposal of the United States. Political warfare would play an even more crucial role in America's effort to penetrate the Iron Curtain. As we have already seen, while preparing PPS 38 Kennan was engaged in formulating the administration's position toward what he considered "an integral part of [U.S.] foreign policy."[82] Kennan's important role in the development of America's clandestine capabilities has been the subject of much debate since it surfaced during congressional hearings in the 1970s. Kennan has tried hard to distance himself from this past. Yet, before passing judgment on his activities, it is important to realize that many analysts considered political warfare a powerful new weapon in the administration's foreign-policy arsenal. Government officials longed for the development of psychological-warfare techniques capable of influencing the policies of foreign governments without resort to overt diplomatic threats or military action—and the academic community was eager to advise the government about these opportunities. America's leading universities, most notably MIT, Harvard, and Columbia, undertook a number of government-sponsored psychological-warfare projects. Among the most important proponents of political warfare were Walt W. Rostow, Henry Kissinger, McGeorge Bundy, and Nelson Rockefeller.[83] Political warfare played a crucial role in stabilizing Western Europe during 1947 and 1948, and may have saved Italy altogether from falling into the Soviets' grasp. Therefore it was neither unusual nor surprising that U.S. policymakers—including

Kennan—would be enthusiastic about political warfare, particularly if it could resolve the cold war peacefully. The key, he would write, was to keep "the situation flexible and to make possible the liberation of the satellite countries in ways which do not create any unanswerable challenge to Soviet prestige." Political warfare offered the most propitious method.[84]

If American policy were to succeed, it was critical that the administration develop a non-provocative method to liberate the satellite states. "Finlandization" notwithstanding, the only other acknowledged possibility was the potential influence of a united and reformed Germany. In October 1949, Kennan and Robert Tufts suggested to Secretary of State Dean Acheson that newly independent Eastern European states could fall under the sway of a reunited and reconstructed Germany.[85] Germany would represent "an independent third force" between the Soviets and the United States, offering the satellite states a "place to go without going over to the United States."[86] Aside from this vague and somewhat perplexing suggestion, Kennan does not offer either in PPS 38 or elsewhere an unambiguous answer to this crucial dilemma. No other options were discussed until he realized the full impact of the Tito-Stalin break.

Scholars have long considered the Truman administration's support for Tito a logical extension of Kennan's policy.[87] In fact, the opportunity presented by Titoism was different from Kennan's original conception of liberation. Whereas Kennan hoped that stable state-to-state relations would continue to exist between a liberated Eastern Europe and the Soviet Union, Tito's defiance of Stalin's authority resulted in a fundamental break of party-to-party and state-to-state relations, producing a grave challenge to Soviet prestige and authority. Kennan fully recognized the strains that the Soviet-Yugoslav break placed on the Soviet bloc and the opportunities it presented the United States for exploitation. Consequently, Kennan abandoned the Finnish model of Soviet–Eastern Europe relations for a third variant: the liberation of communist nations from Soviet domination. Yet, regardless of the opportunity, Kennan did not believe that liberation would long succeed if the United States failed to transform Soviet national security policy as well.

Alteration of Soviet Concepts of International Affairs

Kennan understood the risks that accompanied any effort to undermine Soviet power in Eastern Europe. "We cannot be sure," he observed, "that at some point in this process the Russians will not choose to resort to violence of some sort: i.e., to forms of military re-occupation or possibly even major war, to prevent such a process from being carried to completion."[88] It was important, therefore, that the United States radically shift Soviet foreign policy to accept inclusion in a world where Eastern Europe was not under its absolute domination and international revolution no longer its chief goal.

Again, Kennan does not explain how to accomplish this transformation. He merely argues that the key to altering Soviet foreign relations was through power, not logic. He admits that:

> There is no reasonable prospect that we will ever be able to alter the basic political psychology of the men now in power in the Soviet Union. The malevolent character of their outlook . . . their repudiation of the possibility of permanent peaceful collaboration, their belief in the inevitability of the eventual destruction of the one world by the other: these things must remain, if only for the simple reason that the Soviet leaders are convinced that their system will not stand comparison with the civilization of the West and that it will never be secure until the example of a prosperous and powerful western civilization has been physically obliterated and its memory discredited.[89]

America's objective was to develop a strategic policy and create conditions that would make clear to the Kremlin what actions would and would not be to their advantage—and compel them to make the necessary changes. The focus of this strategy was to discredit communist ideology and to force the Soviet Union to publicly accept stable relations with the West, regardless of the potential domestic ramifications. Kennan argued that a similar modification in Soviet policy had taken place during World War II; it did nto last long enough, however, to have an enduring effect on the postwar policies of the Soviet Union.[90]

If the United States could establish "analogous situations" and maintain them for a longer period, "then they might have a permanent modifying effect on the outlook and habits of Soviet power." The generational changes Kennan observed in "The Sources of Soviet Conduct" played an essential role in this strategy. Kennan believed that a significant turnover in party leadership would soon occur, most likely with the death of Stalin. If the United States could coerce the Soviet leadership to transform its foreign policy from confrontation to accommodation before this changeover, the next generation of leaders might adopt the new framework as the Soviet Union's rightful foreign policy. Such a transformation might end the ideological divide between the Soviet Union and the West without global war and reduce U.S.-Soviet differences to "what might be considered normal dimensions."[91] Kennan stressed, however, that he was not calling for the overthrow of the Soviet regime. Focusing American efforts on toppling the Soviet government, he warned, would lead to the conclusion that "our objective with respect to the Soviet Union is eventual war," since "it could be argued that this is in turn an objective unrealizable by means short of war."[92]

While his position seems unambiguous, Kennan's thinking on this matter actually was far more nuanced. We have seen that Kennan understood the potential for a communist collapse in the USSR and believed that the United States should try to eliminate "concepts inconsistent with world peace and stability regardless of the impact on the internal stability of the Soviet regime." Furthermore, he stressed that it was not the responsibility of the United States:

> to calculate the internal developments to which the adoption of such concepts might lead in another country, nor need we feel that we have any responsibility for those developments. If the Soviet leaders find the growing prevalence of a more enlightened concept of international relations to be inconsistent with the maintenance of their internal power in Russia, that is their responsibility, not ours. We are entitled to let the chips fall where they may in terms of internal developments.[93]

By twisting the argument as such, Kennan could maintain that while it was not the *objective* of U.S. policy to overthrow the Soviet government, this might well be the *consequence* of the strategy. This begs the question of what the difference is between a policy unambiguously designed to overthrow the Soviet government and a policy which it is understood may cause the collapse of Soviet power but is not explicitly intended to do so. A fine line separated Kennan's strategy from outright support for revolution. This issue was not merely a matter of semantics, but would play an important role in later debates concerning the intent and parameters of U.S. cold war objectives.

The Policy Established

Kennan sent "U.S. Objectives towards Russia" to Lovett on 18 August. Lovett immediately approved the document and transmitted it to the NSC, where it was denoted as NSC 20/1 and given to the NSC Staff for consideration in the formulation of the NSC 20 series. The next day Max Bishop sent copies of the draft to Charles Bohlen and John Hickerson for review.[94]

While discussion of Kennan's paper proceeded, the State Department still needed to respond to Forrestal's request for political guidance in preparing the 1950 defense budget. Therefore, on 24 August Kennan asked Admiral Souers to submit PPS 33 to the NSC in addition to NSC 20/1.[95] On the 25th, PPS 33 officially became part of the NSC 20 series as NSC 20/2.[96]

In accordance with Forrestal's earlier request, the NSC Staff combined both NSC 20/1 and NSC 20/2 into one overall statement, a move that Kennan strongly opposed on the grounds that the topic was far too broad for one paper. "If it is really desired that a paper be written which would attempt to set forth the bases of U.S. foreign policy from the standpoint of national security," Kennan informed Lovett, "I should prefer to sit down . . . and draft another paper on this subject."[97]

Meanwhile, the various State Department offices submitted their appraisals.[98] Paul Nitze, then of the Treasury Department, considered the draft "an excellent presentation of the situation" and strongly supported its adoption as national policy.[99] The Bureau of Near Eastern Affairs also gave its concurrence.[100] John Hickerson, the director of the Office of European Affairs (EUR), and Sam Reber, also of EUR, offered the only significant dissent. While stating that he was in "general accord with the conclusions contained in the NSC 20 series," Hickerson expressed serious reservations that the United States might not be able to change Soviet national security policy without the removal of the regime. Hickerson asked, "Can we seriously expect such a change in a Communist regime?"

> Any such change obviously would be a change in tactics and not a change in their dogma. I raise the question therefore of whether this statement as it stands is not tantamount to saying that we want to seek as an objective the substitution of another form of government for the Communist regime in Russia.[101]

Reber concurred, expressing "considerable skepticism in U.S. ability to modify Soviet behavior." While largely disregarded at the time, the fear that no real change in Soviet policy could occur absent a change of regime would become the basis for Charles Bohlen's repudiation of Kennan's strategy in 1952.[102]

By late October, concern was beginning to mount within the Policy Planning Staff over certain aspects of the emerging policy statement. George Butler warned Kennan that the draft did not "bring out clearly your idea that the basic Soviet objective and the most dangerous threat is political rather than military domination" and that it overstated Soviet potential capabilities without adequately factoring in the challenges and vulnerabilities facing the Soviet government.[103] Kennan, however, was already struggling with the NSC Staff over their proposed revisions. Just before the draft's final submission to the NSC, Max Bishop wrote Kennan assuring him that the staff had "taken care of practically all of the points raised in your notes on the earlier draft."[104] While the other staff members still resisted some of the wordings that Kennan proposed, Bishop felt that for the most part he had been successful in "getting them to accept the basic ideas you wanted to put across."[105]

After reviewing both Kennan's original draft and that produced by the NSC Staff, Carlisle Humelsine, director of the Executive Secretariat at the State Department, assured Kennan that only a few minor differences existed.[106] By the end of November, the NSC draft was ready to present to the National Security Council, where it was approved as NSC 20/4 on 23 November and signed by President Truman the next day.

Many historians significantly underrate the importance of NSC 20/4.[107] NSC 20/4 was in fact the definitive statement of U.S. objectives in the cold war and the document to which all subsequent Truman administration studies would refer for guidance. Contrary to much scholarship, NSC 68 would reaffirm—not supplant—the policy objectives elaborated in the document.[108] Five years later, Robert Cutler, the special assistant for national security affairs in the Eisenhower administration, reviewing the Truman administration's national security policy, pointed to NSC 20/4—not NSC 68—as its definitive policy statement.[109]

NSC 20/4 stressed that Eurasia must not fall into the hands of hostile powers, and accepted Kennan's argument that the Soviets sought political rather than military aggrandizement. The document focused, however, on the steps necessary to eliminate the Soviet threat altogether. NSC 20/4 committed the United States to a struggle against the Soviet Union "using all methods short of war," to reduce "the power and influence of the USSR to limits which no longer constitute a threat to the peace, national independence and stability of the world family of nations," while compelling a "basic change in the conduct of international relations by the government in power in Russia, to conform with the purposes and principles set forth in the UN charter."[110] These objectives were identical to those developed by Kennan in "U.S. Objectives towards Russia."

The policy aimed for the independence of Eastern Europe, the revival of nationalist sentiments amongst the peoples of the USSR, abandonment of Kremlin efforts to subdue the non-Soviet world, and the development of "situations" which would "compel" the Kremlin leadership to fundamentally alter its national security policy.[111] The paper demonstrated that American strategists believed the cold war could be resolved only with dramatic concessions on the part of the Soviets, up to and including the abandonment of their core national security beliefs. Finally, given American superiority in the overall strategic balance of power, the administration specified no date by which to achieve these objectives. We shall see that the development of Soviet atomic weapons would fundamentally change this calculation and lead to a vast expansion of American military capabilities and political-warfare efforts—not to change the objectives of NSC 20/4, but to ensure their achievement.

Part Three: The Policy Implemented

Yugoslavia: The First Defection

The June 1948 break between Tito and Stalin introduced the possibility of communist nationalism within Eastern Europe and thus had a profound influence on Kennan's formulation of U.S. national security policy. Previously, most observers considered it highly unlikely that Soviet-supported communist leaders could act in defiance of Stalin and survive. Tito's success offered an opportunity to the nascent American political warfare establishment.

The fact that Tito would break with Stalin was itself quite a surprise. Kennan best expressed the opinion of the U.S. government when he characterized Tito as nothing more than "a bird dog which has been so well trained that it has been taught to heel and no longer go on the leash."[112] The split between the two communist nations came as a complete shock, although the American *chargé d'affaires* in Belgrade, John M. Cabot, warned that the Yugoslavs "might not always follow Russian instructions."[113] The State Department continued to ignore embassy warnings of a potential split as late as June 1948.[114] It was not until 28 June, when the Cominform angrily denounced and expelled the Yugoslav Communist Party, that the State Department realized that a rupture existed within the communist world.[115]

Kennan immediately prepared an analysis of the situation and on 30 June presented the Policy Planning Staff with a document which would "guide American policy into 1949."[116] Under Secretary of State Lovett immediately gave his approval and submitted the policy paper for NSC discussion.

Kennan recognized that the Tito-Stalin break had created a new set of concerns for U.S. foreign policy. Although he warned that it would be an "undignified error" for the West to consider Tito a "friend" just because of his defiant stance, Kennan argued that the break was significant because:

> A new factor of fundamental and profound significance has been introduced into the communist movement by the demonstration that the Kremlin can be successfully defied by one of its own minions. By this act the aura of mystical omnipotence and infallibility which has surrounded the Kremlin power has been broken. The possibility of defection from Moscow, which has heretofore been unthinkable for foreign communist leaders, will from now on be present in one form or another in the mind of every one of them.[117]

Kennan warned that the administration must approach this opportunity with caution and avoid two extremes. First, the West must not "beseech" Tito's favor lest the Soviets exploit this to "arouse feelings of disgust and revulsion throughout the international communist movement and among Tito's own followers." Such a policy would serve only to weaken Tito's support and make him susceptible to a Soviet-inspired coup d'état, devastating the possibilities for the liberation of Eastern Europe. "If, on the other hand," Kennan warned, "the Western world is too cold toward Tito . . . and repulses any advances that may be made toward closer association with the West, this will be used by the Moscow communists as proof that foreign communists have no alternative but to stay with Moscow."[118]

Kennan favored a policy of moderation toward Yugoslavia, whereby the "United States [would] quietly hold open for Tito a door through which he might pass when he should choose to do so."[119] The United States would welcome Yugoslavia's independence; however, it would continue to recognize that the Yugoslavia's internal regime "continued to be one which is deeply distasteful to our people and that as long such a regime exists, Yugoslav-American relations can never take on quite the cordiality and intimacy which we would wish." If Yugoslavia sought closer ties with the West, the United States "would not stand in the way . . . provided Yugoslavia is willing to adopt a loyal and cooperative attitude in its international relationships."[120] This constituted the basis of an implicit international bargain between the West and Yugoslavia. The West would accept the Yugoslav regime and be willing to develop normal relations provided the Yugoslavs demonstrated an independent foreign policy. The onus rested with Tito; however, the backing the Yugoslav delegation provided the Soviets at the July Danubian Conference in Belgrade nearly cost him Western support.[121]

This show of unity was short-lived. By December 1948 the Soviets began a full-scale operation to force Tito from power. They initiated a powerful propaganda campaign denouncing the "Fascist Tito clique," amassed ground forces on the Yugoslav border, and declared an economic blockade, ending all supplies of raw materials while prohibiting trade with Cominform countries. These actions dispelled any doubts as to the reality of the rupture and the seriousness of Tito's plight.

Kennan urged the Truman administration to support Tito's regime more actively. In PPS 49 "Economic Relations between the United States and Yugoslavia," Kennan recommended a series of steps designed to ease U.S. economic restrictions against the country. He feared that a collapse of Tito's regime might crush the hopes of nationalist communists in the other satellite nations. He repeated that "it is in the obvious interests of the United States that 'Titoism' continue to exist as an erosive and disintegrating force operating within the Kremlin's power sphere."[122] Kennan opposed any attempts to force Tito to relax the police-state atmosphere within Yugoslavia for fear that this would serve only to undermine his internal control. "Much as we may dislike him," Kennan explained, "Tito is presently performing brilliantly in our interests in leading successfully and effectively the attack from within the communist family on Soviet imperialism. Tito in being is perhaps our most precious asset in the struggle to contain and weaken Russian expansion. He must be allowed to prove on his own communist terms that an East European country can secede from Moscow's control and still succeed."[123]

This did not mean that the United States would cease its opposition to continued Yugoslav support for other communist insurgencies. U.S. policy toward Yugoslavia had to juggle between providing Tito enough aid to prevent the collapse of his regime and continuing to apply sufficient pressure to force him to abandon his assistance to the Greek guerrillas. By late 1949 it seemed that this juggling act had succeeded. Tito retained power despite a coup attempt, the Yugoslav foreign ministry began to publicly oppose the USSR, and the border between Yugoslavia and Greece was closed, dealing a serious blow to the hopes of the Greek communists.[124]

Yugoslavia's stabilization convinced the Truman administration that it was possible to undermine Soviet power in Eastern Europe. On 1 March 1949, the Policy Planning Staff met with American ambassadors from Eastern Europe and the Soviet Union and representatives from the State Department's Eastern European division to prepare a general policy statement for Eastern Europe. George Kennan stated that the purpose of the meeting was "to determine what are the weak spots on which to hammer relentlessly and also to determine whether we want in the first instance some form of Titoism." Former ambassador to the Soviet Union Walter Bedell Smith argued that the Russians greatly feared Titoism. Smith strongly supported fostering Titoism in the other satellite nations, contending that "the United States does not fear communism if it is not controlled by Moscow and not committed to aggression."[125] While many shared Smith's sentiments, others expressed the concern that the world community might misinterpret U.S. support for nationalist communist forces as general approval for communist regimes. The session ended with agreement that while the short-term goal of U.S. policy was the creation of non-Stalinist regimes, the ultimate goal of U.S. policy remained the liberation of the satellites altogether.

Kennan agreed that the encouragement of other nationalist communist leaders was the most logical first step in rolling back Soviet power. He told Acheson that he did not see "any possibility of a popular revolt in the eastern satellites," but believed that the real tensions existed for the present satellite leaders, who "are terribly worried about their relationship to Moscow."[126] The "germ of Titoism is growing," he offered; "no one speaks of it but it is in everyone's mind."[127] Kennan speculated that the subject "may be taboo even in the Politburo itself." He felt that "Stalin may mistrust everyone now and that it is too awkward a subject to be discussed dispassionately and thoroughly." "It may very well be," he concluded, "that the natural evolution that takes place in totalitarian states kills the youthful vitality which gave birth to it, and thereby makes it impossible later to handle effectively such problems as Tito."[128]

Increasing evidence of inter-party conflict between the Soviets and Poland, Bulgaria, and Albania made those nations the most likely to follow the Yugoslavs' path. Kennan was particularly intrigued by indications of a break between the Polish leadership and Moscow: the absence of a Polish representative at Stalin's birthday celebration, the lengthy meetings between the top three leaders of the Polish Communist Party and Soviet representatives, and the ascension of Soviet Marshal K. K. Rokossovskii to Polish minister of defense.[129] This, he explained, meant that a power struggle was taking place at the top of the Polish party, a struggle that the United States could influence through the "judicious use of covert operations applied at the appropriate time."[130]

Robert Joyce and John Paton Davies wrote a new Policy Planning Staff paper outlining U.S. policy toward the region.[131] Both men worked throughout the summer of 1949 and on 25 August submitted PPS 59 "United States Policy toward the Soviet Satellite States in Eastern Europe" for review by the S/P.[132] The document recapitulated many of the points made at the March staff meeting. Davies and Joyce emphasized the need to intensify efforts to reduce and eliminate "dominant Soviet influence in the satellite states of Albania, Bulgaria, Czechoslovakia, Hungary, Poland, and Rumania."[133] By themselves, these states were "of secondary importance;"[134] the primary threat posed by the Soviet occupation was their use as a staging ground for a Soviet invasion of Western Europe. By reducing Soviet control over these countries, the United States could ameliorate the threat to its European allies.

The report echoed the conclusion of the Policy Planning Staff meeting that supplanting Stalinist control with "schismatic communist regimes" was a necessary first step toward the elimination of Soviet power in Eastern Europe. Joyce and Davies added a new wrinkle to the argument, however. While the ultimate eradication of communism remained the clear preference, they maintained (incorrectly) that only Czechoslovakia had any experience with democracy, while the rest had long histories of authoritarian rule.[135] Thus, the intermediate policy of eliminating Soviet domination without necessarily overturning the communist regimes would alleviate some of the oppression suffered by the peoples of Eastern Europe.

It was one thing to argue that the creation of nationalist regimes was an important first step in achieving U.S. goals. It was quite another, however, for the two staff members to explain how this could be accomplished. Their assessment of Tito's successful break with Stalin highlighted a crucial problem with the whole enterprise: except for Yugoslavia, the Soviet Army had established all the other satellite regimes, and until these occupations ended it would be difficult (if not impossible) for nationalist forces to come to power. Tito had a loyal army, secret police, and party apparatus that he could rely upon to maintain power against Stalinist revanchism—instruments possessed by no other Eastern European leader. Nevertheless, Kennan questioned whether "an outfit as suspicious of itself as is Communist Russia [can] maintain control of a number of states for any length of time."[136]

Therefore, while one might presume that a step-by-step approach to weaning the Eastern Europeans away from the Soviets could succeed, as a practical matter it would be next to impossible so long as the Soviet Army remained in occupation. It was for this reason in particular that Charles Bohlen did not consider the prospects for further Titoist heresies promising. Unlike Kennan, who believed that the possibility existed for a Polish-Soviet break along the Yugoslav lines, Bohlen argued the reverse, that the Soviets were in the process of cementing their control over the satellite leadership and "don't care how tough they have to be to accomplish that purpose."[137] He contended that given Poland's strategic importance throughout Soviet history, Stalin and the rest of the Soviet leadership would never let Poland go. "They don't intend to pamper the Poles," he pointed out, "or stand for any nonsense from them, and they want the Poles to know that." The same held true for the rest of Eastern Europe.[138]

Despite this obvious dilemma, a conference of U.S. chiefs of mission to Eastern Europe unanimously endorsed the conclusions of the report.[139] The chiefs all recognized the distinct position of Yugoslavia within the communist world and agreed with Bohlen that "there was no prospect at this juncture of a successful attempt to emulate Tito's actions."[140] Yet the replacement of subservient Eastern European regimes with autonomous nationalist communist regimes seemed a logical interim step until such time that the establishment of true democratic regimes was possible. The chiefs agreed that economic pressures coupled with the proper use of the Voice of America and Radio Free Europe were the most readily available weapons to undermine Soviet power in Eastern Europe. A VOA-RFE campaign emphasizing the relative freedom of Yugoslavia and the economic benefits the Yugoslavs had gained since their liberation from Stalinist control—compared with the servile status and economic depravation of the rest of Eastern Europe—would be the most effective method to stimulate nationalist forces and to pressure the satellite governments into weaning themselves from total Soviet control.

In practice, the distinction between nationalist communism and democratic revolution in the satellite states was more apparent than real. As Bohlen pointed out, the Soviets considered the loss of a satellite state to Titoism at least as unacceptable as the loss of a satellite state to democratic revolution. In fact, the Kremlin might have considered Titoism even more threatening since Titoism challenged its leadership of the world communist movement while a democratic revolution would not represent such a threat. Kennan best described this problem by comparing the Communist Party and the papacy. "For the communists, as for the Pope," he argued, "there is no way of dealing with heretics other than by excommunication—your whole ideology falls apart if you permit to exist in the fold heretics who attack it. The Titoists seem to have discovered this weakness in the Communist armor."[141]

The push for Titoist heresies throughout the East bloc was not an evolutionary approach to the retraction of Soviet power, but instead an attempt to foment communist-led anti-Soviet uprisings throughout the region. Titoism seemed to be the most promising method for the United States to break up the Soviet bloc, since nationalist communist leaders did exist and were more likely to possess the necessary strength to break from Stalin's embrace than democratic revolutionaries. This, however, highlighted an incongruity within Kennan's thinking, as it was a fundamental premise of NSC 20/1 that the United States expel Soviet power from Eastern Europe without damaging Russian prestige. The reaction of the world community certainly demonstrated that the Tito-Stalin break threatened Soviet prestige at both party *and* state level. How could the Soviets accept so many challenges to their authority, as Kennan believed was occurring, without considering them a diminution of their supremacy within Eastern Europe?[142]

Although President Truman personally approved NSC 58/2 on 21 December 1949, the administration did not consider the document to be a significant policy paper. The 1949–1951 purges of suspected nationalist leaders throughout Eastern Europe provided convincing evidence that the Soviets would not tolerate a nationalistic communist regime any more than they would tolerate a non-communist regime. By 1951, the extent of these purges forced Under Secretary of State James Webb to conclude that:

> Events since the winter of 1949 lead to the conclusion that the USSR will react as strongly to the prospect of the emergence of Titoist regimes in the satellite nations as it will to the direct threat of the creation of non-communist regimes. There would seem no apparent purpose to be served, therefore, in limiting United States policies to the promotion of schismatic communist regimes as an interim objective in the satellite area.[143]

A 1952 NSC Senior Staff review of U.S. policy toward Yugoslavia concluded as well that "the encouragement of communist heresy in the satellites, as an intermediate stage between Kremlin domination and democratic freedom, had been proven to be an unrewarding and unrealistic policy." Charles Bohlen was in complete agreement with the Senior Staff's conclusion and called for a reexamination of NSC 58/2.[144] It did not matter that the administration would not complete this reexamination, as world events demanding new policies quickly overtook NSC 58/2. Within a few months NSC 68 and later NSC 10/5 would replace NSC 58/2 as de facto policy guidance toward Eastern Europe, followed shortly thereafter by a host of new NSC directives which would make clear that engendering communist heresy would no longer be the sine qua non of U.S. policy. These new directives demanded increasingly aggressive strategies to achieve U.S. objectives in Eastern Europe, efforts that would seek to destabilize the communist structures of power themselves.

Albania: The First Attempt at Rollback

One alternative to Titoism was the infiltration of Eastern European countries with small-scale paramilitary forces. President Truman's approval of NSC 10/2 gave the OPC the green light to develop underground resistance forces to destabilize the satellite states of Eastern Europe. The communist regime of Albania's Enver Hoxha provided the first prime target of opportunity for Western paramilitary action. Plausible deniability, however, would significantly restrain the potential use of this option.

Both the United States and Great Britain had employed paramilitary forces to assist underground resistance movements in occupied Europe during World War II. These activities included the insertion of trained commandos who would join the native resistance forces and train them to sabotage vital military, political, and economic targets. The United States and Great Britain hoped to modify this concept for use in the cold war; however, plausible deniability drastically reduced the extent of possible Western assistance to these movements behind the Iron Curtain. For starters, both governments refused to insert Western agents to assist in developing underground resistance groups, considering their possible capture a disaster; consequently, both nations agreed to infiltrate units composed solely of refugees trained by Western intelligence. To maintain the clandestine nature of these operations, even the training programs had to be circumscribed; hence the refugee commando units inserted into Albania were seldom fully prepared for their arduous missions.[145]

Nevertheless, the East bloc refugees were highly motivated and the Truman administration had little difficulty in recruiting volunteers. In fact, many refugees had spent the war fighting not only the Nazis but also the Soviet Union as part of underground resistance movements that had emerged in the aftermath of the German invasion of the USSR. The German occupations of the Baltic nations, Ukraine, Byelorussia, and large swaths of Russia gave rise to nationalist—though often fascist—movements that did not immediately cease operations after the end of World War II. According to the Russian historian Dmitri Volkogonov, the western regions of the USSR were "engulfed in partisan warfare which threatened to spread to the surrounding territory. . . . After the expulsion of German forces from the western Ukraine and the Baltic region, armed detachments carried on the fight against the Soviet regime. On several occasions, Stalin ordered Beria to finish off the 'outlaws in the shortest possible time,' but he could not imagine that it would continue for a full five years after the end of the war, most vigorously in the western Ukraine."[146]

The United States was fully abreast of the Kremlin's problems. The investigative journalists Christopher Simpson, John Loftus, and Mark Aarons demonstrate that with the onset of the cold war the American government became especially interested in using émigrés against the Soviet Union.[147] While it was beyond the West's ability to aid them in their military struggle against Stalin, American and British intelligence services actively participated in helping thousands of Soviet bloc refugees to escape and, consequently, to be used in clandestine Western operations. Many émigrés worked for Radio Free Europe and Radio Liberation; others served as U.S.

intelligence agents and parachuted into their home countries to spy for the United States.[148]

The most famous paramilitary operation occurred in Albania.[149] British and American planners considered Albania, wedged between Greece and Yugoslavia, susceptible to outside intervention and a possible candidate for rollback. The British launched the first destabilization campaign in early 1946. Its aim was to support a royalist anti-communist group in central Albania and organize a guerrilla movement that would gain enough popular support to start a civil war and overthrow the Hoxha regime. The British dropped a few émigré units into Albania in 1947, but the main action did not start until 1949 after the British had received the approval of President Truman and began to coordinate their efforts with the OPC.[150]

For two years from the spring of 1949, the cold war allies infiltrated team after team of "free" Albanians by air, sea, and land. They were recruited in Germany, Italy, Greece, and Egypt under the umbrella of the "Committee of Free Albanians," ostensibly organized by the bodyguards of Albania's exiled King Zog. Almost every mission failed, however. Teams sent across the border from Greece ran into police ambushes. Police met teams landing from rubber craft at the beach. Albanian troops somehow knew the location of planned parachute drops and awaited the insurgents. Often the émigrés escaped capture only because the transport plane missed its drop zone. A few radio operators who did seem to establish a toehold were later discovered to be under the control of the Albanian secret police.[151] It was clear to Western intelligence that communist agents had infiltrated the Albanian émigré movement. What Western intelligence did not know at the time was that Britain's Kim Philby also informed Soviet intelligence of the operation. Assigned to the British Secret Intelligence Service in Washington, Philby acted as liaison between British intelligence and the Federal Bureau of Investigation, CIA, and OPC. Philby quickly gained the confidence of Washington's intelligence elite, including the likes of James Jesus Angleton, the soon to be famous CIA counterintelligence taskmaster, and thus gained access to the highest secrets, including details about the Albania mission.[152] Consequently, these operations were doomed even before they began.

Despite these failures the United States continued to try to overthrow the Hoxha regime, largely inthe belief that Albania's proximity to Western influence made it a ripe target of action. Furthermore, the Korean War, the rise of McCarthyism, and growing popular discontent with the Truman administration's foreign policy created a political climate that required some breakthrough. Finally, these operations cost the United States little, and exposed only the Albanians to any danger. The CIA eventually ceased these efforts in 1954 partly because of the public embarrassment caused by the Albanian government's show trial of several captured guerrilla leaders and partly because of the realization that Albania was of little significance to the Soviets' hold on Eastern Europe.[153]

Yet the early failures to topple Hoxha pointed out the significant problems with the West's approach, namely that the limits imposed to maintain plausible deniability undermined covert efforts behind the Iron Curtain. When the Truman administration embarked on the use of covert action in the cold war, it considered plausible deniability an essential component of any operation. Consequently, U.S. support had to be limited to ensure that if an operation were uncovered, the foreign government under attack could not link it with the United States. Therefore, the guerrilla units that crossed into Albania comprised teams of a handful of individuals who received only a modicum of training, yet were charged with contacting and recruiting members of their own villages much as teams under British direction did during World War II. The same villagers recalled, however, that British officers normally accompanied these paramilitary units and that the Royal Air Force flew missions supplying them with food, arms, and money. The absence of British and American advisors caused sympathetic Albanians to doubt whether their recently returned compatriots did indeed serve under Western leadership.[154] They would not risk their lives unless they knew that the British and Americans would return. For the Americans and the British to return, however, both nations would have had to risk the capture of their agents and the loss of plausible deniability. It was clear that the type of guerrilla forces necessary to inspire the native populations to open rebellion required significant—and undeniable—American support. CIA director Walter Bedell Smith brought this problem to the administration's attention in 1951 when he warned that "somewhere in the process it becomes pointless to attempt to deceive the enemy on U.S. participation, just as it would have been naïve for the USSR to expect the U.S. to believe it had no part in supporting and directing the Greek Communist guerrilla operations."[155] Consequently, American policymakers considered it extremely dangerous for Western intelligence agencies to engage in such efforts during peacetime.

Yet these were certainly legitimate activities during times of war and by 1950 American covert policy shifted toward this posture. Guerrilla forces behind the Iron Curtain controlled by the OPC would support the Defense Department's preparations to retard a Soviet military advance in Europe.[156] Meanwhile, the State Department began preparation of a new type of covert strategy, one that could both maintain plausible deniability and destabilize the Soviet regime.

In the five years since the end of World War II the United States had made considerable progress in shifting its policies from war to cold war. The Truman administration had began the reconstruction of Western Europe, successfully defended it from the massive Soviet efforts to destabilize the region, and created a new bureaucracy to oversee the conflict. It also began to attack Soviet power behind the Iron Curtain, first by exploiting the rift between the Kremlin and Yugoslav leader Tito, then by attempting to foment insurrection within Albania.

These early attempts to roll back Soviet power in Eastern Europe were not as successful, however, as the psychological-warfare campaigns in Western Europe. Although Tito survived all Soviet attempts to oust him from power and return Yugoslavia to the Stalinist fold, the Yugoslavian situation was unique and could not be replicated elsewhere in Eastern Europe. Furthermore, Stalin's brutal suppression of other nationalist-leaning communist authorities demonstrated that he would do everything in his power to prevent further Titoist heresies. The failure to incite an uprising in Albania also exposed the weakness of peacetime exploitation of paramilitary forces. What the administration needed was a new approach to undermining Soviet power, an approach that would enable the United States to attack the Soviet Union directly, destabilize its administrative apparatus, and undermine its ability to suppress revolt.

The events of 29 August 1949 accelerated this need. The development of atomic weapons by the Soviet Union and its likely ability to strike the continental United States fundamentally transformed the strategic environment of the cold war. The Soviet Union would now become a truly global adversary with the capability to destroy the bastion of the West—the economic power of the United States. The cold war had entered a new phase; it was now apparent that the very survival of the United States might depend on its ability to eliminate the Soviet threat.

[2]

Intensifying the Offensive: Atomic Weapons, Strategic Uncertainty, and NSC 68, 1950–1951

The explosion of the Soviet Union's first atomic bomb on 29 August 1949 shattered the strategic foundation of NSC 20/4 and led directly to an extensive reevaluation of the Truman administration's national security strategy. An analysis prepared at George Kennan's behest concluded that by 1954 the USSR would possess the nuclear capability to attack and destroy the American mobilization potential and prevent U.S. retaliation in kind.[1] The Truman administration's national security planners feared that the Kremlin would soon acquire the power to disarm the United States, occupy Western Europe and the Middle East, and destroy the coalescing international economic system.

American national security policy was in crisis. The growing Soviet first-strike capability (as perceived by administration planners in 1950) grievously threatened U.S. strategic ambitions and policy objectives.[2] President Truman's key advisors recognized that global war during a period of American strategic vulnerability would be so disastrous that they needed to reconsider any policy that risked conflict—particularly one aimed at coercing the Soviet regime into abandoning its international ambitions. This was one of the most critical issues facing the new Policy Planning Staff director Paul Nitze and a key inspiration for NSC 68.

Many cold war scholars argue that NSC 68 led to a fundamental restatement of American cold war policy, expanded American vital interests beyond capabilities, and committed the United States to endless limited warfare along the Eurasian periphery.[3] Others contend that NSC 68 changed Truman administration policy from defensive containment to rollback.[4] NSC 68 neither expanded the scope of U.S. objectives nor changed American strategy from defensive containment to rollback. In fact, it reaffirmed the already offensive objectives of NSC 20/4 but stressed that significantly greater efforts were needed to achieve them in light of the threat of global war.[5]

Yet in reaffirming existing cold war policy, NSC 68 fundamentally altered two of George Kennan's strategic assumptions: that the mobilization base would continue to act as a deterrent to Soviet military aggression and that no peak period of danger existed which could threaten the achievement of American objectives. Threat of a Soviet nuclear attack against the continental United States had ended America's long-standing position as the wartime arsenal of democracy; henceforth, national security planners would consider forces-in-being the most important determinant of military strength.[6] Given the concentration of American military and economic targets, officials believed that the growing Soviet stockpile would make a war-winning strike possible, meaning that a peak period of danger might become a reality in 1954. If America sought to roll back Soviet power and peacefully transform the strategic basis of Russian policy it had to rebuild its military capabilities and intensify its efforts at developing more effective psychological-warfare strategies to subvert communist power while maintaining plausible deniability. Aided by the shock of the Korean War, the Truman administration would embark on a fourfold rise in defense spending, a substantial increase in U.S. covert activity, and the creation of the Psychological Strategy Board to coordinate these efforts.

Part One: NSC 68 and the Implications of the Soviet Atomic Threat

The First Estimates

Initially, administration planners did not view the Soviet atomic capability with great alarm. Its likely effect on world public opinion was their primary concern. Would a negative popular reaction in Europe force America's NATO allies into neutrality, or a similar reaction within the United States compel the administration to redouble efforts toward disarmament?[7] The State Department's Office of Intelligence Research prepared the first post-detonation analysis on 30 September 1949 and concluded that Soviet possession of the atomic bomb would not result in a realignment of the world balance of power, but might exacerbate existing international tensions.[8] Support for neutrality within the non-aligned countries and among some European nations might increase but not to a level threatening American policy. Simultaneously, OIR postulated that in some areas of Western Europe Soviet possession of the atomic bomb might actually spur greater defense collaboration with the United States.[9]

These intelligence analysts did not anticipate significant changes in either the military balance of power or Soviet international policy. America would retain its position of superiority until the Soviet atomic stockpile matched that of the United States in both warheads and delivery systems, which OIR felt would not occur until the distant future. As a result little change was expected in Soviet foreign policy other than increased efforts to brandish their new capability in order to undermine Western European support for NATO.[10]

Despite his agreement with the intelligence estimate, George Kennan believed that the growth rate of the Soviet atomic stockpile would determine the long-term viability of any analysis. There was little possibility of the State Department "accurately estimating Soviet intentions without regard to their capabilities," he surmised, "since the whole tempo and reach of United States foreign policy was obviously affected by the extent and reach of Soviet power."[11] Consequently, Kennan requested that the Joint Chiefs of Staff analyze the Soviet threat "assuming their possession of given numbers of the atom-bomb, e.g., 10, 50, 100, etc."[12]

Kennan had already developed misgivings about the possible impact of the USSR's atomic capability on U.S. security. He considered America's nuclear strength to be a "wasting asset" and believed the growing Soviet stockpile would soon nullify the ability of the United States to deter a Soviet conventional attack against Western Europe. "We are so behind the Russians in conventional armaments, and the attraction of the atomic bomb to strategic planners has been such," he warned Dean Acheson, "that we are in danger of finding our whole policy tied to the atom bomb."[13] Kennan concluded that the United States must wean itself from its strategic overreliance on nuclear weapons even if that "would require a state of semi-mobilization, involving some form of compulsory military service."[14] Along with greater defense preparations he recommended that the United States restart arms-control negotiations with the Soviets, including a public disavowal of developing the hydrogen bomb.[15] Paul Nitze, the new deputy director of the Policy Planning Staff and Kennan's eventual successor, agreed, contending that these arguments made "conventional armaments and their possession by Western European nations, as well as ourselves, all the more important." He further argued that an effective civilian defense program might reduce the public's fear of Soviet retaliation to an American atomic strike.[16] Nitze remained confident, however, that the likelihood "of a total war started deliberately by the Soviets is a tertiary risk."[17] Acheson was not averse to Kennan's proposals. He too felt that it might be possible to use the threat of an atomic arms race to start a series of negotiations that could provide the momentum necessary to overcome differences on other issues.[18] Acheson would never realize these opportunities in 1949, however, or at any time during his tenure as secretary of state, as he focused his attention and energies on the dramatic changes caused by the fall of China to Mao Tse-tung and the Korean War.

A new intelligence report disrupted the State Department's deliberations and transformed the administration's understanding of the Soviet atomic threat. On 20 January 1950, the Joint Chiefs of Staff issued Joint Intelligence Committee (JIC) report 502 "Implications of the Soviet Possession of Atomic Weapons." The conclusions of this report directly contradicted the September OIR estimate and profoundly altered the way officials within the U.S. government viewed the significance of the Soviet atomic capability.[19]

The new estimate made it abundantly clear to Acheson and his new Policy Planning Staff director Paul Nitze (who had replaced Kennan in January 1950) that an appropriate American response required a careful analysis of the new international environment. On 31 January 1950, President Truman authorized both Acheson and Secretary of Defense Louis Johnson:

> to undertake a reexamination of our objectives in peace and war and of the effect of these objectives on our strategic plans, in the light of the probable fission bomb capability and possible thermonuclear bomb capability of the Soviet Union.[20]

Acheson and Johnson immediately assembled a study group composed of members of the State Department Policy Planning Staff and the Department of Defense Joint Strategic Survey Committee, with Nitze serving as director of the State-Defense Team.[21] The study group also received outside assistance from a number of leading experts, including Robert Lovett, Robert Oppenheimer, Harvard president James Conant, and nuclear physicist Ernest O. Lawrence. On 29 March 1950, after nearly six weeks of work, the State-Defense Study Group circulated two reports, a long version entitled simply "State-Defense Staff Study" and a shorter "Report to the President." On the recommendation of the Joint Chiefs of Staff, President Truman also received the lengthy State-Defense study. That study would become NSC 68.

JIC 502 and the Growing Threat of War

The State-Defense Team immediately adopted the conclusions of JIC 502 and made them the foundation for the strategic analysis in NSC 68. This new estimate charged that the United States would face the possibility of total defeat in the aftermath of a Soviet surprise attack when the Soviet atomic stockpile grew to some two hundred weapons, transforming the administration's original attitude of mild disquiet into stunned disbelief.[22]

The JIC's estimate was a response to Kennan's request that the Joint Chiefs examine the impact of Soviet atomic capabilities according to various stockpile levels, "10, 50, 100, etc."[23] JIC 502 concluded that when the Soviet stockpile reached fifty deliverable atomic weapons [by mid-1951] the USSR would be able to destroy the national command center and some of the nation's largest cities, causing nearly one million casualties and significant delays in the mobilization of American industry.[24] The Soviet attacks would aim to neutralize the Strategic Air Command's most important installations, disrupt the planned strategic offensive, and destroy essential ports of embarkation for the overseas projection of American forces. Although the study reaffirmed the ability of the United States to recover and mobilize its military capabilities for war, its authors feared that the worldwide psychological effect of the attack would undermine NATO and even cause weaker U.S. allies to bandwagon in favor of the USSR.[25]

An attack during 1952 when the Soviets could deliver one hundred atomic bombs would cause substantial losses for American industry and U.S. atomic retaliatory capability. It would result in the "removal of United States opposition to the expansion of Soviet power in Europe and Asia" and a further weakening of the non-Soviet world's will to resist Soviet encroachments. Despite the enormity of the assault, however, the report contended that the "backbone of the nation's capacity for war production still would not be broken."[26]

Such would not be the case in 1954, when the JIC feared that the Soviets would have the capability to deliver two hundred nuclear warheads to the continental United States, giving them the ability to launch a decisive attack against both U.S. industrial potential and retaliatory capability. Such an attack would "delay indefinitely the industrial and military mobilization of the United States, Canada and the United Kingdom," reduce the total mobilization capacity of the United States by up to 50 percent—and by nearly 100 percent in vital strategic industries—and cause total casualties of more than ten million people in the United States alone. In short, by mid-1954 the Soviets might be able to defeat the United States in global war with one surprise nuclear attack, an event so devastating that the psychological impact on the rest of the world would virtually extinguish resistance to Soviet encroachment.[27]

The threat of a surprise atomic attack transformed the U.S.-Soviet strategic relationship, upsetting what in 1948 had been a stable balance of power based upon preponderant mobilization capabilities. A "tremendous military advantage would be gained," the study warned, "by the power that struck first and succeeded in carrying through an effective surprise attack." Not even the overwhelming superiority of the American nuclear stockpile could reduce the fear of a Soviet surprise attack. JIC 502 established a premise that, by 1952, would become the fundamental axiom of the surprise-attack school of thought in the United States. The study concluded that:

> Today the world power balance favors the Allies, because of the superior atomic weapon capability of the United States and the superior Allied eco-

> nomic potential for support of a major war. . . . The Soviet Union is now making and will continue to make aggressive use of time to . . . equalize the scales of power. To achieve this balance, it is not necessary that the Soviet Union have as many bombs as the United States, it is only necessary that it have sufficient bombs to inflict serious or critical damage to the United States and its Allies.[28]

"Sufficiency" and not "equality" had become the crucial factor in defining the balance of power in the nuclear age. The Soviet Union would possess a significant first-strike advantage over the United States when it developed the capability to destroy a specific set of economic and military targets, even though numerically the U.S. atomic stockpile would remain vastly superior. While this hypothesis was not central to JIC 502, it would become a central fixture of American strategic thought for the remainder of the decade.[29]

JIC 502 is one of the most important strategic studies ever produced. It demonstrated that for the first time since the early years of the republic a foreign power immediately and directly threatened the survival of the United States. Not even the fear of Eurasia's conquest by a single power equaled the danger posed by the new Soviet atomic capability. The vulnerability of America's mobilization base meant that its half-century wartime advantage over its Eurasian adversaries was at an end. No longer could the Truman administration rely upon the vast superiority of the U.S. mobilization potential as a deterrent to Soviet military aggression and as a rationale for a small peacetime military establishment. The atomic capability of the Soviet Union threatened to prevent the United States from reprising its role as the "arsenal of democracy" in global war; instead the United States would have to build substantial peacetime military forces to close this window of vulnerability, thus militarizing the cold war. JIC 502 forced a reassessment of the conclusion in NSC 20/2 that the United States would not have to base its military rationale on a year of maximum danger. Finally, the report created grave doubt whether—given the growing danger of war—a policy of subversion behind the Iron Curtain was in the national security interest of the United States.

Reactions to JIC 502

The Joint Chiefs of Staff viewed JIC 502 as vindication of their demands for a significant increase in military spending and immediately approved the study as its official position.[30] Both the Air Force and Army representatives to the Joint Ad Hoc Intelligence Committee concluded that the United States must assume that the Soviet Union would automatically initiate a military attack against the West once it possessed a sufficient stockpile. Only the Navy refused to commit itself to any definitive conclusions.[31]

The implications of the report, particularly its total refutation of the earlier OIR estimate, stunned both State Department and CIA analysts. Mose Harvey, the State Department's representative to the Joint Ad Hoc Intelligence Committee, declared that he and the rest of OIR were "struck—not to say dumbfounded—by the implication that with the placing of *a* number . . . of bombs on target in the U.S., U.S. power of retaliation in kind could be destroyed." Harvey and his staff declared that they simply could not believe the estimate was correct. It was inconceivable that the Soviet Union might soon have the military capability to defeat the United States with one decisive attack and without suffering retaliation.[32] Consequently, representatives from both the State Department and the CIA rejected the armed services' conclusion that the Soviets would automatically attack when they possessed a sufficient stockpile.

On 10 February, the CIA presented its rebuttal to JIC 502.[33] The agency agreed that the development of Soviet atomic weapons had altered the strategic balance of power. It asserted, however, that other military variables, in addition to the fundamental precepts of Leninist-Stalinist doctrine, indicated that its atomic capability would not change the willingness of the Soviet Union to initiate war deliberately. "It would be essential," the agency argued, for the Soviets to be "virtually certain of attaining surprise . . . virtually certain that effective U.S. retaliation could be prevented . . . [and] possess more effective means of delivery than the TU-4. The Soviets could be sure of none of these."[34] While the agency recognized that the risk of war would increase should the Soviet Union believe it could launch a decisive nuclear strike, it doubted that the USSR could safely arrive at such a conclusion. The report stressed that Soviet ideologists expected the USSR to emerge victorious from the cold war due to capitalism's ultimate collapse and not through global war. Taken together, the risk of war and capitalism's inherent weaknesses allowed the CIA to conclude that the atomic bomb did not substantially change the nature of the Soviet threat.

The service representatives and, surprisingly, even OIR harshly rejected the CIA's report. Air Force intelligence denounced the document as "dangerous as an intelligence basis for national policy." Furthermore, the CIA's calculations did not diminish the strategic dilemma posed by Soviet atomic capabilities. The Air Force accused the CIA of failing to appreciate:

> whether the acquisition of an atomic capability has provided the Soviet Union for the first time in history with a clear-cut capability that would enable them to win the war against the U.S.; and whether under conditions of atomic warfare, the lack of instantly available American military power vitiates the importance of the great American war *potential*.[35] (Emphasis in original)

Army intelligence agreed that extant Soviet capabilities were the most important consideration, insisted that the administration consider JIC 502 as the official estimate, and demanded that ORE 91-49 be withdrawn.[36]

The most surprising reaction came from OIR, whose representatives repudiated the report with the same vigor as the service departments. Mose Harvey characterized the CIA report as a "hodgepodge of argumentation based upon an incomplete reading of Russian history and Soviet doctrine as 'proof' that the USSR would never deliberately resort to war. This, however, was so faulty that refutation was automatic with even a cursory examination."[37] Harvey's dissent was not restricted to matters of ideology alone and included an admission that the State Department was itself becoming concerned with the implications of a potential Soviet first-strike capability. It had been easy for the State Department to contend that the Kremlin would not deliberately initiate war so long as the Soviet Union did not possess the capability to devastate the continental United States. Now that the Soviets possessed atomic weapons and the estimated capability to initiate a successful first strike against the United States by 1954, the foreign-policy community would have to take a more conservative approach in appraising the likelihood of war.

OIR maintained that there was no immediate risk that the Soviet Union would attack the West. The blockade of Berlin in addition to other provocative moves persuaded it, however, that the Soviet Union would not be deterred from employing all available means to achieve its objectives. Therefore, the most legitimate method to judge Soviet intentions was the "pragmatic test of whether or not such action would, at a given moment, appear advantageous to the Soviet Union."[38] Harvey concluded that:

> Prior to Soviet development of an atomic weapon, all evidence indicated that the preponderance of strength enjoyed by the United States in consequence of its over-all economic superiority and its atomic monopoly made unlikely a Soviet estimate that it would be to the advantage of the USSR to resort to military action. Soviet development of an atomic weapon may have decisively changed this situation, particularly if surprise employment of the weapon could sharply reduce retaliatory action or make it impossible.[39]

Due to the failure of ORE 91-49 to establish an acceptable intelligence estimate, the Joint Ad Hoc Intelligence Committee shelved discussion of Soviet political intentions and instead decided to pursue a truncated estimate highlighting the Soviet atomic threat. This effectively reduced the State Department and CIA to a secondary role on the committee panel since, as Harvey contended, OIR was "dependent on the services for an estimate of the *military* consequences" and was in "no position to challenge their expertise."[40] Yet by excising Soviet intentions from an analysis of Soviet capabilities the new estimate reshaped how the United States calculated the likelihood of war. Subsequently American national security planners would focus primarily on the threat posed by Soviet military capabilities and less on political calculations surrounding a decision to go to war.

The outcome of this effort was ORE 32-50 "The Effect of the Soviet Possession of Atomic Bombs on the Security of the United States." This report affirmed the conclusions of JIC 502, contending that Soviet atomic capabilities had raised the likelihood of war and placed the United States in "increasing jeopardy."[41] Its most important and far-reaching determination was that deterrence was not an automatic outcome of the presence of two nuclear stockpiles. The Joint Ad Hoc Intelligence Committee wrote that:

> With the continued development of the Soviet atomic stockpile and Soviet defense capabilities against atomic attack, the United States superiority in total numbers of atomic bombs will no longer in itself be a strong deterrent to war.[42]

The implications of this judgment appalled George Kennan. For the past several years, Kennan had argued that any estimate of potential Soviet actions would be meaningless without a discussion of *both* political intentions and military capabilities.[43] Only a few months earlier he had published an essay in the March 1950 issue of *Reader's Digest* contending that since Stalinist doctrine presaged communism's ultimate victory through the "the inner contradictions of the capitalist system" and not world war, the Soviet atomic bomb neither appreciably threatened U.S. security nor changed Soviet political calculations.[44]

Not surprisingly, Kennan considered the CIA's estimate "a thoughtful and generally competent appraisal of Soviet intentions and objectives" and expressed his "shock and outrage" that the State Department's analysts would reject the CIA's effort and attempt to replace it with "an inferior statement" without consulting either Charles Bohlen or himself. He complained to Bohlen that "if you and I know enough to advise the Secretary on such matters, we know enough to be consulted before the department gets opinions off the top of its head" and promised to raise the issue with W. Park Armstrong, Secretary Acheson's special assistant for intelligence.[45] Kennan waited until the Joint Ad Hoc Intelligence Committee produced ORE 32-50 and on 20 June wrote Armstrong a memo lambasting OIR for ignoring his views. He "flatly disagreed" with the committee's contention that U.S. atomic capabilities were susceptible to a Soviet nuclear strike. He argued that:

> Provided we keep our own atomic attack forces in a proper state of readiness and dispersal, which is not difficult to do, the damage we should be able to do in the Soviet Union is not affected by whether the Russians have bombs themselves or not. The bomb is not a defense against the bomb except in a very limited degree.[46]

Mose Harvey replied that he completely agreed with Kennan. "As individuals," he explained, "we in OIR continue to have as much personal faith as anyone else that this estimate [JIC 502] simply cannot be right." Yet he felt that OIR was in no position to disagree with the military's conclusion that an attack of two hundred atomic bombs upon the continental United States could destroy both American industry and U.S. retaliatory capability—meaning in essence that the atomic bomb "could be a defense against the bomb." He was not free to dismiss the JCS's position on such matters "simply based upon faith."[47]

Due to his consternation over JIC 502, Harvey sought out the opinions of higher authorities within the State Department when the report was first issued. Because Kennan was touring South America, he presented the JIC report to Paul Nitze, who agreed to discuss the matter with the military.[48] Kennan's disagreement with the JCS estimate was not shared by the Policy Planning Staff, however, which started its work on NSC 68 during the first week of February, roughly at the same time that the Joint Ad Hoc Intelligence Committee debates reached their climax.

Nitze's exposure to the JIC's estimate did not have the effect Harvey had desired. Instead of rejecting the document, Nitze and the Policy Planning Staff were profoundly affected by the prospect that a surprise Soviet attack could disrupt U.S. war mobilization and prevent atomic retaliation—so much so that they made this estimate the foundation of NSC 68. The effect was immediate: whereas Nitze had argued in December that the likelihood of general war was a "tertiary risk," by February he admitted that the possibility of war seemed "considerably greater than last fall."[49] Nitze's position had shifted so far that he now accepted the Air Force's contention that the Soviet Union might choose to achieve its international ambitions through military force. "For this reason," he argued, "there appears no reason to assume that the USSR will in the future necessarily make a sharp distinction between military 'aggression' and measures short of military aggression."[50]

Nitze and the Policy Planning Staff recognized the importance of this estimate to U.S. national security policy. Nitze had strongly supported Kennan's elucidation of U.S. national security objectives as well as his analysis that as long as the Soviet Union lacked the capability to launch a decisive attack against the North American industrial complex, it would not resort to war to achieve its objectives.[51] Consequently, the United States need not prepare for conflict by a specific date. This was now no longer the case.

NSC 68 was the product of this anxiety. Nitze and the State-Defense Team argued that the danger of military defeat immediately threatened Western security as well as America's continued efforts to liberate Eastern Europe, increase nationalist tensions within the USSR, and successfully transform Soviet national security doctrine as dictated by NSC 20/4. NSC 68 outlined four possible responses to this new threat. After dismissing a continuation of the status quo, isolationism, and preventive war, the Study Group argued that the only viable solution was to build a "preponderance of power," a combination of political, economic, and military strength such that the United States could deter Soviet expansionism, roll back Soviet power, and eliminate the Soviet threat without war. If war did occur, U.S. preponderance would enable the country to survive an initial Soviet strike and still have sufficient forces-in-being to defend its key commitments, namely Western Europe, Japan, and the Middle East, as it recovered and built the forces necessary for victory. Meanwhile the United States would develop the hydrogen bomb and escalate its political-warfare efforts to undermine the Soviet bloc.

Without a significant military buildup, the Soviet Union could launch a devastating nuclear strike on the United States, occupy Western Europe, and present the United States with what Policy Planning Staff member Robert Tufts would later call "reciprocal containment"—a geopolitical debacle whereby the Soviets expelled the United States from the Eurasian continent.[52] Only with a significant military buildup could the United States avoid this disaster and shield its intensified efforts to achieve its national security objectives.

The intensification of U.S. national security efforts under NSC 68 has led to the general misconception that the NSC directive supplanted George Kennan's analysis in NSC 20/4. Paul Nitze is criticized either for applying containment to regions of the world (most notably Southeast Asia) not considered vital to U.S. interests or for abandoning containment altogether and adopting a policy of rollback. Both views are incorrect. No policymaker from 1950, even the report's harshest critics, believed that NSC 68 ushered in a new national security policy. Nor would the Eisenhower administration view NSC 68 as a replacement of NSC 20/4. Nor for that matter did George Kennan in 1950 ever express a concern that the State-Defense Team had supplanted his policy objectives. In fact, unlike many important government officials, Kennan prepared no formal assessment of NSC 68. Given Kennan's acerbic temperament—as demonstrated by his response to JIC 502—had Nitze truly dismissed his policies, he surely would have responded with a scathing rebuttal, as did many other officials at the time.[53] Furthermore, while Charles Bohlen rejected the State-Defense Team's analysis of the Kremlin's priorities, he considered their conclusions "unassailable" and not a refutation of NSC 20/4.[54] As historian Melvyn Leffler argues, NSC 68 simply called for "more, more, and more money to implement the programs and to achieve the goals already set out."[55] It would not be until 30 September 1950 that President Truman would approve a significantly abridged version with its most controversial elements expunged.[56] Most of this six-page document simply reproduced the conclusions of NSC 20/4, demonstrating the continued predominance of this policy paper. The remaining section stressed that the United States needed to build preponderant military power to deter the threat of global war, shield an all-out political and psychological offensive to destabilize the Soviet bloc, and achieve these objectives before Soviet nuclear capabilities made continued aggressive risk-taking behind the Iron Curtain too hazardous.

The one substantial difference between NSC 20/4 and NSC 68 was the latter's requirement that the United States shift its deterrence posture from reliance upon mobilization potential to reliance on forces-in-being. The immediate objective was to build adequate military capabilities to support the cold war effort; otherwise the United States faced a possibly disastrous situation in 1954. "By acting promptly and vigorously in such a way that this date is, so to speak, pushed into the future," the authors of NSC 68 argued, "we would permit time for the process of accommodation, withdrawal, and frustration to produce the necessary changes in the Soviet system."[57] Yet the mobilization of American military power was itself only part of the solution to the Soviet threat. Also required was a vastly expanded political-warfare effort to achieve U.S. objectives. The State-Defense Team enunciated this point by declaring that "the military buildup is a shield behind which we must deploy all of our non-military resources in the campaign to roll back the power of the USSR and to frustrate the Kremlin design."[58] The military buildup was not an end in itself but a means to achieve the objectives of American policy.[59]

NSC 68 and the Intensification of Covert Action

NSC 68 reconfirmed the administration's national security objectives as established by NSC 20/4, but called for much more aggressive measures to achieve them. It led to a massive expansion of the covert program established in NSC 10/2 well beyond what the OPC had previously been able to undertake.[60] On 18 April Robert Joyce of the Policy Planning Staff met with Assistant Director Frank Wisner's top aides (Wisner was in Japan) to explain the meaning of NSC 68 and the nature of the new covert program being demanded of the OPC.[61] Joyce stressed that the State-Defense Team called for an "intensification of affirmative and timely measures and *operations by covert* means in the fields of economic warfare and political and psychological warfare with a view to fomenting and supporting unrest and revolt in selected strategic satellite countries."[62] In doing so the United States could "reduce the power and influence of the Kremlin *inside* the Soviet Union and other areas under its control. The objective would be the establishment of friendly regimes not under Kremlin domination."[63] Joyce informed Wisner that the NSC expected OPC to prepare a budget anticipating a "major effort in the field of covert operations" over the course of the next six years.

On 7 October, Lieutenant General Walter Bedell Smith replaced Roscoe Hillenkoetter as CIA director. He quickly recognized that the covert program demanded of OPC greatly strained the agency's resources. Smith informed the NSC that "although the accumulation of missions already undertaken by CIA, to say nothing of those now proposed to CIA, may transcend the original intentions of NSC 10/2, the NSC 68 series leaves little doubt that it is our national policy to conduct covert operations on a very large scale."[64] One CIA study described the situation as such:

> Such broad and comprehensive undertakings as delineated by NSC 68 could only be accomplished by the establishment of a worldwide structure for covert operations on a much grander scale than OPC had previously contemplated. It would be a task similar in concept, magnitude, and complexity to the creation of widely deployed military forces together with the logistical support required to conduct manifold, complex, and delicate operations in a wide variety of overseas locations.[65]

These operations were so extensive that they threatened to overwhelm the capability of the CIA to carry them out, leading to the creation of new interdepartmental structures to assist in the allocation of resources to the CIA. Nevertheless, the new operations significantly intensified U.S. efforts to destabilize the Soviet bloc. Therefore, while NSC 68 reaffirmed the objectives of NSC 20/4, it abandoned the evolutionary approach encapsulated in NSC 58/2.

Part Two: The Psychological Strategy Board and the Renewed Political Offensive

NSC 68's massive escalation of the responsibilities and requirements of American political-warfare activities forced the Truman administration to create a new interdepartmental structure, the Psychological Strategy Board, to coordinate these efforts. With the establishment of the PSB on 4 April 1951, the Truman administration inaugurated a new era in covert action, expanding the existing planning for psychological warfare well beyond that conceived by the OPC. So extensive and ambitious was the planning for covert and psychological warfare that it may be considered strategic in nature; that is, the framers of the plans designed them not only to fight, but also to win, the cold war.[66]

The Truman administration considered aggressive covert action the key to achieving U.S. objectives before the time that Soviet atomic capabilities threatened to make them too risky. As discussed earlier, such activities included propaganda, economic warfare, sabotage, demolition, "subversion against hostile states," and support for underground resistance forces and guerrilla movements, and were the prime methods to win the cold war. Administration strategists intended to foment revolutionary activity within the Eastern European satellites and sought to undermine communist power even within the Soviet Union.

Because of the potential hazards, the U.S.-Soviet balance of power heavily influenced development of these operations. As Kennan observed, "we cannot be sure that at some point in this process the Russians will not choose to resort to violence of some sort: i.e., to forms of military re-occupation or possibly even major war, to prevent such a process from being carried to completion."[67] Since the release of JIC 502, the growth of Soviet nuclear capabilities had come to be the principal consideration in calculating the risk of war. If the balance shifted too far in favor of the Soviet Union, the risk of war would become too great for the United States to undertake such aggressive actions. Consequently, the successful mobilization of preponderant military power was crucial to the level of risk-taking called for in NSC 68.[68]

Establishment of the Psychological Strategy Board

The State-Defense Team's call for a political offensive to wrest the cold war initiative from the Soviet Union went far beyond challenging the Soviet Union in the "contested areas" of the world (i.e., Western Europe, Asia, and Africa). It included a direct challenge to communist domination of Eastern Europe and the USSR. NSC 68 proposed an:

> intensification of affirmative and timely measures and operations by covert means in the fields of economic warfare and political and psychological warfare with a view to fomenting and supporting unrest and revolt in selected strategic satellite countries.[69]

By calling for outright revolt in the satellite regions, the State-Defense Team changed the focus of U.S. policy in Eastern Europe from encouraging Titoist heresies to supporting anti-communist forces. While NSC 68 did not officially supersede NSC 58/2, it established a parallel policy for Eastern Europe, thus creating a new and superior mandate for heightened activities behind the Iron Curtain. Questions regarding coordination remained, however.

The move toward greater centralization of the psychological war effort had already been set in motion before the onset of the Korean War.[70] The bureaucratic tug-of-war between the departments of state and defense during 1948 and 1949 resulted in the inability of the various agencies to coordinate their psychological-warfare activities and respond effectively to the growing virulence of Soviet propaganda campaigns. The failure to harmonize these activities, coupled with the increased commitments caused by NSC 68 and the Korean War, led to the consensus that a single organization should oversee these efforts.

The State Department tried to fill the gap by creating in August 1950 the

National Psychological Strategy Board. Richard Barrett, assistant secretary of state for public affairs, became the NPSB's first chairman and directed a committee composed of representatives from Defense, CIA, the National Security Resources Board, and the European Cooperation Administration. The State Department intended the NPSB to coordinate American psychological-warfare activities while simultaneously reinforcing the department's control over the whole apparatus. The State Department was so determined to consolidate its control over psychological warfare that it prepared a study which—if approved—would have concentrated all peacetime and wartime planning in the hands of the secretary of state.[71]

This paper, entitled NSC 74 "Plan for National Psychological Warfare," received strong opposition from the armed services, who saw it as an usurpation of their wartime military prerogatives, an especially sensitive issue when U.S. forces were fighting on the Korean peninsula. The Defense Department argued for the creation of an interdepartmental committee answerable only to the president and NSC. The State Department replied that the proposed committee would compete with its responsibility to formulate foreign policy.[72]

It was clear that only President Truman could break the logjam. Therefore on 4 January 1951 Truman ordered Frederick J. Lawton, director of the Bureau of the Budget, and Admiral Sydney Souers to develop a plan for the establishment of an interdepartmental committee. These proceedings were so contentious that it took several months of extensive negotiation before Truman could issue a presidential directive. Finally, on 4 April President Truman announced the establishment of the Psychological Strategy Board. Truman's directive called for the creation of a "board of directors" (referred to simply as the board) composed of the under secretary of state, deputy secretary of defense, the director of central intelligence, and a representative from the Joint Chiefs of Staff, as well as a presidentially appointed director. Two members of the PSB staff would have permanent seats on the board, with personnel from other agencies called to participate as needed. The board would report directly to the National Security Council on its activities and "on its evaluation of the National psychological operations, including implementation of approved objectives, policies and programs by the departments and agencies concerned." Psychological operations included all activities (excluding economic warfare) envisioned under NSC 59/1 ("The Foreign Information Program and Psychological Warfare Planning," 9 March 1950) and NSC 10/2; that is, information and propaganda campaigns along with covert paramilitary activities.[73]

The State Department's Opposition to the PSB's Mandate

The establishment of the PSB led to another significant struggle: defining the organization's jurisdiction. Far from precisely determining the fledgling agency's responsibilities, Truman's directive embroiled the PSB in a conflict with the State Department that would hinder covert planning throughout the final two years of the administration.

The battle over the PSB's mandate revolved around two competing views: an expansive interpretation supported by the CIA and a limited definition proposed by the State Department.[74] The CIA argued that the PSB should have sole authority over all matters of foreign-policy conduct short of formal hostilities and must ensure that "'cold' war objectives and strateg[ies] are formulated and that our 'cold' war weapons are effectively employed in carrying out these strateg[ies]" to fulfill the "aims and purposes of NSC 68."[75] Brigadier General John Magruder, senior consultant to the OPC representing the secretary of defense, helped elucidate the CIA's position. In a memo dated 21 May 1951, Magruder stated that "the functions of the PSB begin where the functions of the National Security Council leave off." According to the general, the NSC was responsible for the promulgation of broad national policy objectives while the PSB was charged with devising and implementing the necessary planning. Once the board approved a program, it would give the responsible agencies a set of tasks. Magruder believed that the principal missing factor in psychological operations to date was a grand strategy similar to that developed by the Combined Chiefs of Staff in World War II. It was the duty of the Psychological Strategy Board to fulfill this role.[76]

The CIA encouraged the PSB to adopt as wide a mandate as possible. Consequently, during a meeting on 26 July 1951 the Psychological Strategy Board's temporary staff decided that the PSB would "run the cold war" and "get up the master plan to defeat the Kremlin." The board declared its job to be the one "Harry Hopkins had under Roosevelt."[77] The next day the PSB staff approved a definition of psychological operations declaring that:

> 'Psychological Operations' is a cover name to describe the systematic application in peace and in war, by the departments and agencies of the Government, of all elements of U.S. national power for the attainment of fundamental national objectives.

Charles Burton Marshall of the State Department's Policy Planning Staff warned that the expansive view threatened to usurp that department's mandate as chief formulator of U.S. cold war policy. Marshall considered the CIA's proposal nothing less than a "fundamental—indeed, an implicitly revolutionary—shift of authority in the entire organization of the Executive Branch" and claimed that the board not even need answer to the president, let alone the respective agencies.[78] If the PSB exercised its understanding of the president's directive the board would be able to exert influence in every activity except those involving "hot" war and overt economic warfare.

Marshall countered that the primary objective of psychological strategy should be first "to prosecute measures primarily designed to serve the national interest by acting upon the minds of other peoples" and second "to ensure, in the planning and execution of activities in concurrent fields of action . . . the taking of maximum practicable advantage of all opportunities to serve the national interest." Paul Nitze echoed Marshall's concern when he bluntly warned PSB director Gordon Gray "to just forget about policy, that's not your business; we'll make the policy and then you can put it on your damn radio."[79] According to Nitze the PSB mandate should be limited to:

(1) Primary authority in ensuring among all agencies concerned maximum of effectiveness and unity of objective in regard to activities set forth in NSC 59/1 and 10/2;
(2) Secondary authority to see that full account of psychological factors—that is, aspects having impact on the mind, will, and morale of foreign peoples—is taken in the planning and execution of other activities bearing on the field of foreign relations, including the planning of the national objectives themselves.[80]

Nitze considered the PSB so threatening to the State Department's jurisdiction that he asked Acheson to "challenge" Gray to secure an immediate resolution of the problem. Acheson replied that "he saw no reason for forcing the issue at this point" but commanded Nitze to make clear to all parties that "we are ready for any showdown anytime the other people want to force it."[81]

Wallace Carroll, a highly respected psychological-warfare expert for the World War II Office of War Information (OWI) and a famous journalist, sharply attacked the Policy Planning Staff director's demand, arguing that one of the very handicaps of American efforts in psychological-warfare planning was the "persistent notion that psychological warfare is word warfare—more particularly, radio warfare."[82] Previous strategic plans were often frustrated, he explained, for the very reason that they were limited to "radio warfare" with operatives becoming little more than "long distance editors." Carroll argued that radio-based psychological warfare merely tried to put the best face on events, but the real purpose of psychological warfare was to make events happen.[83]

Carroll warned that a narrow interpretation of the PSB's mandate would serve only to weaken the U.S. psychological effort and miss opportunities to make significant gains against the Soviets. He suggested that the agency adopt as its mandate an aggressive long-range covert plan of attack designed to inspire the administration to take the necessary steps to achieve U.S. national security objectives. The board must be careful not to focus too much attention on short-term operations instead of long-term strategy, he warned, as "there will remain a danger that the Board will one day find itself hitched to the machinery of word warfare."[84]

The PSB's director, Gordon Gray, interpreted the president's directive as mandating a central role for his agency in the "formulation and promulgation, as guidance to the departments and agencies responsible for psychological operations, of overall national psychological objectives, policies, and programs." The PSB would determine the overall strategic concepts and their priority. The board would then establish an overall strategic psychological plan, worked out by panels composed of government officials and experts from the academic community. The plan needed to be sufficiently detailed that the PSB could assign to designated departments and agencies the various responsibilities for operational planning and timetables for the preparation of each plan. The PSB would not take part in the particulars of formulating policy or organizing operations; the former would remain the purview of the State Department and the NSC, while the latter was the responsibility of the particular agency. In other words, the PSB would take overall guidance from the policy objectives approved by the NSC, develop the psychological warplans, and then hand the plans to the relevant agencies for implementation, remaining involved only to assist in coordination and evaluation of the effort.[85] Although his directive should have reconciled the views of the State Department and the CIA, Gray's compromise did not end the battle over the mandate for long. The differences between the Policy Planning Staff and the PSB over the correct interpretation of NSC policy would again reopen the mandate dilemma.

Walter Bedell Smith, Covert Operations, and the "Magnitude" Problem

The mandate controversy was not the only dispute to emerge during the board's formative period. When Walter Bedell Smith established his authority over the Office of Policy Coordination as of 12 October 1950, he unwittingly assumed responsibility for the OPC's international covert operations, which had been vastly expanded by the intensification of U.S. cold war efforts under NSC 68. So extensive had OPC operations become that they actually surpassed those of the CIA, and consequently exceeded the CIA's administrative capacity. Smith was concerned that these added responsibilities overextended the agency's limited resources and would undermine its primary function of collecting intelligence. In the meantime, Smith faced growing demands from the Joint Chiefs of Staff for the CIA to continue reorienting most of its covert paramilitary resources toward the retardation of Soviet military advances in case of global war.[86] Smith decided that only the president and the NSC could resolve these issues. Therefore, on 8 May 1951, Smith submitted a memorandum to the NSC appealing for "specific guidance in order to define the scope and pace of covert operations" in the cold war and in establishing the level of assistance to be rendered to the military in time of global war.[87]

Smith needed NSC guidance regarding not only increased support for the CIA, but also to resolve the dichotomy between NSC 68 and NSC 58/2 over the scope of the covert operations themselves. NSC 68 had established as national policy support for "unrest and revolt in certain strategic satellite nations." Smith understood this to mean that the role of covert operations and psychological warfare was to "rollback the perimeter of Soviet power and ultimate[ly] frustrat[e] the Kremlin design."[88] This seemed to repudiate the policy of first encouraging Titoist heresies within the satellite states and then creating democratic governments. Consequently, "to what extent," Smith asked, "will the United States support counter-revolution in the slave states?"[89]

Never a strong proponent of covert operations, Smith had even less respect for psychological warfare. He realized, however, that the administration considered both important to the achievement of U.S. objectives and that he could hope only to moderate this policy.[90] Yet, by early 1951, covert activities had increased in accordance with the greater demands placed upon them by NSC 68, prompting Smith to contend that "the policies established by NSC 68 have never been spelled out in terms of a specific covert program directive to [the] CIA." He believed that without a significant increase in assistance, the growing magnitude of covert operations would "divert an ever increasing share of the time and attention of key CIA personnel from the basic intelligence mission of the Agency, with the attendant risk that such missions will not be adequately accomplished."[91]

Smith further requested that the NSC resolve the dispute between the CIA and the JCS over the purpose of covert operations behind the Iron Curtain. With the United States at war with both North Korea and China, the Joint Chiefs of Staff contended that the expansion of covert operations under NSC 68 should be used to accelerate preparations for war in Europe. The JCS submitted a memo to the NSC on 28 March 1951, arguing that the CIA should give top priority to preparations for the retardation of a Soviet military advance across Europe.[92] Smith strongly disagreed with the JCS position and argued that unless the Joint Chiefs could guarantee that their demands were consistent with national policy, the NSC should reject them. Shifting the CIA's focus from peacetime achievement of U.S. national security objectives to the retardation of Soviet military advances across Europe, he explained, would terminate the CIA's peacetime efforts to roll back Soviet power from Eastern Europe since the only way to maintain the availability of these assets for war was to prevent their peacetime exposure.

Smith recommended that the NSC initiate a comprehensive review of the subject, including a judgment as to which agency would hold the greatest responsibility for these operations. If the CIA was to be made responsible, then provisions should be made for (1) joint planning with the military authorities; (2) specific guidance with regard to dual cold war and military missions; (3) coordination with the political leadership, especially the State Department; and (4) the provision of personnel and of administrative and logistical support. Finally, Smith suggested that when issues involved the interests of both the State Department and Defense Department, the PSB should provide the required guidance.

In response, NSC executive secretary James Lay established a Special Committee of the NSC Senior Staff chaired by Paul Nitze and including Frank Nash of the Defense Department, Admiral T. E. Woolridge of the Joint Chiefs of Staff, and William Jackson, deputy director of the CIA.[93] The Special Committee recommended that the NSC approve the immediate expansion of the OPC and the intensification of its activities and reaffirm the responsibility and authority of the DCI for the conduct of covert operations.[94] It charged the PSB with responsibility for determining the desirability and feasibility of particular operations, their scope, pace, timing, and priorities, and coordinating support for the CIA from the departments of state and defense.[95]

The Special Committee's response was not what Smith had sought. The memo of 27 June committed the CIA to conduct covert operations on a very large scale, without adequately resolving his concerns about the effect of this increase on the CIA's intelligence-gathering capabilities. Yet the Special Committee did reaffirm Smith's overall authority under NSC 10/2 and accepted the need for the State Department and Defense Department to provide the necessary resources.[96]

On 15 August, the JCS responded to the Special Committee report with their own study entitled "The Scope and Pace of Covert Operations."[97] The military now accepted much of the argument presented by the Special Committee, including the belief that "a well planned national program of covert operations, vigorously prosecuted, might conceivably be the major contribution to the attainment of the national objectives vis-à-vis the USSR without resorting to war." The JCS suggested that the PSB develop a strategic concept and national program consistent with national military planning. The JCS report then recommended a review mechanism that significantly expanded military influence in operational planning.[98] The Special Committee recognized what the JCS was attempting to do with its proposed set of procedures and summarily rejected them at a committee meeting on August 28.[99] The Special Committee then transmitted a final draft for NSC approval.

The JCS's obstructionism was not due to its opposition to U.S. covert efforts to roll back Soviet power from Eastern Europe, but was instead a method to gain a larger voice in cold war decisionmaking. In fact, Joint Chiefs of Staff chairman Omar Bradley strongly supported covert action as a method to win the cold war without escalation to global war. Bradley made this position clear in a memo to then secretary of defense Marshall on 15 January 1951. Bradley argued that the United States must:

> develop an integrated and coordinated over-all economic, political, psychological, and national military program including a plan for the United States and its allies against Kremlin dominated communism and its aggressive tactics, designed to wrest the initiative from the Soviet Union to force the USSR on the defensive and ultimately, to reduce to impotence the threat of Kremlin dominated communism. This plan should include affirmative measures of economic, clandestine, subversive, and psychological character to foment and support unrest and revolution in selected strategic satellite countries and Russian political divisions. The objective would be the establishment of friendly regimes not under Kremlin domination. Such action is essential to engage the Russians' attention, keep the Kremlin off balance, and force an increased expenditure of Soviet resources in counteraction. In other words, it would be the current Soviet cold war techniques used against the Soviets, and must be carried out with full acceptance of the risk of war.[100]

President Truman approved the Special Committee's draft as NSC 10/5 "Scope and Pace of Covert Operations," on 23 October 1951.[101] The paper called for an intensification of covert operations "in general order of emphasis to":

> A. Place the maximum strain on the Soviet structure of power, including the relationships between the USSR, its satellites, and Communist China; and when and where appropriate in the light of U.S. and Soviet capabilities and the risk of war, contribute to the retraction and reduction of Soviet power and influence to limits which no longer constitute a threat to U.S. security.
> B. Strengthen the orientation toward the United States of the peoples and nations of the free world, and increase their capacity and will to resist Soviet domination.
> C. Develop underground resistance and facilitate covert guerrilla operations in strategic areas to the maximum practicable extents consistent with [paragraph] A, and ensure availability of these forces in the event of war for utilization in accordance with the principles established by the National Security Council including whenever practicable provision of a base upon which the military may expand these forces on a military basis in time of war within active theaters of operations.

President Truman reconfirmed Smith's authority as director of central intelligence to coordinate the covert political offensive. Furthermore, he ordered the Psychological Strategy Board to develop an overall strategic concept to guide the national psychological program and link U.S. national security objectives with available covert resources. The PSB, with Smith as its chairman, received responsibility for determining the desirability and feasibility of the political-warfare programs and establishing the scope, pace, timing, and priority of these covert operations, and the power to ensure the adequate provisioning of all operations by the departments of state and defense. With his approval of NSC 10/5, President Truman gave his blessing to an enormous intensification of the administration's covert offensive to destabilize communist control throughout the Soviet bloc.[102]

Developing a Strategic Concept

Following President Truman's approval of NSC 10/5, PSB director Gordon Gray assembled a team of psychological-warfare specialists to commence work on the most crucial element of NSC 10/5: the overall strategic concept for cold war operations. The "Director's Group" was comprised of six permanent members who were responsible for devising the plan.[103] Its chairman was Rear Admiral Leslie Stevens, a sixty-one-year-old aeronautics expert who had represented the Joint Chiefs of Staff as senior consultant for the OPC and previously served as a naval attaché at the U.S. embassy in Moscow from 1947 to 1950.[104] Stevens was renowned for his National War College lectures regarding the need for a sustained and organized national strategy to defeat the Soviet threat.[105] He also held the post of JCS representative to the PSB until his ascension to the Director's Group. Among the other names considered for membership were George Kennan and James Burnham, rollback's most vocal public proponent.[106] While full-time membership was impossible due to President Truman's decision to nominate him for the post of ambassador to the Soviet Union, Kennan did consult with the Director's Group until his departure for Moscow in May 1952.[107] Burnham, on the other hand, was already working with the Republican Party for the 1952 presidential elections. The final composition of the Director's Group included Admiral Stevens, a geophysicist named Palmer Putnam, Wallace Carroll, William D. Kennedy, a vice president at Ford Motor Company, Yale Soviet specialist Frederick Barghoorn, and Lieutenant Colonel Tobias R. Philbin.

At its first meeting, the Director's Group agreed that its primary responsibility was to determine the programs necessary to achieve the objectives established in NSC 20/4.[108] On 13 November, the Director's Group presented Gray with a preliminary strategic concept.[109] This draft established specific worldwide objectives planned according to three phases: short, medium, and long range, to be approved by the director of central intelligence, under secretary of state, and deputy secretary of defense. The draft called for an intensified covert and psychological effort to induce a Soviet withdrawal from East Germany, end the division of Germany, and rapidly incorporate a united Germany into Western Europe. It also proposed psychological operations in the Far East aimed at separating Manchuria from China and turning China into "basically a rice-growing agricultural society incapable of exercising any major force of its own beyond its traditional borders." Regarding the USSR, the Director's Group focused its strategies on the Kremlin and the Soviet military. Covert action would include operations to overwhelm the Soviet power structure and control mechanisms and foment tensions between the Communist Party and the Military High Command. The long-range objective included "frustrating the historic power plans first outlined by Peter the Great [that] will involve the breakup of the USSR into separate national component states."[110]

The Director's Group created short-range plans—i.e., intended for completion within the first year—to rectify the U.S. positions in the Middle East and the Far East, as well as offensive operations to strike Eastern Germany, Poland, Czechoslovakia, and Bulgaria.[111] In addition, the United States would initiate psychological-warfare operations directly against Soviet territory, although the PSB strategists concluded that capabilities for direct action were limited in the early period. Finally, the Director's Group ordered a series of studies to determine how best to exploit minority dissatisfaction within the USSR and the role of defectors in U.S. policy, as well as to review current Soviet policies toward land and industrial ownership.[112]

A second group of planners—Palmer Putnam, William Kennedy, and Gordon Gray's assistant Robert Cutler—prepared a summary version of the national strategy paper for PSB approval.[113] Their paper requested agreement on the scope and pace of covert operations necessary to achieve NSC 20/4 objectives. They stressed that the United States would be entering a critical period in the cold war between 1953 and 1955, when "the Soviet may be able to deal the U.S. a crippling (atomic) blow" and "towards the end of this period, the U.S. economy will be bearing what economists consider the maximum possible strain [due to the military buildup]." Therefore, the board needed to design a strategy to achieve U.S. national objectives "prior to this critical period." The board ordered the departments of state and defense to provide the necessary information by 1 February 1952 so that operational planning could begin immediately.[114]

Kennedy, Putnam, and Cutler stressed that the PSB must weigh all projects, proposals, and plans against the risk of war with the Soviet bloc. They defined this risk as "greatest when the Soviet is convinced that it is falling behind in its chances for political survival and for winning a war." The United States could "accept greater risks of war as our defenses are strengthened" and "mount operations against the Soviet Union or its satellites with less risk of war in direct proportion to the effects achieved by those operations first executed." "Success of any operations," they argued, "will lessen the power of the Kremlin."[115]

The PSB directed the State Department and the CIA to turn over all plans and projects, whether approved or not, designed to meet the following objectives: "to strengthen the U.S. position in each country outside the Iron Curtain; to mount psychological war[fare] designed to detach each of the satellites from Moscow; to mount psychological war[fare] designed to eliminate the threat from the Kremlin." Furthermore, these agencies would be responsible for assessing the relative priority of the project and its feasibility, manpower and logistical requirements, and time schedules. After three meetings and numerous informal reviews, Gray sent a version of this paper to various members of the departments of state, defense, and CIA for comment.

The State Department reacted with outrage to the proposals of the Director's Group. C. B. Marshall viewed them as another attempt by the PSB staff to usurp the policymaking function of the department. He fired off a memo to Nitze arguing that the PSB staff's approach "stems from a misunderstanding of the nature of foreign policy . . . derived from the faulty logic that foreign policy objectives are measurable time scales like military objectives and that a government can achieve control of the factors that bear on its national situation in the same sense that a commander can control the factors that bear on a tactical situation."[116] Accusing Gray's staff of seeking to make themselves the "general staff" for cold war operations, Marshall advised Nitze to reject Gray's request for information regarding the department's efforts to subvert the Soviet bloc, arguing that the demand could "only be fulfilled by telling everything that is known or suspected in the field of foreign policy."[117] Assistant Secretary of State H. Freeman Matthews agreed and promptly attacked the PSB for trying to determine whether the State Department's actions "in relation to the Soviets was the proper and correct thing."[118] Due to this growing controversy, Admiral Stevens requested the presence of various agency representatives—Charles Bohlen and Paul Nitze for the State Department, John Magruder for the Defense Department, and Frank Wisner, the newly promoted deputy director of plans for the CIA—at all future Director's Group meetings.[119]

On 5 December, the Director's Group and PSB deputy director C. Tracy Barnes met with Bohlen, Nitze, Wisner, and Magruder to discuss the draft strategic concept. Gray stated that his staff intended the paper to be a "working draft . . . to serve as a basis for discussion between the group and representatives of the agencies involved" and to establish the level of resources required to implement NSC 10/5.[120] Bohlen questioned whether it was at all possible to have an overall strategic plan. He reiterated Marshall's concern that while the paper focused on psychological strategy, "it asks for studies on basic policy and would have the effect of causing a review of all basic national policy; policy with a capital 'P.'"[121] Nitze argued that the PSB must realize that the subversion of Soviet power and influence was one of several national objectives but not the most important. He considered "the preservation and development of our own system and point of view; preservation and development of a climate in which our system can survive and develop; and mitigating the danger of war" as the three superior national objectives.[122] He and Bohlen agreed to discuss the paper with Assistant Secretary of State Matthews in order to prepare the State Department's response.

Magruder, Wisner, Bohlen, and Nitze met with the Director's Group on 18 December to review its progress in revising the strategic concept paper. The State Department insisted that the various departments agree to the framing of the covert objectives, arrive at a common understanding of the limitations imposed upon formulating a strategic plan, and determine the available methods of attack.[123] Three days later Admiral Stevens prepared a draft statement—derided within the PSB as the "Bazoo" paper for the intense debate it provoked—establishing what he hoped would be the accepted method of formulating a psychological strategy. Stevens—adopting Nitze's formulation—recognized four limitations to U.S. political-warfare strategy. First, these efforts had to be "consistent with preservation of our way of life and institutions; second, not involve an undue risk of precipitating general war; third, not break up our alliances; and fourth, not bring about an unmanageable or hostile milieu with which we would have to cope in the future."[124] Stevens argued that the administration could organize the psychological campaign geographically—i.e., by dividing the Soviet-dominated areas into various regions. Alternatively, it could be organized according to particular instruments, ranging from military and paramilitary action to political revolution and coup d'état, or by creating enforceable settlements and simply denying the Soviets the opportunity to enhance their power. Stevens concluded that it might be best to combine all the approaches: selecting the area of greatest opportunity and using the most effective strategies and capabilities accessible to U.S. agencies.

Interagency haggling forced Stevens to redraft this paper eleven times before all parties were willing to consider it an acceptable statement of the problem.[125] The State Department and the PSB agreed that a special working committee called the Strategic Concept Panel comprising representatives from the State Department, the Defense Department, the CIA, and the PSB would assume responsibility for writing the strategic concept paper. The panel included Admiral Stevens as chairman, Frank Wisner, John Magruder, Charles Bohlen, Paul Nitze, and Charles Stelle. Even George Kennan consulted with the panel prior to his departure for Moscow.[126] The State Department considered this a significant victory in its struggle to rein in the fledgling PSB. Nitze apprised Acheson that the PSB "capitulated on all fronts as regards the thesis that [it] should create a master plan for the overthrow of communism."[127] While this reflected an exaggerated sense of bravado, he was correct in saying that the State Department and not the PSB would be the principal force behind the attempt to promulgate a strategic concept to resolve the cold war.

The New Psychological Warfare Program

Although a strategic concept had yet to be approved, the National Security Council had offered enough guidance in its various policy papers for the agencies to formulate a "packet" of short-range psychological-warfare and covert operations designed to destabilize the communist governments of Eastern Europe and the Soviet Union. Recently declassified documents suggest that the Packet comprised a significant number of operations designed to attack the political structures of Eastern Europe and the USSR. In fact, one government study reported that the Packet "evidences the fact that the CIA-OPC is principally engaged in developing a world-wide covert apparatus" that was "an obvious prerequisite to the successful execution of NSC 10/2 and NSC 10/5 missions."[128]

Administration planners considered the disruption of the Soviet power structure an essential first step in the liberation of the satellite states and the destabilization of the USSR. It was clear that citizens of communists states have, as Charles Bohlen emphasized, "no power of action unless and until [the] state apparatus of control is near collapse."[129] Truman administration officials did not wish to inspire the populations of Eastern Europe and the Soviet Union to revolt before schisms emerged within the region's governments. In striking contrast to their successors in the Eisenhower administration, the Truman administration—and Bohlen in particular—contended that such a policy would be both "useless" and morally indefensible since it would lead to the kind of brutal suppression for which Stalin was notorious. Instead, U.S. political warfare would engage in "spoiling operations" designed to weaken the central organs of power by exploiting the chief weakness of these regimes: namely the "jealousy and paranoiac suspicion [with]in the ruling groups." The goal was to instigate, using "disinformation and deception" and by "compromis[ing] important officials," conflicts between the party and secret police, the army and secret police, and the army and the party. Only a covert strategy could succeed since any public declaration would formally commit the U.S. government to the liberation of the satellite states, offer false hopes to the peoples of the Soviet bloc, and give the Soviets "justification for more extreme measures of control."[130]

Such activities included the paramilitary operations employed in Albania and attempts to contact the remaining anti-communist groups in Eastern Europe and the USSR, as well as a number of activities that have become known only in the last few years. Starting in late 1994 the U.S. government has declassified documents detailing operations designed to undermine Soviet control in East Germany and induce defection of key Soviet bloc officials.[131] Other operations were intended to incite a power struggle within the Politburo and unrest among Soviet nationalities in the wake of Stalin's death in order to undermine the Soviet power structure by exploiting its highly centralized nature. These new strategies sought to provide a new impetus to the covert program while simultaneously maintaining plausible deniability.

Most documentation regarding these operations remains classified. Yet tantalizing hints indicate that they were only a portion of a much broader covert effort that has yet to emerge. Enough material is available, however, to demonstrate that U.S. covert strategy had shifted from its singular focus on developing paramilitary guerrilla movements to a much more nuanced strategy employing new techniques designed first to weaken Soviet power and then to inspire the satellite nations to revolt when the time was right.[132] Although NSC 10/5 reaffirmed the use of paramilitary forces in retracting Soviet power from Eastern Europe, the administration realized that due to the limitations imposed by plausible deniability they would be best employed either during war or in the midst of a major power struggle within the Kremlin, when it might be more difficult for the Soviet leadership to respond to a popular uprising. Prior use would only expose these forces and lead to their destruction, as had happened to the British and American efforts in Albania.

Identifying and Exploiting Soviet Vulnerabilities

While analysts disagreed over the nature of the Soviet threat, there was agreement that the Soviet regime represented an occupying force with little public support within Russia. The communist regime was, in the words of one PSB official, "a colossus with feet of clay" vulnerable to a decisive psychological-warfare offensive.[133] The problem remained that this "colossus with feet of clay" possessed an extensive military and security apparatus that had ensured the party's control of the Soviet Union through a civil war, Lenin's death, the struggle for power between Leon Trotsky and Stalin, and World War II. The security apparatus infiltrated Russian society so successfully that many analysts considered constructing the organization necessary for a revolt impossible.[134] Therefore the United States would have to rely upon instigating a "revolution from above" within the security and administrative apparatus, which became the principal targets for U.S. psychological warfare.

Administration planners identified four possible methods to undermine Soviet power within Russia.[135] First, the United States would seek to incapacitate the administrative structure of the Communist Party and state offices. The Stalinist structure of authority itself was the target under this scheme. The crucial role of the Soviet security forces in Stalin's drive to ensconce both the power of the party throughout the Russian empire and his control of the party is well known. Political-warfare specialists believed that the Great Terror of the 1930s, the extermination of the kulaks, and the purges of high-ranking military officers created an atmosphere that forced officials to avoid displaying individual initiative and assuming greater responsibility out of fear of receiving blame for potential errors. Consequently, lower-level officials frequently referred important decisions to higher decisionmaking levels. By manufacturing problems of a sufficient magnitude and introducing them at the lowest decisionmaking levels, analysts believed it was possible to overload the Soviet state, delay the making of key decisions, and encourage a breakdown of the Stalinist power structure in Russia.

A second strategy was to increase the incidence of defection to the West. Strategists believed that the defection of any official—the higher the rank the better—would weaken the top leadership's confidence in the loyalty of its subordinates, belie its claims to the moral superiority of communism, and—if followed by subsequent defections from the same department—force party leaders to question the reliability of that institution to the state. The goal was to incite a significant number of defections from both the military and security apparatus and shake the party's faith in their allegiance. Analysts hoped that this would result in a new round of purges and reduce the party's abilities to suppress dissent.

A third method was to use disinformation against high-level Soviet leaders, particularly Politburo members, in order to intensify their mutual distrust and induce a power struggle at the apex of the Communist Party. Officials considered this strategy a potentially effective means of disrupting Soviet control in the days immediately following Stalin's death, when the feelings of mutual insecurity within the Politburo would be at a maximum.[136]

Finally, experts devised strategies to accentuate the unreliability of both the Eastern European satellites and Chinese military and political organizations. Encouraging Titoist deviations as discussed in NSC 58/2 remained one possible, though increasingly unreliable, method. Analysts devised schemes to reduce the Soviet Union's confidence in the East German Communist Party and the reliability of the Soviet armed forces stationed close to the border with the West. Meanwhile, operations continued to detach Albania from the Soviet bloc and to spread disinformation to the Soviet leadership regarding the possible Titoist intentions of the Chinese communists in order to prompt another schism within international communism.

While an enormous amount of material remains classified, the U.S. government has released a portion that demonstrates the intensity with which the Truman administration tried to destabilize the Soviet bloc. The discussion below will provide a preliminary history of these plans and projects from documents now available.

Operation Overload and Delay

The near total centralization of authority in the hands of the party and the security apparatus represented the Achilles' heel of Soviet power and the principal target for American efforts. While the Stalinist power structure ensured that little chance existed for a "revolution from below," it also guaranteed that the highest rungs of power would handle the greatest portion of all problems. Analysts believed that the more complex and controversial an issue, the more likely that the lower strata would submit the problem to higher authorities for resolution. This belief lay at the foundation of a strategy designed to cripple the decisionmaking apparatus of the Soviet system, overloading the Soviet Politburo with numerous problems, weakening their internal control, and delaying implementation of their worldwide ambitions.

Operation Overload and Delay was the progeny of Project TROY, a State Department–sponsored study of political warfare organized by MIT in collaboration with Harvard University and the RAND Corporation. Although constituted with the limited mandate to discover better means of defeating Soviet jamming of U.S. radio broadcasting into the Soviet bloc, the project members decided that the problems with U.S. radio warfare could be resolved only as part of a full-scale review of U.S. political-warfare strategy.[137] Included in the study's review was an invaluable discussion of Soviet vulnerabilities and their susceptibility to psychological attack, analysis which would later serve as the basis for many projects, Overload and Delay being one such undertaking.

The principal architect of Overload and Delay was MIT psychologist Alex Bavelas. Bavelas argued that the degree of Kremlin domination made it difficult to influence specific groups within Soviet society. "The extent of authoritarian rule . . . ," argued Bavelas, "cannot be underestimated." The Politburo even selected local leaders throughout the Soviet Union, tantamount to a president's cabinet approving the election of county leaders in the United States. Furthermore, the system was devised so that higher-level decisionmakers invariably reviewed every official's actions, with the power to annul "incorrect" decisions. Too many "incorrect" decisions would not endear an official to the party hierarchy. According to one intelligence report, in 1946 alone the Soviet Politburo purged 64 percent of the local executive committee chairmen during their first year in office.[138] These control mechanisms provided an invaluable opportunity to attack the Soviet system as a whole.

Bavelas concluded that few Soviet officials would be willing to make decisions or to express attitudes on any question that had not been already addressed by the highest authority. Absent such guidance, it would be nearly impossible to distinguish between matters of major or minor importance. For instance, a question of textbook selection in Leningrad that reached the

Central Committee attracted the attention of Stalin himself, and according to Bavelas led to a "sweeping reorganization of the entire school system." According to another account, the Politburo reviewed the production and morale reports of a Stalingrad factory every five days for a protracted period. A defector wrote that the Politburo spent hours discussing a small contract made by one of the minor Soviet importing firms. This state of affairs, Bavelas argued:

> leads to an operational atmosphere which has been called 'vested confusion.' The bulk of the personnel exhibits a great unwillingness to take single steps or to make obvious decisions which, however sound they may appear to be, can easily be 'incorrect.' They found it much wiser to refer such problems upward for guidance.[139]

Bavelas concluded that the result of "vested confusion" was the funneling of vast amounts of information and problems to higher decisionmaking levels. How much information made its way up the ladder was the question. Bavelas pointed out that lower echelons of the Soviet power structure could safely pass judgment only on issues of a repeat nature. Since any non-doctrinaire approach—or even the very expression of initiative itself—could result in censure and arrest, a substantial amount of information and requests for decisions flooded the highest echelons of the Soviet government on a daily basis. The purpose of Overload and Delay was to find the straw that could break the Stalinist system's back. Bavelas described the approach in this manner:

> Our most effective program of attack upon a system should be directed at those weaknesses which could not be corrected without seriously reducing the power held by these few at the top. We might, for instance, take actions which would result in a serious overloading of the top levels by a crippling increase in the number of problems referred upward for a decision. How far could the Soviet system go in increasing the decision-making powers at the lower ranks before it fell below the critical level of centralized control for maintaining a dictatorship? We should explore all the input points available to us, as we deliberately embark on a program for increasing them, particularly at the lower levels.[140]

Bavelas specified two approaches to overload the Soviet system: first, increase the number of input points, particularly at the middle and lower ranks, and second, create complex and unpredictable situations requiring action. One way of producing more input points was to bypass established procedures in dealing with Soviet agencies. Bavelas used the example that in dealing with the Soviet trade monopoly, American businessmen, acting on their own initiative, developed new input points by cabling the same information to both the foreign office and the Moscow office of the Soviet agency, contradicting established procedure. The home office, unaware of the sleight of hand, accepted the transaction without checking with the foreign office, very likely resulting in embarrassment and possibly censure for these officials.[141]

The rationale for creating complex and unpredictable situations, Bavelas concluded, was to create as many conditional situations as possible. "Instead of being faced with a 'yes' 'no' situation it should be faced with 'yes, if so, and so, and so, and so,' 'no, if so, and so, and so,' 'but maybe after all.'" U.S. agencies must try to make all decisions as complicated as possible for the respective Soviet agency, guaranteeing that Soviet officials would refer the issue to higher authorities. The embargo status of a commodity, for instance, should not be predictable over the course of a long period. It should always appear as if it might change, thereby forcing the Soviets to plan their actions against an "ever-shifting and unpredictable background." This situation should increase the number of bad guesses that would not only be inconvenient for the economy but "deadly to the individual involved."[142]

A crucial problem Bavelas did not address was how the numerous U.S. government agencies would be able to coordinate such an extensive operation without engaging in the type of bureaucratic contests that had hindered the development of strategy since 1948. Nevertheless, evidence exists that the Truman administration did try to implement Overload and Delay. Unlike many of the other operations, Overload and Delay has very little paper trail by which we may trace its development. In fact, only scattered references exist in the declassified literature indicating that the CIA put into effect the ideas of Project TROY. Allen Dulles referred to Overload and Delay during an interdepartmental committee meeting overseeing the establishment of the PSB. In this memo Dulles writes that one of the warplans ready for discussion was "implementation of project 'OVERLOAD and DELAY' of the Project TROY report."[143] PSB staff member John Sherman mentioned Overload and Delay in a memo to Deputy Director of the PSB C. Tracy Barnes discussing new procedures for the handling of different psychological warplans. The memo states that the new procedures

> apply more to the containment type plans for taking the initiative in the so-called contested areas around the periphery of the Soviet orbit such as the Far Eastern, Middle Eastern, and European plans now being developed than it will apply to plans of direct attack against the Soviet Union such as MIDRIB, OVERLOAD, and DELAY.[144]

It can be assumed, therefore, that the Truman administration tried to implement plans established by Project TROY; evidence does not as yet exist detailing exactly how it tried to accomplished this objective, however. Fortunately, more documentation exists regarding other newly declassified operations.

U.S. Policy toward the Use of Defectors, Exiles, and Refugees

Exploitation of Soviet and satellite defectors was one of the most promising methods to both discredit communist propaganda and undermine the legitimacy of the regime.[145] Defectors offered the best source of intelligence on actual conditions within the Soviet Union, including the state of military preparedness, the attitudes of various segments of the population to the present regime, and other potential vulnerabilities. Moreover, they offered firsthand assessments of the effectiveness of political-warfare operations. Defectors also provided broadcasters for the Voice of America, Radio Free Europe, and later Radio Liberation, and covert operatives willing to infiltrate their homelands.[146]

While American political-warfare strategists had long recognized the potential utility of Soviet defectors, the administration realized its full impact with the dissemination of the SPONGE reports. The authors of the SPONGE reports based their analysis on the results of extensive interviews conducted by Frederick Barghoorn—a Soviet studies specialist at Yale University—submitted to the State Department in May 1950.[147] Barghoorn's interviews of Soviet-bloc refugees confirmed that the Soviet leadership viewed defection as a grave threat to its authority. And, despite the measures taken by Soviet authorities, he concluded that it was possible to stimulate more high-level defectors.

Defectors warned Barghoorn that it was essential that the United States use its various radios, particularly the Voice of America and Radio Free Europe, to provide disgruntled Soviet officials with the hope that a better life awaited them if they defected. Devising methods to convince officials of significant rank to defect was the problem, for the life of defectors, refugees, and escapees was difficult. It was common for defectors to remain restricted to refugee camps in Germany for long periods before American officials brought them to the United States. The worst possible disaster for Western propaganda was a despondent defector who decided to return to the Soviet Union.[148]

Thanks to George Kennan the SPONGE reports were not lost amid the tumultuous first weeks of the Korean War. Kennan considered Barghoorn's report "one of the most interesting ever filed with the Department on Russian matters" and urged Dean Acheson to study it despite the gravity of the international situation.[149] Kennan believed that NSC guidance was essential to exploit this opportunity properly.

Therefore, in October 1950, the National Security Council ordered the NSC Senior Staff to prepare a policy paper regarding defection. On 18 April 1951, the council approved NSC 86/1 "United States Policy on Soviet-Satellite Defectors." Today NSC 86/1 remains classified in full. Portions were inadvertently released when the U.S. government declassified Operation Engross, "A National Psychological Plan with Respect to Escapees from the Soviet

Orbit: Phase B." According to Operation Engross, the long-range objective of U.S. policy was "to contribute to the achievement of general U.S. objectives and aims with respect to the USSR as stated in NSC 20/4, particularly by placing the maximum strain on the Soviet structure of power through threatening the regime's control of its population." Additionally, the United States would seek to benefit from increased access to intelligence, use of propaganda, and denial of valuable personnel to the Soviet Union and its satellites, and by spreading "increased disaffection and confusion within the Soviet and satellite regimes."[150]

The newly established Psychological Strategy Board assumed control of the defector program. The board organized a steering committee to oversee development of strategic projects, ensure coordination with national strategic objectives, and consider all sources to provide desperately needed funding. Part of the funding crunch was resolved with the allocation of one hundred million dollars from the Mutual Security Agency's budget—known as the Kersten Amendment to the Mutual Security Act—giving the MSA and its director Averell Harriman extensive influence over the program.[151]

During the steering committee's first hearing, the PSB's director, Gordon Gray, highlighted past problems and stressed the need to move rapidly in developing a plan to manage the defector problem before defection ceased being possible. Gray ordered the steering committee to define solutions to the extra problems regarding refugees and defectors and to develop an official government policy.[152]

Two months later the steering committee presented PSB D-18a at the sixth meeting of the Psychological Strategy Board. The committee decided to split the defector problem into two parts: Phase A would determine the best means to settle, employ, and care for current escapees; Phase B would develop strategies to entice more defectors and escapees and better utilize them in covert operations against the Soviet bloc.[153]

The plan proposed in PSB D-18a called for the State Department to assume the principal focus of efforts to settle refugees and defectors and coordinate with the Mutual Security Agency, which would provide the 4.3 million dollars needed to fund the escapee program. It encouraged these agencies to take advantage of "private" organizations—such as the National Committee for a Free Europe—and recommended that the military liberalize conditions under which escapees could be recruited.[154]

With the approval of Phase A, a panel representing the PSB, the State Department, the Defense Department, the NATO Standing Group, JCS, Army, Navy, Air Force, CIA, MSA, and the Bureau of the Budget set out to tackle Phase B. It reaffirmed that the objective of U.S. policy was to reduce Soviet power "by application of psychological and other pressures to the . . . population resources under its control," and to "enhance the power of the United States and the pro-democratic world by selective acquisitionand utilization of the human resources of the Soviet orbit."[155] These terms of reference remained intact as the administration approved the final plan on 17 December 1952.[156] The United States would entice potential Soviet-orbit escapees with offers of asylum and assistance in building a constructive life in the West. It made a priority of inducing the defection of high-level Soviet officials except when such defections threatened to undermine intelligence operations. Finally, the plan called for the development of military forces composed of East bloc defectors under the leadership of high-level émigrés and incorporated into the U.S. military.[157]

With the election of Dwight Eisenhower, this plan lost its relevance. The Eisenhower administration considered PSB D-18a insufficient and would develop new strategies to use exile groups, not only in the clandestine services but also in the organized military units that made up the Volunteer Freedom Corps.[158]

U.S. Plans to Exploit the Death of Stalin

Overload and Delay and Operation Engross were plans aimed at undermining Soviet power over a period of years. The death of Stalin offered the possibility of immediate and dramatic change within the Soviet system. With the structure of Soviet power centered on one man, it was natural that most Soviet specialists would believe that Stalin's death offered the best hope for fundamental change. In "The Sources of Soviet Conduct" George Kennan considered the post-Stalin succession as potentially the most critical period for the long-term survival of the Soviet power structure.[159] Kennan argued that the next leadership change could "take place quietly and inconspicuously, with no repercussions anywhere" or it might "unleash, to use some of Lenin's words, one of those 'incredibly swift transitions' from 'delicate deceit' to 'wild violence' which characterize Russian history and may shake Soviet power to its foundations." Kennan warned that if "anything were ever to occur to disrupt the unity and efficacy of the Party as a political instrument, Soviet Russia might be changed overnight from one of the strongest to one of the weakest and most pitiable of national societies." Opinion was unanimous that the United States must develop the techniques to exploit Stalin's passing and weaken the Kremlin power structure in order to prevent an orderly transfer of authority.

The authors of Project TROY were among the first to assemble such a strategy. They called for the establishment of an expert staff responsible for correlating the predictions of the leading Sovietologists as to the various political scenarios likely to arise in the aftermath of Stalin's death. These scholars would try to anticipate the possible constellations of power that might assume control of the party. For instance, Stalin's death might lead to a triumvirate of Molotov, Beria, and Malenkov; or Beria, Bulganin, and Molotov. Bulganin backed by the armed forces might seize power alone, or Beria supported by the security services might emerge as the new leader. It would be the staff's responsibility to prepare a psychological warplan designed to create the maximum confusion possible in order to undermine the new leadership's ability to consolidate its hold over the country. Given Stalin's age time was of the essence, and "failure to have a strategy worked out might permit the consolidation of power under a new dictator, and we might have to wait another quarter of a century for another opportunity."[160]

Each plan would employ many of the same techniques used by other psychological-warfare plans. These plans would "take advantage of the Russians' historical willingness to believe that a deceased ruler has not in fact died."[161] American agents would plant the disinformation that a new power clique in Moscow murdered Stalin, or that the army or security services murdered Stalin. Other stories would claim that Stalin was in fact still alive—possibly "living in Georgia to persuade Georgian nationalists not to kill all Russians in Georgia; in Georgia to seek refuge from Russian nationalists; in Central Asia, in Siberia, a prisoner of the MVD in the Kremlin, etc."[162]

Other disinformation would state that high-level party officials had fled abroad to live off money previously deposited in foreign banks, that major Soviet Army units in Germany had defected upon receiving orders to invade West Germany, and that there were conflicts between army and MVD units in various parts of the country. Agents would sabotage the major industrial establishments and power plants located within the home regions of various party officials. Western sympathizers would spread rumors that directors of collective farms had been murdered, or that peasants had seized control of the Machine Tractor Stations. Finally, "consideration should be given to limited sabotage of power plants, refineries, and spreading crop and livestock diseases for the purpose of giving some substance to the rumor campaign."

Project TROY lead directly to PSB D-24: "Program of Psychological Preparation for Stalin's Passing from Power," code-named CANCELLATION, approved by the PSB on 1 November 1952.[163] The paper was less a plan, however, than an understanding of the problems that Stalin's death might pose.

PSB D-24 reaffirmed the view that Stalin's death might "touch off a split in the top leadership . . . it may also lead to the crystallization of present dissatisfaction among various groups in the Soviet population which feel themselves discriminated against." The authors warned, however, that Stalin's death could also result in changes which might not be favorable to the United States, such as a regime even more hostile to the West, a general war, or a general collapse so great that it could spread instability worldwide. Given the stakes involved, the report's authors contended that the administration must thoroughly examine each prospect in the event that it was possible "to pave the way, to a modest extent, for their eruption in desirable forms."[164] The report recommended that the United States continue to collect all available intelligence information so that a panel of experts might determine the potential constellations of forces that might arise in the aftermath of Stalin's death and prepare contingency plans for these possibilities. This suggestion rankled some within the State Department as being far too speculative for policy guidance.[165]

When Stalin did in fact die, in March 1953, Dwight D. Eisenhower's cold war advisor C. D. Jackson would criticize the report for having not prepared the U.S. government for the occasion. Consequently, the Eisenhower administration replaced PSB D-24 with a new strategy document—one that nevertheless would rely upon the findings of the Project TROY report.

As much as any previous event in the history of the country, the development of nuclear weapons by the Soviet Union transformed the strategic foundations of American national security policy. The Soviet atomic capability ended the century-long immunity of the United States from direct attack. It also ended the nation's half-century-long reliance on its vast mobilization capacity to either deter a Eurasian rival from initiating a global war or defeat that challenger should war come. Once the USSR built a sufficient stockpile of nuclear weapons, the United States faced the prospect of losing World War III at its outset.

The Truman administration could no longer count on the slow, methodical approach George Kennan proposed to resolve the Soviet threat. Paul Nitze and the State-Defense Team developed a new, more intensive strategy to achieve Kennan's policy, a strategy premised upon the United States turning its economic potential into "preponderant power" and significantly escalating its psychological-warfare efforts to destabilize the Soviet bloc. Time was now of the essence: the United States needed to weaken Soviet power and resolve the cold war before the Soviet Union's new atomic capability could devastate the United States in a surprise attack.

In making their case, Nitze and his colleagues felt they needed to exaggerate the Soviet menace to gain the administration's full support for their vast mobilization program. Yet in doing so they exposed their new strategy to Charles Bohlen's devastating challenge, which would dramatically transform the administration's effort to resolve the cold war.

[3]

Redefining Policy: Charles Bohlen and the Retrenchment of 1952

Charles Bohlen returned from his two-year tour of duty as minister in the U.S. embassy in France on 25 July 1951 and immediately relieved George Kennan of his position as counselor to Secretary of State Dean Acheson. Much had changed since Bohlen had last served in Washington, D.C. The NSC 68 mobilization of American military power had commenced. President Truman had approved the escalation of the psychological-warfare program to achieve the liberation of Eastern Europe and the destabilization of Soviet power and the PSB had begun to devise the strategies necessary to achieve these objectives. The strategic assumptions of NSC 68 seemed to have become fully ensconced in American national security policy.

Despite the claims of recent scholarship, Bohlen strongly supported Paul Nitze's contention that U.S. security required a sustained, massive military buildup and considered the conclusions of NSC 68 "unassailable."[1] Nevertheless, he had expressed reservations regarding the State-Defense Team's analysis of the Kremlin's willingness to risk war to achieve its objectives. In particular, Bohlen disagreed that the nuclear balance of power was the sole influence on the Soviets' calculations. He felt that the desire to maintain power was the principal motivation of the Soviet leadership and that they would take no risks that might threaten their survival. Although important, he did not consider this problem of a sufficient magnitude to revise NSC 68 in May of 1950, but upon his return from France Bohlen would raise the issue with Nitze.

Despite the unusually esoteric nature of Bohlen's criticisms, they would in fact force a fundamental transformation in America's cold war strategy. By positing that the Kremlin would take no action that might undermine its domestic control, Bohlen concluded that the Soviet Union was impervious to the pressures George Kennan believed necessary to compel it to abandon its international ambitions. Furthermore, he contended that no amount of military power—not even preponderant power—could coerce the Soviets into changing their aspirations. In fact, the objectives of NSC 20/4—and a resolution to the cold war itself—required nothing short of the removal of the Soviet regime, a capability the United States did not possess.

Consequently Bohlen would propose a new strategy, called "the doctrine of rational hope," which emphasized the consolidation of the free world, maintenance of a survivable nuclear retaliatory force capable of threatening Communist Party control of the Soviet Union, and awaiting the development of significant weaknesses within the Soviet state that the United States might exploit. In essence, Bohlen enunciated and received administration approval for a true policy of containment. Therefore, while Bohlen is remembered largely for his role as President Franklin Roosevelt's interpreter during the Yalta Conference and later as ambassador to the Soviet Union, scholars must consider him as important in the development of American national security policy as either George Kennan or Paul Nitze. Bohlen would in fact lay the intellectual foundation for U.S. policy for the rest of the cold war.[2]

Part One: The New National Security Policy toward the Communist Bloc

NSC 114: The First Review of NSC 68

On 12 July 1951, President Truman ordered the NSC Senior Staff to review the world situation and estimate the status of the military buildup in light of the Korean War. While Truman intended the review to satisfy a request for information from the Bureau of the Budget, it opened a debate that resulted in the formulation of a new strategy to achieve U.S. objectives toward the Soviet bloc.

The NSC Senior Staff presented the first draft of the review, NSC 114, to the council on 27 July.[3] Immediately it surprised the national security establishment by charging that despite the mobilization efforts, the military power of the United States had deteriorated significantly relative to the USSR since the completion of NSC 68. The report criticized both the projections of NSC 68 and the low level of implementation carried out by the various agencies. The Senior Staff concluded that despite the American buildup:

> The danger to our security is greater now than it was in April 1950. It is greater now than it was then thought it would now be. Fifteen months ago 1954 was regarded as the time of maximum danger. It appears that we are already in a period of acute danger which will continue until the United States and its allies achieve an adequate position of strength.[4]

While the report concluded that the United States and its allies were struggling to attain the force levels envisaged in NSC 68/4, new intelligence estimates indicated that Soviet strength had actually increased in both absolute and relative terms. Particularly alarming was the new estimate that Soviet atomic capabilities were growing at a substantially greater rate than anticipated in NSC 68. NSC 114 estimated that the Soviet Union would have the capability to launch a decisive surprise attack against the North American continent by 1953—rather than 1954.[5] The danger had become so acute that the Senior Staff warned that the Soviets might feel confident enough to consider "preventive action" (preventive war), if they could not forestall Western rearmament through political intimidation—a possibility that the administration took seriously.[6] Even if the Soviet Union shied away from such an extreme act, the growing disparity in the balance of power provided it with greater flexibility to engage in much more aggressive actions along the Eurasian periphery, actions ranging from political intrigue in Iran to direct military action on the scale of the Korean War. The NSC Senior Staff concluded that the nation needed to take still greater efforts to redress this situation, more than those envisaged even in NSC 68.[7]

Bohlen's Challenge to NSC 68

Although Charles Bohlen had returned from his assignment as minister in the U.S. embassy in Paris only several days before the Senior Staff distributed the draft paper, he recognized his long-awaited opportunity to challenge the interpretation of Soviet motivations made in NSC 68. Beginning with a 28 July memorandum to Nitze and continuing throughout the remainder of August, Bohlen argued that the administration needed to introduce more precision in its assessment of Soviet intentions. He strongly and repeatedly emphasized that his criticisms were "not designed to supplant the main thesis of the NSC 68 series, i.e., the vital necessity of a buildup of U.S. force and of our allies,"[8] admitting that "I am not in any position to comment on the parts [of NSC 114] dealing with our current programs, their status, adequacy, execution, etc." He stressed that the need for a buildup would continue "as long as the Soviet regime continues in power, or until there is so fundamental a change in its present structure as radically to alter the entire world situation."[9] He felt, however, that the imprecision of the State-Defense Team's analysis of Soviet motivations undermined the long-term rationale of the buildup, placing it "at the mercy of a traditional shift in Soviet tactics."[10] Bohlen focused his critique on two points: that Stalin's most important objective was world domination and that Soviet calculations for war were determined solely by balance-of-power considerations.

Bohlen argued that NSC 114 perpetuated the "mistaken analysis" first presented in NSC 68: that the Soviets operate as a "mechanical chess player engaged in the execution of a design fully prepared in advance with the ultimate goal of world domination."[11] Rather, the principal Soviet goal was to maintain the power of the communist regime in Russia; therefore, the Kremlin would take no risks that might endanger its authority. World war, especially if it entailed atomic retaliation against the USSR, would pose the most significant threat to the survival of the Soviet system. This did not mean that Bohlen considered the likelihood of war low. To the contrary, he contended that the Soviets would continue to probe and challenge the United States wherever possible. Instead, he rejected the contention that Soviet leadership might act in accordance with a specific schedule, i.e., that they might go to war by "deliberate calculation at such and such a date."

Bohlen disagreed with the Policy Planning Staff's use of the "doctrine of the decisive blow" to determine a specific date when the Soviet Union might launch an atomic strike against the United States.[12] Bohlen argued that policymakers must carefully distinguish between a "serious and continuing risk of war growing out of the present situation" and "a firmly held belief that war will probably start by deliberate Soviet calculation at such-and-such a date."[13] He was especially dismissive of the NSC Senior Staff's efforts to portray the Korean War as evidence of the Kremlin's global ambitions. Bohlen emphasized that he did not believe that a North Korean attack indicated a greater willingness to accept the risk of war on the part of the Soviets.[14] On the contrary, the war was a major blunder the Soviets did not anticipate, not he concluded, the result of their "relentless pursuit of the Kremlin design."[15] "If the atomic equation is regarded as controlling," Bohlen wrote, "then logically the Russians would go to very great lengths to avoid anything that could lead to a serious risk of general war before this equation . . . was sufficiently balanced in their favor."[16] He was so emphatic on this point that a few weeks later he wrote Acheson that Korea actually disproved the accuracy of the analysis in NSC 68. If the strategic balance of power guided Soviet behavior, he wondered, why would they have accepted the risk of armed action prior to their possession of a decisive nuclear capability?[17] Finally, Bohlen reminded his audience that the Soviets had actually threatened the survival of the United States prior to their detonation of the atomic bomb and had in fact been "preparing for possible war with the U.S. . . . well before 1950."[18]

Throughout August and September the Policy Planning Staff met with Bohlen in order to clarify his critique of NSC 68. Bohlen made clear that he did not challenge the need for a substantial military buildup, but that he disagreed with the characterization that the Soviets were functioning according to a "carefully laid out blueprint" that raised the prospect of a deliberate Soviet attack on the West. Henry Koch, one of the S/P representatives in these meetings, believed that the original drafters of NSC 68 had not envisioned such a design. He readily admitted, however, that many people in

Washington were in fact acting under the assumption that the communist leadership had a timetable for world conquest, an assumption that threatened to undermine the construction of a stable national security policy.[19] Koch concluded that:

> Though it may be necessary for the administration to over-simplify Soviet intentions in appealing to Congress and the people for support of the defense program, it is nonetheless important that we in the Department and on the National Security Council do not become 'hoisted by our own petard.' We do not want to find ourselves in the position of the gambler at the race track who spread rumors about the excellent chances of a broken-down nag in order to improve the odds on the horse which he considered the likely winner who at the last moment . . . shifted his bet from the winner to the nag who crossed the finish-line last.[20]

Whether Soviet nuclear developments provided the USSR with the capability of destroying both American industry and retaliatory power remained the chief disagreement between the two sides. Bohlen contended that the Soviet Union would not launch a nuclear first strike if it could not destroy American retaliatory capabilities since the counterattack might destroy the communist regime's control of the country. Koch agreed, and concluded that much work was needed to determine the extent of the Soviet nuclear threat.[21]

Despite the intensity of his challenge and the respect Koch accorded him, Bohlen's criticisms of NSC 68 had, in fact, broken no new ground. Nearly all the points that he raised had already been made by numerous government officials the year before. George Kennan among others had already opposed the notion that the nuclear balance of power solely determined Soviet decisionmaking regarding the likelihood of war, a position that the State-Defense Team had already come to accept. Robert Hooker of S/P responded to the numerous criticisms on this point by arguing that NSC 68 neither predicted war by a certain date nor asserted that the nuclear balance of power was the sole determinant of Soviet behavior.[22] Hooker had emphasized during the preparation of NSC 68 that the "study group would itself be the first to refute any claim that the study represents the ultimate in wisdom or provides all of the answers to the extremely complex and difficult problems involved." Furthermore, he had denied that NSC 68 predicted the Soviets would go to war in 1954.

> If a 'yes' or 'no' answer to the question as to whether we anticipate that Russia will strike in 1954 and we should prepare to mobilize by that date is needed, the answer should be in the negative. However, a careful reading of the paper cannot lead to the conclusion that we do anticipate such a Russian attack except under a number of qualifying conditions and assumptions.[23]

In fact, the Ad Hoc Committee established by President Truman to review the conclusions of NSC 68 determined that "NSC 68 did not call for complete preparation for war, but primarily for a posture of defense sufficient to enable the U.S. to deter a direct Soviet attack, and to achieve ultimate U.S. objectives short of war."[24]

Even Bohlen's reading of NSC 68 was suspect, as he was wrong on his two most significant criticisms. First, the State-Defense Team, using the intelligence estimates provided by JIC 502, premised its strategic analysis on the belief that a Soviet attack at the level of two hundred atomic weapons could destroy both American retaliatory capabilities and mobilization capacity, undermining his criticism of the State-Defense Team's analysis of the Soviet Union's motivation to strike the United States. Second, while Nitze and his staff did argue that the ultimate Soviet goal was domination of the world, they fully recognized that the Soviets would take no efforts that would undermine their accomplishments to date. They argued that "the fundamental design of those who control the Soviet Union and the international communist movement is to retain and solidify their absolute power, first in the Soviet Union and second in the areas now under their control."[25]

Consequently, Paul Nitze, who had spent most of 1950 fending off these attacks to his policy paper, grew frustrated with Bohlen's criticisms. He recognized that while Bohlen may have been fully supportive of the military buildup, opponents such as Secretary of Defense George Marshall and Deputy Secretary of Defense Robert Lovett, both of whom believed that only a slower pace would maintain public support, might conflate Bohlen's arguments with their concerns about the viability of the buildup.[26] Bohlen's critique could not have come at a worse time, since he was arguing that considerations regarding the domestic strength of the regime influenced Soviet foreign policy more than the strategic balance of power. If Bohlen's viewpoint became established policy, then Marshall and Lovett could argue that there was no longer a need for a rapid mobilization of the scale supported by Nitze.[27]

Therefore, on 22 September Nitze harshly criticized Bohlen's approach in a long memorandum submitted to Acheson, arguing that their debate seemed more concerned with form than content. "I assume from his memorandum . . . ," Nitze argued:

> that Chip [Bohlen] would be agreeable to the inclusion in NSC papers of a general statement of Soviet intentions to the effect that the Soviet Union is 'a heavily armed great power, which by its basic doctrine and the form of its state organization is implacably and unappeasably hostile to the United States and other free countries.' What Chip appears to object to is an attempt to analyze Soviet intentions beyond these very broad generalizations. Surely the State Department has an obligation to give somewhat more precise guidelines for dealing with the problems confronting the U.S. Government.[28]

Nitze pointed out that both he and Bohlen agreed that the Soviet Union possessed significantly superior military capabilities, was "implacably and unappeasingly hostile" to the free world, and sought to aggrandize its world influence whenever possible. Nitze concluded that if the "implacably hostile" USSR possessed "dangerously superior relative capabilities," it would act opportunistically:

> Then it seems the unavoidable conclusion is that the U.S.S.R. will exercise their capabilities at any time and place they conceive to be favorable to them. I do not consider this to be a 'metaphysical' analysis of Russian intentions, and do think it supports the view that the U.S.S.R. has an impulse to an extension of their authority and the objective of removing all serious threats to them which, in the long run, would amount to domination of the world.

Bohlen responded with an equally testy rejoinder. After accusing Nitze of trying to cloud the debate with extraneous issues he declared: "*The only issue here is whether or not the NSC 68 analysis of the Soviet Union is sufficiently accurate to serve as a guide for U.S. Government interpretation of Soviet actions and for an estimate of probable future Soviet moves.* My entire position is that it is not; that it is not a true picture of how the Soviet Union operates as I have observed and studied it."[29] Bohlen remained adamant that Soviet actions since April 1950 were not congruent with the analysis in NSC 68, particularly concerning the Korean War. He wrote:

> It must be recalled that NSC 68, the master paper on the Soviet Union, was completed less than three months before the Soviet Union took its most important single action since the close of hostilities, i.e., Korea. Yet NSC 68 would not set anybody's mind to think of the probability of such type action on the part of the Soviet bloc.[30]

Bohlen's attack on NSC 68 and 114 quickly embroiled the NSC Senior Staff.[31] Since distribution of the original draft paper on 27 July, the Senior Staff had struggled to arrive at a set of conclusions acceptable to Bohlen while not straying too far from the original draft of NSC 114. Bohlen's critique placed the NSC Senior Staff in a quandary. Bohlen believed that NSC 114 required such significant revisions that the NSC Senior Staff could not present it to the National Security Council. To write a new policy paper, however, the Senior Staff would need to receive President Truman's personal authorization, and the president had recently warned NSC executive secretary James Lay that the council required the final draft by 17 October.[32] Consequently, the Senior Staff continued to struggle through many long and contentious meetings to hammer out an acceptable policy within the NSC 114 framework.

The Senior Staff discussed the result of these efforts—NSC 114/2—on

25 September and made a significant effort to bridge the opposing sides of the debate.[33] The organization of the document reflects this attempt: the staff divided it into two sections, the first studying the impact of growing Soviet capabilities and the second outlining the aims and objectives of Soviet policy.

Section one reaffirmed Nitze's viewpoint that Soviet military power was growing stronger relative to that of the United States. The Soviets would maintain significantly superior ground forces capable of overrunning most of Western Europe and the Middle East—although the staff estimated that NATO forces might be able to hold key strategic regions in Western Europe after 1953.

Soviet nuclear developments remained the most troublesome aspect of East bloc capabilities. NSC 114/2 repeated earlier predictions that despite U.S. nuclear superiority, the Soviets could be capable of launching a decisive nuclear strike by mid-1953, and rejected the contention that American nuclear superiority would itself be sufficient to deter potential Soviet aggression. Its authors concluded that when the Soviet atomic stockpile could disrupt an American retaliatory strike and seriously damage the U.S. industrial base "the importance of the Soviet stockpile will be entirely out of proportion to the relative size of the two stockpiles." The most important strategic relationship, consequently, was not the balance between the two stockpiles but the relationship between a deliverable stockpile and the number of important strategic targets. Over 40 percent of the U.S. population and over 50 percent of U.S. industry were located in fifty-four major centers, which, given estimated Soviet capabilities and a lack of air defense systems, would be highly susceptible to attack by 1953. The authors of NSC 114/2 did not believe that the Soviets would strike on that date. The most likely date for a deliberate initiation of war was when the Soviets possessed both decisive nuclear capabilities and the ability to crush NATO resistance and prevent the United States from holding areas in Europe. It was imperative that the United States build sufficient forces to deter Soviet military action under any circumstances.

While section one was clearly in accord with Nitze, Bohlen's critique heavily influenced section two. The document accepted Bohlen's argument that the strategic balance of power was not the only determinant of the possibility of Soviet aggression. It argued that while the Kremlin was interested in expanding its power position whenever possible, it would not if such aggression would threaten the maintenance of its authority. Section two continued to warn, however, that Soviet calculations of these risks would be determined by the status of the American military buildup.

Although the conclusions of the report satisfied Nitze, Bohlen remained opposed.[34] He considered the discussion of Soviet aims a "futile and dangerous attempt to indulge in metaphysical speculations on general Soviet intentions."[35] He felt that the drafting committee's efforts to assuage his concerns resulted in a confusing and contradictory explanation of Soviet power. He recommended that the Senior Staff replace a significant portion of the paper with a section explaining the risks faced by the Soviet regime, without ultimately regressing into "complicated ideological considerations."[36] He offered the following statement in particular:

> It would appear sufficient for the justification of our military buildup, as rapidly as it can be done without serious damage to the economies of the free world, to accept as a basis certain unassailable facts concerning the Soviet government and the areas of the world controlled or directed by it. Confronted by a heavily armed great power, which by its basic doctrine and the form of its state organization is implacably and unappeasably hostile to the United States and other free countries, no complicated analysis of ideological considerations is necessary to support the conclusion that the United States and its allies in elementary survival must develop adequate defensive strength—adequate in the sense of being able to hold essential positions against Soviet attack while mobilizing to inflict a military defeat on the Soviet system.[37]

The Senior Staff fiercely debated NSC 114/2. The staff's meeting of 10 October grew so contentious that it took nearly five hours for the group to review only eighteen pages of the report. At one point, PSB representative Robert Cutler and presidential economic advisor Leon Keyserling argued with such intensity that Keyserling stormed out of the room and refused to return. Some concluded that U.S. knowledge of Soviet atomic capabilities was "pretty god-damned sketchy" and that the "date of criticality may even be sooner than expected."[38] The following day Bohlen reiterated that NSC 114/2 required extensive redrafting and with the support of others on the Senior Staff recommended that the administration undertake a full reappraisal. Lay warned him that Truman would not change his 17 October deadline because of the importance of the paper to the formulation of the 1953 budget.[39] Over the course of the next week, Lay arrived at a solution. He would present to the NSC the military requirements outlined in NSC 114/2 as well as some of the revised portions of NSC 114/2, but for informational purposes only. Meanwhile, he requested Truman's authorization for a reappraisal of NSC 68 in light of changes in the world situation over the last eighteen months.[40] The following day Bohlen requested, and received, Acheson's support for the reappraisal.[41] At the 105th meeting of the NSC on 17 October, the council recommended that Truman agree to the reexamination of NSC 68 and 114, which he did the next day.[42] On 24 October, James Lay formed a steering committee composed of representatives of the Defense Department, the CIA, and the Joint Chiefs of Staff to review the military situation while Bohlen would write the review of U.S. national security policy.[43] The reappraisal of NSC 68 had begun.

The New Policy: "The Doctrine of Rational Hope"

On 30 June 1952, after nearly seven months and numerous drafts, Bohlen and the steering committee submitted to the Senior Staff their completed work on the reappraisal of the NSC 68-114 series.[44] The committee separated the document into two parts. Section one—entitled "Bases of Soviet Action"—was written by Bohlen and comprised the views he had been expressing since May 1950, while the Department of Defense prepared part two—"Relative Political, Economic, and Military Capabilities" of the United States and the Soviet Union.

"Bases of Soviet Action" described what Bohlen called the three fundamental features of the Soviet system.[45] First, the USSR was a heavily armed totalitarian state ruled by a small group of men whose minimum objective was to build the strength of the Soviet system so that no power—domestic or foreign—could challenge the authority of their regime. Second, the USSR was "fundamentally and unappeasably hostile" to any nation not under its control and would exploit any opportunity to weaken its enemies and increase its own power position as long as its actions did not undermine the security of the regime. Third, the Soviet leadership was devoid of any "humanitarian, moral or ethical" considerations that would act as a restraint on its actions. Therefore, regardless of the tactical shifts in Soviet policy an imbalance of power in favor of the Soviet bloc represented a critical threat to the free nations of the world.[46]

Its great military power notwithstanding, domestic vulnerabilities limited the threat posed by the Soviet Union. The history of the Bolshevik era, according to Bohlen, demonstrated that "to date no substantial sacrifice has been made for the benefit of the world revolutionary movement at the expense of the regime." This did not mean that the Soviets were not interested in expanding their authority. On the contrary, the Soviet rulers believed that by continuously subduing Western nations they could significantly reduce the threat to their regime. They would not continue with these efforts, however, if it appeared that they would threaten their own political survival. According to Bohlen, the greatest threat the regime faced was another world war that would strain the Soviet Union's economy, undermine control of the satellites, and "alter to the detriment of the party the relationship between party and army." The Soviet leadership would not take general war lightly. On the other hand, if the Soviet Union developed the unquestioned capability to quickly destroy America's warfighting and retaliatory capability, "they would probably take such action," demonstrating Bohlen's acceptance of Nitze's strategic logic. Therefore, the United States needed to maintain a level of military strength demonstrably capable of surviving a Soviet strike and retaliating with such force that the Soviet system would collapse.[47]

While Bohlen was generally optimistic that the threat of global war with the Soviet Union was not immediate, he was entirely dismissive of the prospects of a rapprochement between the two social systems. He argued, as Kennan had nearly six years before, that a hostile environment was a necessity for the maintenance of the Soviet system. The cold war began when the Bolsheviks first took power in 1917 and had to establish an iron grip in order to maintain control at home. To justify the ensuing years of oppression, the revolutionary leaders created the "bogey" of capitalist encirclement: that the capitalist nations intended to destroy the Soviet state through either war or internal uprising. Under no circumstances could the Soviet leadership establish peaceful relations with the West, since doing so would remove the chief rationale for the police state and threaten continuation of its power within the USSR. Consequently, Bohlen concluded that it was impossible for the United States to compel the Soviet leadership to fundamentally change its national security beliefs, a clear repudiation of Kennan's argument in NSC 20/1 and U.S. policy since 1948. The objectives of NSC 20/4 could be attained only with the removal of the Soviet regime. This was a crucial point of opposition between Bohlen and George Kennan. While Kennan felt that successful U.S. efforts to coerce the Soviet Union might very well result in the collapse of the regime, Bohlen argued the reverse: fear of collapse would prevent the Soviet leadership from being coerced into making any such changes to begin with.[48]

Not only did Bohlen challenge the offensive strategy Kennan developed to achieve the objectives of NSC 20/4, he also questioned the political utility of preponderant military power as stressed in NSC 68. He concluded that:

> It does not appear that the developing situation will, in the foreseeable future, require the Soviets to yield interests now held which they regard as important to their security. Nor does it appear likely that an increase to any higher level of strength which the free world could maintain over an extended period would significantly change the prospect. Neither does it appear that there is any prospect, regardless of the level of strength we may achieve, of negotiating lasting settlements with the present communist regime. Our strength may deter deliberate initiation of hostilities by the Soviets or the undertaking of local aggression, but it will not change the implacable nature of communism which dictates that it be hostile to all not under its control.

This paragraph directly challenged the suppositions of NSC 20/4 and NSC 68, that the policies of the Soviet regime could be changed if the United States attained a position of preponderant power. Bohlen concluded that nothing short of the removal of the Soviet regime itself would lead to the achievement of American national security objectives.[49]

Bohlen presented the conclusions of his analysis to the NSC Senior Staff on 8 July, proposing the following national security policy:

> Phase A: completing the consolidation of a free world defensive position which will enable us to stop Soviet expansion in all key areas; phase B: [com-

> petition with the Soviet system] reaching into the indefinite future with an 'element of rational hope' based on confidence in the intrinsic superiority of our system over the Soviet system, which would have a chance to operate in our favor after a military stalemate is achieved. We would of course try to reinforce this latter development by various diplomatic and other pressures, but it is out of the question to try to offer a blue-print: nobody can foresee how the struggle will end.[50]

In other words, the United States would adopt a policy of containment and coexistence: build the liberal international economic order, prevent continued Soviet expansion, maintain a secure retaliatory force capable of destroying the party's control of the USSR, and hope that in the distant future the Soviet system would decay to such an extent that the regime would collapse. Although he believed that "temporary understandings" with the Soviets were possible in "local situations that got a little too dangerous" for both East and West, "there was not much hope" for a long-term settlement with the USSR as long as it remained a totalitarian police state. "We are in for a long, long, pull," lamented Bohlen, before a resolution to the cold war could be possible.[51]

Various Senior Staff representatives expressed alarm at the "defeatist" tone of the new draft policy, a particular concern since "the assumptions of NSC 68 now being discarded seemed to have taken with the leadership, and had apparently made a deep impression on the President himself."[52] Bohlen responded that the element of frustration leading to the charge of "defeatism" was due to the "false expectations, including illusions fostered by the mistaken analysis of NSC 68." He contended that the new policy actually showed that the United States had come a long way in the cold war since NSC 68 "in that we are no longer worried about the possibility of global defeat in war." The crucial difference between the new policy and NSC 68 was the "different diagnosis of Soviet motivation" resulting in the conclusion that "even if we could and did create a situation of marked military superiority as envisaged in NSC 68, it would not be worthwhile because it would not in fact enable us to do what NSC 68 thought it would. The nature of the Soviet system precludes real 'negotiated settlements' of the kind NSC 68 looked forward to."[53]

Charles Noyes of the Defense Department and co-author of NSC 114 claimed that in fact there was no basic departure from the strategy of NSC 68; instead the drafts proposed that "we go steadily ahead as we are now, and merely renounced the prospect of using preponderant military force for coercion."[54] Others demurred, however. Allen Dulles interjected that there were a "number of positive things we could do without having preponderant military strength, and that these should be put into the paper."[55] Dulles's view reflected the feelings of many political-warfare specialists who had long argued that vast military power was not a precondition for aggressive operations against the Soviet bloc. Admiral T. E. Woolridge noted that the JCS considered the main new point in the drafts to be the recognition that the struggle could be lost at points around the periphery and not merely in Europe. Furthermore, although he saw no possibility of ever attaining marked military superiority in standing military forces, he believed a sound defense was possible.[56]

Everett Gleason, deputy executive secretary of the NSC, warned that the new policy risked losing public support for the military programs "if it [the public] is given no serious hope of a final solution to the Soviet problem." Therefore, the meeting concluded with the decision to assign the paper to the NSC Staff assistants in order to present the new national strategy "in somewhat more hopeful language, but with little change in real content."[57] Meanwhile, the Senior Staff would await the responses from other agencies. They would not have to wait long, as within two days the S/P lodged a thunderous reply.

Nitze and the Policy Planning Staff Reply

During July of 1951, it was Paul Nitze and Robert Tufts of the Policy Planning Staff who received the wrath of Charles Bohlen; in July of 1952, these gentlemen gained their recompense. Tufts, a member of the drafting committees for both NSC 68 and NSC 114, warned as early as May 1952 that the new policy papers did not have access to a significant amount of information necessary for the review.[58] He cautioned that "the present draft study is almost wholly irrelevant to the major issues on which this Government must take decisions within the coming months." Tufts considered the study's conclusions "inadequate, misleading in some respects, and inaccurate in others. It would be . . . positively harmful for the NSC to proceed with the consideration of the present draft study with a view to its eventual approval as a reappraisal of NSC 68 and 114 policies."[59]

If Tufts was critical of the early draft policy statement, he was downright contemptuous of the 30 June draft. Tufts warned Nitze that the new draft statement had effectively rejected the central conclusion of NSC 68: the policy of preponderant power. Tufts wrote that the steering committee failed to understand that the pursuit of preponderant power was not simply a matter of budgets but the very basis of international relations itself. All nations, he clarified, search for a level of power that will enable them to influence the international system. "Given the polarization of power around the United States and the U.S.S.R.," argued Tufts, "to seek less than preponderant power would be to opt for defeat. . . . Preponderant power should and must be the objective of U.S. policy."[60] The consequences of failing to produce preponderant military strength prior to a future global war were simple to predict. The West would be swept off the Eurasian continent and a new division of the world would occur: the Soviets would be masters of all the productive capacity of Eurasia, possibly including Japan, while the United States would be relegated to the Western Hemisphere. The edifice of postwar U.S. national security policy, i.e., establishment of the liberal international economic order, would be demolished. The very possibility of this outcome, Tufts feared, might itself be sufficient to entice the Soviets into launching a nuclear attack prior to their ability to eliminate both American industrial production and retaliatory capability. In other words, they would "eat whatever damage we can inflict" in order to acquire Western Europe and establish a new line of "reciprocal containment."[61] Tufts denounced the reappraisal for concluding that:

> We cannot roll back Soviet power nor hope that the successful containment of Soviet power will produce any significant changes in the nature of the Soviet system. The endorsement of the NSC 20/4 and NSC 68/2 objectives is therefore a merely formal endorsement. Our maximum actual objective becomes merely to deter general war and the undertaking of local aggression for an indefinite period of time—probably permanently.[62]

Tufts' criticisms were incorporated into Nitze's memo to Deputy Under Secretary of State H. Freeman Matthews. Nitze dismissed the steering committee's analysis for being "internally inconsistent." He contended that the reappraisal accepted that U.S. military capabilities were significantly inferior to those of the Soviets—and would remain so for "a long time." Yet the steering committee seemed to decide, according to Nitze, that there was nothing the United States could do—or should do—to rectify this situation. Consequently, the administration would have to abandon "any hope of effective air and civil defenses; any attempts at serious negotiation; any attempt now or later to roll back the iron curtain; any attempt to gain preponderant power. The conclusion is that we should accept a long period of relative disadvantage during which we unhopefully wait for the U.S.S.R. to change."[63]

Nitze contended that Bohlen had failed to present evidence that the risk of war and the risk that the United States faced "piecemeal defeat" in the cold war no longer remained great. Furthermore, he believed that the overall capabilities of the West were in fact more than sufficient to maintain a significant military buildup. Finally, Nitze concluded that the only way the United States could attain the objectives of NSC 20/4 was through the development of clearly preponderant power, "probably more power than to win military victory in the event of war." The problem was the free world lacked the necessary direction, organization, and leadership; "if these necessary factors were in place, we can within the next several years gain preponderant power."[64]

Nitze continued that there was a clear hierarchy of national security objectives: strength at the center, strength at the periphery, and the retraction of Soviet power and a change in the Soviet system. Bohlen's rejection of a coercive strategy was dangerous for American policy; "as the free world's capabilities are developed," he contended, "opportunities will arise for inducing or compelling a retraction of Soviet power, not, of course, without any risks but at acceptable risks."[65] While this seemed intended to restore an offensive dimension to American policy, in reality it signaled acceptance of Bohlen's critique and a rejection of the intensification of U.S. psychological-warfare efforts called for in NSC 68. Compare Nitze's statement with Robert Joyce's 18 April 1950 presentation to the OPC where he stressed that the Policy Planning Staff wanted the OPC to prepare a covert strategy capable of "fomenting and supporting unrest and revolt in selected strategic satellite countries."[66] This action would be done in such a way that the United States could "reduce the power and influence of the Kremlin *inside* the Soviet Union and other areas under its control. The objective would be the establishment of friendly regimes not under Kremlin domination."[67] There would be no waiting for the successful containment of Soviet power; the administration would unleash psychological warfare against the Soviet bloc immediately. Consequently, Nitze's hierarchy of objectives represented a significant change from the programs first proposed by NSC 68 and in fact did not differ at all from the strategy proposed by Bohlen. It would serve as the basis for an eventual compromise between the two strategists.

The New Doctrine Approved

The following two weeks saw intensive negotiations between Bohlen's office and Nitze's staff over the draft policy statement. According to one observer, "State is reportedly split right up to the top on the issue and Secretary Acheson is spending hours on end discussing it with his top advisers."[68] Finally, on 30 July, Bohlen and Acheson concluded a compromise policy statement—NSC 135/1—that Acheson supported and President Truman approved in a slightly revised form on 24 September. (The final draft was denoted NSC 135/3.) While in some respects the new policy statement reverted back to the tone of NSC 20/4 and NSC 68, in substance it reaffirmed Bohlen's "doctrine of rational hope." U.S. policy would seek to develop "positive appeals superior to those of communism," block further expansion of Soviet power "even at grave risk of war," and take "all means short of war to induce the retraction of the Kremlin's control and influence and so foster the seeds of destruction within the Soviet system that the Kremlin is brought at least to the point of modifying its behavior to conform to generally accepted international standards."[69] Furthermore, it would remain U.S. policy to build "such strength" sufficient to prevent expansion of the Soviet orbit either "physically or politically" with the ultimate goal of assisting the gradual weakening and decay of the Soviet system, although "no specific time can be established" by which this objective could be achieved.

While nominally in accord with the objectives of NSC 20/4—which is why NSC 135/3 did not officially supersede NSC 20/4—we shall see below that the conclusions of NSC 135/3 were interpreted by the Strategic Concept Panel to mean that while a limited modification in Soviet behavior might be achieved, only the removal of the Soviet regime by war or revolution could fully accomplish the objectives of U.S. policy. Additionally, the document failed to emphasize the need to gain preponderant power, so crucial to the NSC 68-114 series and the key complaint of both Nitze and Tufts. The objective of the free world would be to build such overall strength necessary to confront the Kremlin with the prospect that "a Soviet attack would result in serious risk to the regime." In addition, the United States would seek "to reduce opportunities for local Soviet aggression and political warfare" and to "permit the exploitation of rifts between the USSR and other communist states" and between the communist regimes and their peoples, "thus possibly offering to certain satellite peoples the prospect of liberation without war."[70]

While this declaration seemed in consonance with NSC 20/4 and NSC 68, the authors stressed that as of 1952 U.S. political-warfare capabilities could not achieve the liberation of the satellite states given the strength of Soviet and satellite control mechanisms. Some decay of the Soviet system was essential before covert action could become effective. The document stated that:

> Where operations can be conducted on terms which may result in relative decrease in Soviet power without involving unacceptable risks, the United States should pursue and as practicable intensify positive political, economic, propaganda, and paramilitary operations designed to weaken Kremlin control over the satellites. However, we should not over-estimate the effectiveness of the activities we can pursue within the Soviet orbit, and should proceed with caution and a careful weighing of the risks in pressing upon what the Kremlin probably regards as its vital interests.[71]

The prospects for political warfare, so crucial to U.S. policy from 1948 to 1951, were now questioned. The strategies designed to coerce the Kremlin into altering its policies were inadequate for the much more onerous task of overthrowing the Soviet regime itself. While the United States would continue "to develop our capabilities for assisting revolution,"[72] barring "extraordinary opportunities for exploitation" such as the death of Stalin "such operations cannot be depended upon to reduce drastically the basic threat which the Soviet system poses to the free world."[73]

Despite the Policy Planning Staff's best efforts, it was unable to halt the retrenchment in U.S. policy toward the Soviet bloc. A combination of factors seems to have doomed its position: a lack of expertise to challenge Bohlen's contention that U.S. objectives could be achieved only by the removal of the Soviet regime and growing questions as to the ultimate effectiveness of U.S. psychological-warfare capabilities in achieving policy. Concern was also mounting that in the nuclear age it was impossible to develop the necessary "preponderant power" to shield a U.S. political offensive against Eastern Europe. NSC 135 reconfirmed the proposition first presented in JIC 502 that the absolute number of nuclear weapons possessed by the United States and the Soviet Union was less important than the relationship between a specific stockpile and the number of key targets required to destroy the opponent's warfighting capabilities.[74] Although the United States might hold a massive superiority in deliverable nuclear weapons, given the number and distribution of U.S. economic and military targets the Soviets could soon amass a stockpile capable of achieving a decisive surprise attack in a preemptive strike. According to intelligence estimates, the Kremlin would possess 100 bombs in the thirty to seventy kiloton range by mid-1953, 190 by mid-1954, and 300 by mid-1955. By mid-1955 the Soviet Air Force would include some eleven hundred TU-4 bombers capable of striking the continental United States, albeit on one-way missions. Assuming a worst-case scenario, a Soviet first strike could inflict 9 million casualties in 1953 (12.5 million in 1955), paralyze 33 percent of U.S. industry (66 percent in 1955), and destroy one-quarter of the U.S. retaliatory capability.[75] These facts led to the conclusion that:

> The controlling relationship in the atomic equation appears not to be that of stockpiles to each other, but rather the relationship of one stockpile, plus its deliverability, to the number of key enemy targets, including retaliatory facilities, which must be destroyed in order to warrant an attack. If this latter relationship is controlling, then it follows that the Soviets may achieve what is, in their judgment, a level of atomic strength sufficient to warrant the risk of an all-out surprise attack, even though this level may be inferior—in absolute terms—to the then existing atomic strength of the United States.[76]

Even though the United States possessed a substantial advantage in nuclear weapons in 1953, moving to strategic superiority by 1955, the Soviet nuclear force could be capable of such damage that the incentive to strike first would still exist.[77] The question arose whether strategic superiority was at all possible in the nuclear age, and, if not, what affect this would have on American objectives predicated upon such superiority. This undermined the very foundation of NSC 68: that the United States could build a military shield to deter Soviet action while destabilizing the Soviet empire. Once Soviet capabilities reached a certain level, American superiority would become irrelevant.[78] The possibility that the United States could so deter the Soviets that they would not respond militarily to efforts to destabilize their regime was now unclear. The political implications of this conclusion were sobering.

Because the United States was willing to take all necessary risks, including "grave risk of war," to consolidate the liberal international economic order by securing Western Europe, the Middle East, Japan, and the third world, absolute nuclear superiority remained strategically important. Since the United States was not willing to fight a global war to secure the collapse of the Soviet bloc, however, the extent of America's ability to intimidate the Soviet Union was limited. These new estimates established that the administration had to consider Soviet military counteraction a legitimate threat—regardless of American capabilities—once the Soviet Union's nuclear stockpile reached a certain threshold.

This did not mean that U.S. policymakers anticipated a Soviet first strike. Part of the compromise between the positions of Bohlen and Nitze was agreement that the principal objective of Soviet power was survival of the regime; the Kremlin would take no action that it believed could lead to a collapse of its power at home, such as nuclear war.[79] This compromise, however, also pointed out the obvious problem of U.S. policy: could the United States ever be confident that the Soviet Union would not respond with a preemptive nuclear strike if American political warfare threatened either the Soviets' hold on Eastern Europe or the stability of the Soviet regime itself? This was a possibility that Kennan himself admitted as early as 1948.[80] Bohlen seemed to recognize this dilemma as well when he wrote: "basically we should seek by every means to avoid confronting the Soviet rulers with the apparent choice between maintenance by war or loss of their power in Russia."[81] Now that the administration realized U.S. nuclear capabilities might not deter a Soviet first strike, it was imperative not to incite a war.

NSC 135/1 reshaped the approach by which the United States could achieve the objectives of NSC 20/4. Kennan's strategy of political and psychological coercion, as well as Nitze's doctrine of "preponderant power," was replaced with an approach which differed little from traditional notions of containment.[82] The United States would continue to build an "over-all position of strength" and take all measures necessary to ensure the security of key geostrategic regions around the Soviet periphery. It would abandon, however, efforts to seek preponderant or superior power, and would await the internal disintegration of the Soviet system before aggressively pursuing the collapse of communist power. This strategy, Nitze concluded, resulted in the United States becoming "a sort of hedge-hog, unattractive to attack, but basically not very worrisome over a period of time beyond our immediate position."[83] The effect of NSC 135/1 was to turn the objectives of

NSC 20/4 into a set of aspirations that the United States would try to accomplish, rather than an immediate and tangible set of goals. Consequently, the new policy drastically changed the development of the strategic concept and the psychological-warfare plans to attack the Iron Curtain.

Part Two: A Strategic Concept Is Decided

Rival Versions of the Strategic Concept Paper

Since the key participants in the debates over the administration's national security policy also took part in the preparation of the strategic concept paper, the shift in policy also heavily influenced the development of the strategic concept. By January 1952, the NSC had issued sufficient policy guidance to begin work on the project. The Strategic Concept Panel, composed of Admiral Leslie Stevens, Charles Bohlen, Paul Nitze, Charles Stelle, John Magruder, and Frank Wisner, was assigned the task of establishing U.S. political-warfare strategy in accordance with NSC 10/5 and subject to certain restrictions. The Strategic Concept Panel faced the daunting task of trying to establish operational guidance so that the United States could achieve its objectives before the Soviet Union developed a decisive nuclear capability. Such guidance had to strengthen the U.S. position in countries outside the Iron Curtain, direct efforts to detach each of the satellites from Moscow, undermine the structure of Soviet power within the USSR, and force the Kremlin to abandon its international objectives. These efforts were limited to methods "consistent with our freedoms and our evolving way of life" that did not incur excessive risks of general war, did not alienate U.S. allies, and did not "generate psychological climates unmanageably hostile to the United States."

By late January, it had become evident that the State Department and the CIA were assuming control of the strategic concept paper at the expense of the PSB. By claiming that the paper entered areas of policy, the State Department was able to assume a leading role in the deliberations of the Strategic Concept Panel and restrict the PSB to an advisory capacity. The CIA assumed a superior position to the PSB given the strength of CIA director Walter Bedell Smith, the close friendship between Frank Wisner and Charles Bohlen, and the agency's position as the principal operating arm of U.S. covert warfare.[84] It was no surprise that the State Department and the CIA prepared the four position papers from which the panel would derive the strategic concept. The State Department was responsible for establishing the most desirable approach for each region of the world and for assessing the difficulties U.S. political warfare faced in each area. The CIA would analyze the best methods of attack and existing capabilities for covert action.

Of the four papers produced, two have been declassified: the State Department study assessing the most pertinent areas for attack and the CIA analysis of extant psychological-warfare capabilities.

The State Department paper, written by Charles Stelle of the Policy Planning Staff, suggested that the reduction of Soviet power be divided into two categories: "weakening Soviet power and influence by strengthening the West; and weakening Soviet power and influence in the Communist orbit."[85] Covert operations designed to strengthen the Western position would attempt to destroy communist parties and communist-leaning organizations outside the Iron Curtain. Other operations were calculated to weaken Soviet power and influence within the communist orbit and destabilize the satellite regimes' control over their populations.

Stelle argued that the administration should base its operational planning on three general considerations. First, the effect of successful or unsuccessful operations on communist influence and power; second, the degree to which U.S. capabilities for such operations promised success; and third, the degree to which the undertaking might provoke a military response. The last point was tied directly to the success of the Western military buildup because the risk that the Soviets might respond with direct military action would lessen as the West grew stronger.[86]

Stelle subcategorized covert activity in accordance with the perceived risk of war. The United States could engage in "large scale covert activities" without undue risk of general war in Communist China "south of the great wall," North Korea, and Viet Minh areas of Indochina. After further buildup of Western military strength it could do the same in "Albania, Eastern Germany (after rearmament of Western Germany), Bulgaria, Manchuria, and Non-USSR Central Asia." Lastly, Stelle believed that a significant military buildup must precede sustained covert operations in Finland, Poland, Czechoslovakia, Romania, Hungary, and the USSR.[87]

While Stelle's paper expressed considerable optimism about the administration's ability to undermine Soviet power, the CIA "means" paper demonstrated a growing uncertainty regarding the short-term ability of political warfare to achieve the objectives of NSC 20/4. The study warned, "the liberation of the Russian people is not considered to be a feasible undertaking for the next several years." It regarded the chances of detaching one or more satellites as more feasible but "barring developments not presently foreseen, was not considered a likely near-term possibility." The CIA hypothesized that if a united Germany were successfully integrated into a Western European organization, "some basis may exist for the ultimate evolution of an Eastern European political and economic federation which would not fear the resurgence of a militaristic Germany on one side, and, at the same time, maintain a compatible relationship with the Soviet Union on the other side."[88] The CIA means paper considered further work in this area impossible, however, until the completion of a strategic concept paper.[89]

By March 1952 a split had appeared between those planners who continued to support aggressive covert action and others who had come to accept Charles Bohlen's thesis that diplomatic and psychological coercion was an inadequate strategy to attain the objectives of NSC 20/4. This division was especially evident in two proposed versions of the strategic concept, one prepared by Mallory Browne, director of the PSB's Office of Evaluation and Review, and a significantly revised version of Charles Stelle's paper.

Browne considered the Soviet Union a "colossus with feet of clay" and called for a full-scale psychological-warfare offensive against the Soviet bloc.[90] Like the Director's Group six months earlier, he believed that the satellite nations were the Achilles' heel and that the Soviet regime could be shattered—and Russian domination severed—by the careful preparation of "controlled liberation movements." Browne contended that these goals had to be achieved within five years, as waiting longer might kill hope within the satellite states, but warned that acting "before we were ready to support [revolt] materially . . . would be fatally premature." Browne declared that the United States should consider supporting liberation movements with clandestine military aid. Within two years, the United States could begin a concealed program of arming the growing liberation movements and preparing to support potential uprisings as they occurred. U.S. involvement would be clandestine, or "at least as well concealed as Soviet support of the North Korean attack."[91]

Browne argued that the administration must make two policy changes in order to accomplish these objectives. First, it must publicly reject containment and espouse a policy of "liberation," and second, "scrapping—not necessarily in public but in our strategic planning—the passive wishful thinking of 'coexistence,' and adopting a positive approach that acknowledged the vital necessity of overthrowing the Kremlin regime." Such changes would be "frank recognition of what is really implicit in our existing policy objectives." Browne's beliefs reflected those of a growing number of PSB officials who believed that the 1952 Republican foreign-policy onslaught provided the Truman administration with a unique opportunity to shift to a public offensive against the Soviet Union. They may also have represented a response to Bohlen's challenge. Browne wrote:

> Finally, the fact should be frankly and fully faced, that such a new strategic concept as is outlined above will require a visible and even obvious change in American policy. Under normal circumstances, such a policy change, on a public plane, might be so difficult as to be impractical. But at this time, with a change of President now certain (and perhaps a change of Party as well, per-

> haps accomplished by the accession to the Presidency of such a well-known American symbol as General Eisenhower), there is every reason why there should be a public change of policy. To fail to capitalize on the opportunity thus offered of making and publicizing properly a change, would be to lose a rare occasion to administer both shock tactics to a world body in need of such a stimulating shock.[92]

Browne's strategy paper elicited a number of diverse responses. While former Director's Group member Palmer Putnam agreed that liberation should now be considered the official policy of the United States, many others viewed the recommendation as "undesirable"; to declare public support for a satellite revolt "before we have the capability of providing the necessary military support for our friends might lead to premature action and heavy losses."[93] PSB strategist John Sherman rejected Browne's contention. "Liberation," he argued, "generally connotes the use of force, something intrinsically opposed to U.S. policy" and could seriously mislead world public opinion. Liberation would remain, however, "a valid covert and private goal" of the United States.[94]

Browne's criticisms especially irritated the Strategic Concept Panel, which initially favored a more aggressive approach but had slowly come to accept Charles Bohlen's contention that U.S. objectives could be achieved only through the overthrow of the Soviet regime.[95] The panel members now realized that the United States needed significantly improved political-warfare capabilities to accomplish this new objective, capabilities that would take years to build. Browne's paper, by so obviously aligning itself with the growing Republican critique of the Truman administration's policy, was now out of place within the administration, and presaged a wholesale rift between those strategists who had grown disenchanted with the prospects for achieving U.S. objectives and those like Browne who believed that the Republican campaign had created a window of opportunity to launch the offensive that they had long hoped for.

Stelle's redraft of 30 June demonstrated the growing impact of Bohlen's influence. Stelle had resigned from his earlier optimism to now contend that the cold war would be resolved only by the destruction of the Soviet regime "either by war or successful revolution."[96] Preventive war was of course barred by numerous NSC policy papers, but so was fomenting revolution. He quoted from both NSC 20/1 and NSC 20/4 to argue that the NSC had rejected the overthrow of the Soviet regime as a policy option four years previously. This, however, posed a dilemma: "it is well within the realm of possibility," Stelle argued, "that Soviet power and influence will not in fact be reduced to 'limits which no longer constitute a threat to U.S. security' without either war or revolution." Since both were out of the question, "it was possible," he argued, "that a definitive strategy for operations under

NSC 10/5 may from the outset be impossible of construction." This led Stelle to conclude that work toward a "definitive strategic concept for operations in the covert field [may be] an unproductive effort." Stelle proposed another option, the creation of certain limited criteria against which covert operations could be tested. Such criteria would include a covert operation's effectiveness at reducing Soviet power or strengthening the free world, feasibility, potential risk of war, and flexibility to exploit potential opportunities. While Stelle's alternative solution did not offer much new to the debate, it represented a significant step in what inevitably became the strategic concept paper.

The Princeton Meeting on Psychological Warfare and the 1952 Presidential Campaign

While the Truman administration deliberated the viability of American efforts to roll back Soviet power, the Republican presidential campaign began its assault on the policy of containment. Citing the long and seemingly fruitless war in Korea, the Eisenhower campaign demanded that the United States shift its focus from containment of Soviet expansion to an offensive leading to the ultimate defeat of Soviet communism.

Besides trying to take advantage of voter disapproval of the Truman administration's policy, the Republican foreign-affairs entourage possessed another purpose for its attacks: to prompt the Truman administration into initiating its own political offensive. A growing number of political-warfare specialists, such as Walt W. Rostow of MIT and C. D. Jackson of the National Committee for a Free Europe and an Eisenhower campaign advisor, considered 1952 a defining year for U.S. psychological-warfare efforts. They believed that concerns over the Korean War had opened the door for a national debate on whether American security policy should abandon a defensive posture and initiate a political offensive against the Soviet bloc.

Therefore, on 10–11 May the National Committee for a Free Europe, the sponsoring agency for RFE and RL, organized a meeting on psychological warfare at Princeton University. The meeting brought together experts from academia, private industry, and government with the purpose of writing a statement to be read by either President Truman or Secretary Acheson inaugurating the new political-warfare campaign.[97] Among the twenty-eight attendees were Rostow, Jackson, Frank Altschul, Charles Bohlen, Robert Joyce, Allen Dulles,[98] William Jackson, and George Morgan.[99] The meeting contrasted the viewpoints of those within the government who had grown disenchanted with the possibilities offered by psychological warfare and those within the Eisenhower camp who remained convinced that if properly executed it could be an effective instrument in attaining U.S. objectives. It also demonstrated the great differences of approach between the Truman administration representatives who hoped to roll back communist power by first destabilizing the Soviet and satellite regimes and Eisenhower's supporters who wanted a public campaign to inspire the citizens of Eastern Europe. The ensuing debate was a microcosm of the larger political struggle engulfing the nation during the 1952 campaign.

The working group quickly divided into two camps: those who agreed with C. D. Jackson that "a storm is blowing up in Eastern Europe which a political warfare offensive should exploit," and supporters of Bohlen who questioned the susceptibility of the Soviet bloc to existing U.S. political-warfare capabilities. The protagonists of aggressive psychological warfare maintained that RFE and RL had made great strides in developing the capacity to influence action in Eastern Europe, citing one instance in which RFE broadcasts into Czechoslovakia led to a "buying panic" amongst Czech consumers. So successful were RFE broadcasts into Czechoslovakia that Jackson believed the country ripe for revolt.[100] The United States, Jackson argued, was at a crossroads. "We must either go forward or backward in Eastern Europe, since the people there have been given hope by RFE but will throw in their hand if there is no follow-up. . . . If we do not go forward, RFE had better go out of business."[101] For Eisenhower's camp the solution was obvious—a major political-warfare offensive capable of "winning World War III without having to fight it."[102] It was now time, C. D. Jackson stressed, for the United States to launch an overt psychological-warfare offensive in Eastern Europe, initiated by a public statement of policy, on the belief that "major accomplishments can be produced in that area by political warfare short of shooting." By doing so the United States could energize its cold war efforts and shift the struggle in the West's favor.[103]

Bohlen led the attack against many of Jackson's contentions. He challenged the assumption that the Truman administration had neglected political warfare, arguing that it had been "engaging in it since 1946 at least." He warned that public statements of the sort that Jackson supported had a "constant difficulty" since support for political warfare in one area had to be "adjusted to the response of a great variety of audiences in other areas." Furthermore, he counseled against maintaining the "considerable illusion" that pervaded talk of political warfare, namely that it could be handled as if it were a military offensive. Bohlen felt it highly unfortunate that so much military vocabulary had crept into the language of the psychological-warfare specialists. In regular warfare, he argued:

> You have both an absolute commitment and relatively tangible and calculable factors, whereas in so-called political warfare such fixed points are generally absent. Hence demands for formulating "strategy" and taking the "offensive" are apt to imply a basic misunderstanding of what is possible. Everybody agrees of course that you ought to seize the initiative when you can, but the problem is what initiative will really be effective.[104]

The proposed statement declared that it was U.S. policy to support cooperation among Western European nations, to support the entrance of the satellite states into the world family of nations "as soon as their national liberties are restored," and to strive for the democratic unification of Germany. It further stated that the West did not want an arms race with the Soviet Union, yet must maintain the necessary strength to shield the free world from Soviet domination. The United States stood ready to participate in an "effective and enforceable program for the control and reduction of armed forces and armaments." In pursuing these objectives, the United States would not seek to impose its cultural, social, economic, or political patterns on any country.[105]

Bohlen remained unconvinced that the statement would have a positive effect. He informed Under Secretary of State David Bruce that both he and Robert Joyce tried to point out to the RFE supporters the great difficulties involved in making the type of statement they wanted, and that it "was certain that no statement affecting Europe could be made" prior to resolution of the German situation. Bohlen expressed concern that the attitudes and beliefs of the RFE operators and their supporters in the National Committee for a Free Europe would convince other officials that the statement could appreciably improve the position of the United States in the cold war. Bohlen wrote:

> It is my impression, which Bob Joyce shares, that the extremely intelligent and energetic people backing NCFE and RFE are encountering the problems inherent in an operation of that kind in technical times of peace and are perhaps somewhat naively thinking that a policy statement will somehow or other be the magic wand to cure those problems. As you know, the problem is much deeper and is not too different from what this and other Western Governments are encountering in trying to look ahead in their foreign policies. I put in this caution merely because we in the Government should understand that the problems and activities of these groups which we support will not in any sense be solved by a statement of this nature if it should be found appropriate for future use.[106]

The Policy Planning Staff also considered the Princeton statement an ill-advised attempt at political warfare prepared in total ignorance of the significant national security deliberations taking place. John Ferguson wrote that the statement reflected a hubris regarding U.S. capabilities to influence events behind the Iron Curtain. He considered the gap between capabilities and rhetoric such that:

> It would be unwise to state that 'it is a basic tenet of American policy that political independence shall be restored' to the Eastern European countries unless, at a minimum, we are simultaneously prepared to undertake the expansion of U.S. and allied military capabilities required to back up this policy.[107]

Even the Psychological Strategy Board discounted the potential of the statement. PSB representative George Morgan supported issuing a balanced statement which took into consideration Bohlen's criticisms and which also carefully thought through what capabilities the United States possessed to accomplish its goals. This was especially important, argued Morgan, since new estimates had arrived indicating that "the Soviet system has perfected new techniques of slavery which make revolution well nigh impossible." Despite C. D. Jackson's assurances that "he did not really mean that political warfare should be conducted without a sober estimate of capabilities," Morgan concluded that:

> This meeting on the whole was another serious symptom of the rising tide of public pressures for a spectacular political warfare offensive based partly on unrealistic conceptions of what political warfare can achieve, partly on the American urge to get going even if we don't know whither, partly on desperation.[108]

C. D. Jackson and Walt Rostow were deeply disappointed with the opposition from the Truman administration and believed that their opponents displayed a singular lack of appreciation for the potential uses of psychological warfare in the cold war struggle. To win the battle for world public opinion, any American psychological-warfare effort had to portray the United States as a peace-loving nation whose only objective was the liberation of the satellite peoples from tyranny. Hence the declaration that liberation would not come by force of arms but would in fact be coupled with arms-control provisions, which appealed directly to a Western European public skeptical of American intentions and fearful that U.S. policy could lead to war in Europe.[109] Rostow would later write that the Princeton meeting was a "historic" moment in defining the utility of political warfare for the United States. As we shall see below, Jackson, Rostow, and others realized that the future of political warfare would have to wait for the next administration.[110]

A week after the Princeton meeting *Life* magazine published John Foster Dulles's article "A Policy of Boldness," the seminal foreign-policy statement of the Republican campaign.[111] The future secretary of state castigated the Truman administration for upholding a "negative, futile, and immoral" foreign policy that abandoned more than five hundred million people of non-Russian nationality to the fate of Soviet domination. Dulles proposed a two-track strategy that would threaten the Soviets with "massive retaliation" if they continued to encroach on the free world while simultaneously initiating a political offensive to roll back Soviet power in Eastern Europe. By crystallizing the debate between the public perception of the Truman administration's national security policy and the rising school of thought that called for aggressive actions to free Eastern Europe, the article served as the focal point of the Republican presidential campaign platform of 1952. Given the deep divide between Republican and Democratic foreign-policy belief systems and the cool reception given to the Princeton statement by the Truman administration, the article was seen as a declaration of war between the two camps.

A few weeks after the publication of "A Policy of Boldness," Bohlen penned a scathing rebuttal that went unpublished.[112] He rejected Dulles's strategy as being "misleading and dangerous if applied to all situations." It would not be suitable in areas where aggression starts locally and there is no direct Soviet or Chinese military involvement. Applications in these areas would be foolhardy since they would threaten world war without evidence of involvement by the USSR, which would be essential to garner support from both the allies and American public opinion.[113]

Bohlen saved most of his venom for Dulles's views on liberation. He dismissed the notion of publicly renouncing the use of force in liberating the satellite states while simultaneously believing that through the "dynamic force of our ideals" the United States could "produce the equivalent results of the use of armed force." Bohlen considered this to be:

> cruel and misleading and tends to create in the minds of the American people that there is a cheap and easy way of dealing with the menace of the Soviet bloc. It reveals ignorance, real or assumed, of the nature of the Communist totalitarian regimes. It is a very clear example of what might be called the subjective approach to the harsh realities of the world we live in by pretending that the situation is different than it is.[114]

The Princeton statement and Bohlen's reaction to the Dulles article showed just how wide a divide now existed between the supporters and detractors of psychological warfare.

PSB D-31: The Strategic Concept Paper

On 5 August 1952, the Strategic Concept Panel presented its first draft strategic concept paper, designated PSB D-31 "A Strategic Concept for a National Psychological Program with Reference to Cold War Operations under NSC 10/5."[115] PSB D-31 reaffirmed U.S. efforts to retract Soviet power and influence and to fundamentally change Soviet international behavior by undermining the USSR's domestic power structure as codified by NSC 20/4. Demonstrating the adoption of Bohlen's analysis, the study concluded that the United States could achieve these objectives only by toppling the Soviet regime. PSB D-31 concluded that:

> In the absence of hostilities, the cold war can be expected to continue in one form or another as long as the Soviet Union, which is to say the Bolshevik Party, adheres to the aims and methods which it has pursued ever since its ac-

> cession to power, within as well as outside the Party. . . . The overthrow of the Party by war or successful revolution appears to be the only certain means of forcing such changes [as dictated by NSC 20/4]. One is excluded, and the other so far beyond our current capabilities as to be presently unfeasible.[116]

The Strategic Concept Panel announced that it could not arrive at a definitive strategy as required under NSC 10/5. Instead, it offered an interim strategy that determined the role of covert operations in the continuing cold war struggle. The panel stressed that the United States should "continue to develop our capabilities for assisting revolution," improve "existing techniques," and embark on a "major program for the development of new techniques and approaches." Meanwhile, the administration would streamline its covert activities to achieve three goals:

1) Weakening the Kremlin control over the internal assets of the Soviet-controlled bloc, and increasingly occupying the Kremlin with problems within this area,
2) Direct action to reduce subversive Soviet influence in those areas of the free world that are the most threatened thereby,
3) Covert manipulation of key elements in unstable countries of the free world to increase the stability and utility to the objectives of U.S. foreign policy of those countries.[117]

PSB D-31 specified four categories of covert action to meet these three objectives. First, it proposed that the CIA develop the necessary operations to eliminate the communist parties operating throughout the free world. Second, it called for greater efforts to detach Albania from the Soviet orbit. The Strategic Concept Panel contended that Albania remained vulnerable to aggressive covert efforts that maintained plausible deniability by using only exiled Albanian personnel. Furthermore, it asked the CIA to prepare a feasibility study that included an assessment of the likelihood of cooperation with Great Britain, Yugoslavia, Greece, and Italy. Third, the document stressed the need to intensify covert efforts "to breed suspicion and dissidence within the communist system." It argued that:

> The inherent suspicion and lack of mutual trust and confidence within the communist system and our own experience in exploiting them gives ground for the belief that we would be able to increase this suspicion far beyond what we have hitherto accomplished, to the point of the systematic removal or elimination of personnel in important and effective positions.[118]

Fourth, it highlighted the need to disrupt Soviet and Eastern European economies in order to reduce the economic and military potential of the Soviet bloc. The document pointed to Czechoslovakia as the most vulnerable satellite economically and therefore the key target of opportunity for these operations.[119] The strategic concept paper explored no covert actions aside from these limited operations.

The strategic concept paper, the product of over six months of deliberations, and to which so much hope had been attached, concluded that a peaceful solution to the cold war along the lines expressed in NSC 20/4 could be achieved only with the overthrow of the Soviet regime. This conclusion paralleled the rejection of Kennan's strategy as the operative strategy to achieve the objectives of NSC 20/4 and demonstrated the final acceptance of NSC 135/1 as national security policy. The administration could achieve those objectives only through revolution, a capability it did not possess. While the panel stressed that the government should reassess the interim strategy on an annual basis, few failed to realize that the document represented a significant change in the administration's covert policy. The strategic concept was an extension of Bohlen's "doctrine of rational hope": if the United States continued to develop the free world and contain Soviet expansion, perhaps in the distant future a modification of Soviet aims and methods could lead to an acceptable solution to resolve the cold war. Though it did call for greater efforts to increase dissidence within the Soviet Communist Party and to continue to detach Albania, these operations were not considered capable of meeting the requirements established by NSC 10/5. Consequently, the paper represented the end of an era in psychological warfare; the enormous hopes and aspirations of 1948–1951 were replaced by a quiet acquiescence in the conclusion that the United States had yet to develop the means to achieve its basic national security policy objectives.

On 4 August, the Strategic Concept Panel met for the last time to review the final draft of PSB D-31, with Admiral Stevens, Frank Wisner, Charles Bohlen, Paul Nitze, Charles Stelle, Robert Joyce, George Morgan, and John Magruder in attendance.[120] Stevens, Bohlen, and Nitze were particularly pleased with the effort, with Bohlen declaring that it represented significant progress "over the illusions current in the field last autumn." Bohlen and Nitze further modified the draft to prevent its application to overt psychological operations, principally VOA, RFE, and future RL broadcasts, so that these activities would not come under the rubric of the PSB. The view among the others at the meeting showed similar agreement. Wisner was particularly supportive of the analysis since it was the first paper to offer high-level guidance for CIA activities. Nitze presented the paper to Under Secretary of State David Bruce on 26 August and argued in his cover memo that the most important outcome of the exercise was the impossibility of arriving at a definitive strategic concept for the resolution of the cold war.[121]

Reactions to the strategic concept paper within the PSB were sharply divided. A number of members like George Morgan and Director Raymond Allen had come to accept the notion that limits existed to U.S. psychological capabilities, particularly regarding the possibility of subverting the Soviet regime. In his cover memo to Under Secretary of State Bruce, Deputy Secretary of Defense William Foster, and CIA director Walter Bedell Smith, Allen wrote: "compared to the hopes with which the project was launched, the outcome represents a disillusion which can be salutary, and corresponds to a similar trend of national policy thinking reflected in NSC 135/1." He accepted the conclusion that the United States did not possess the requisite capabilities for action, but disagreed that an "interim strategic concept" offered the best short-term solution. The director declared that because of PSB D-31 the department would intensify efforts to build the requisite capabilities "to assist revolution." Allen had already been working on a project that would coordinate the efforts of the PSB with those of the best social scientists in the country in an effort to build the necessary political-warfare techniques. As the draft strategic concept paper was being disseminated, Allen declared in a general memo to all PSB members that:

> Our efforts over the coming years to avoid a continuing stalemate with the USSR, will depend in large part upon our success in developing novel, non-military means of changing the intentions of the present regime in the USSR, or in bringing about a situation in which it can be supplanted. Since according to present evidence these means are yet to be conceived, it is essential that we direct our research efforts along the most promising lines.[122]

One such study was the Soviet Vulnerabilities Project under the direction of Walt W. Rostow of MIT. We shall see below that Rostow's group rejected the Strategic Concept Panel's conclusion that it was impossible to determine a strategic concept for cold war operations.

Many of the previous members of the Director's Group were aghast at the conclusion reached by the Strategic Concept Panel. Palmer Putnam considered the paper "dangerously, perhaps fatally, unrealistic" and useless as a strategic concept. The paper lacked "any sense of urgency," any estimates of when the Soviet Union would possess the capabilities to "annihilate the U.S.," any proposals to create a firm stalemate, any proposals to exploit such a stalemate, any efforts for a significant increase in intelligence, any proposals to keep the public informed of cold war issues as called for in numerous NSC documents—in short, a coherent overall approach.[123] Edmund Taylor, director of the PSB's Office of Plans, opposed the plan even more vociferously. He charged that by offering guidance solely to the covert elements in U.S. cold war strategy and ignoring the interrelationships with economic, diplomatic, military, and overt psychological warfare, the strategic concept paper:

> is not only setting the clock back to pre-PSB days, it is setting it back to pre-OSS days, for we learned during the war that neither propaganda nor covert operations are really effective unless they are coordinated with each other and integrated into general strategy.[124]

In full agreement with Taylor was PSB deputy director C. Tracy Barnes, who had had deep misgivings about the project since its inception. Barnes warned former PSB director Gordon Gray as early as 11 January that Admiral Stevens was not up to the challenge of handling the State Department.[125] State, Barnes accused, was not at all interested in creating the type of strategic concept initially described in NSC 10/5, and was preventing much work from being done. Consequently, Barnes came to fear that the project would in fact accomplish little.[126] At one point Barnes asked Gray to intervene with Walter Bedell Smith on the PSB's behalf. Gray spoke with Smith to offer his assistance in completing the project but was informed by Smith that the project was well under his control, and Gray's offers of help were acknowledged without comment.[127]

By the time of the August release of the strategic concept paper, Barnes had grown so disenchanted with the future of the PSB that he had begun talks with Frank Wisner about becoming chief of political and psychological warfare (formerly assistant director of the OPC) within the Planning Directorate at the CIA.[128] The failure of the panel to arrive at a true strategic concept, as well as the appointment of former ambassador to Moscow Alan Kirk as the new PSB director—which Barnes interpreted as a "sellout" to State—confirmed Barnes's suspicions that the PSB lacked any further usefulness and resulted in his formal resignation from the agency.[129]

Gordon Gray had come to a similar conclusion regarding the future of the PSB. Soon after leaving the agency to resume his position as president of the University of North Carolina, Gray wrote a report to President Truman explaining the history of the PSB, the debates regarding its mandate, and providing a number of policy recommendations.[130] Gray realized that the PSB was poorly organized to achieve the results originally intended, primarily because either the Defense Department or the State Department could veto any initiative, and concluded that the PSB should be incorporated into the NSC rather than remain an interdepartmental organization. Despite making a direct appeal to President Truman, Gray's proposals received little reaction from the administration, a point that forced him to accept that he "wielded little, if any, influence."[131]

Wallace Carroll agreed with both Gray and Barnes that the PSB was quickly becoming a "fifth wheel" within the administration.[132] Yet he rejoined that the only thing to do was "to take the longer view, as Bobby Cutler points out." Carroll argued that little could be done within the present administration to "improve the mechanism or results." He remarked, however, that "I am sure that in the perspective of a few more months we may be able to offer much more useful suggestions to those who follow after, even if we have to do so by indirect means."[133]

Gordon Gray obviously agreed with Carroll as on 16 June he wrote John Foster Dulles in response to his article "A Policy of Boldness." In a rather self-aggrandizing fashion, Gray remarked that he was in firm agreement with Dulles, claiming that "I argued very strongly during the period that I served as Director of the Psychological Strategy Board that containment was not enough. However, I am not sure that I succeeded in convincing anyone but myself and my associates in the staff of the Board."[134] The growing prevalence among the PSB hard-liners to secretly attach themselves to the Eisenhower-Dulles bandwagon presaged a full-scale shift of these operatives to positions within the future administration. These disgruntled men would form the core of the renaissance of support for covert activity in the Eisenhower administration.

While Gray, Carroll, Cutler, Barnes, and Taylor were certainly correct that the State Department's motivation was to aggrandize its own power at the expense of the PSB, their charge that the State Department forestalled efforts to develop an aggressive foreign policy was at best spurious. As we have seen, the State Department had been at the forefront of developing a national security strategy premised on the independence of Eastern Europe and the destabilization of Soviet power. It was George Kennan who formulated these objectives, and it was Paul Nitze who called for the very intensification of the means to achieve these objectives that led eventually to the formation of the PSB. It was only with the rejection of coercing changes from the Kremlin leadership and recognition that preponderant power could not be achieved in the nuclear age that the administration shifted its policy. Only war or revolution would lead to a definitive conclusion to the cold war, and it was the opinion of the Strategic Concept Panel that the United States did not have the political-warfare capabilities to peaceably attain its national security objectives. Nevertheless the document reiterated the need to "continue to develop our capabilities for assisting revolution." It was only then that Bohlen was able to convince a hostile Policy Planning Staff that the only realistic U.S. policy was containment and coexistence. With the acceptance of Bohlen's "doctrine of rational hope" the time had come for a reexamination of the psychological-warfare program.

Part Three: Retrenchment of the Psychological-Warfare Program

The "Magnitude" Issues Revisited

Bohlen's challenge also had significant ramifications for the covert program developed in 1951 and assembled into the CIA "Packet." The Packet was designed to achieve the objectives of NSC 10/5: to place the maximum strain on the Soviet structure of power, retract its power and influence, orient the free world toward the United States, and develop resistance and guerrilla operations behind the Iron Curtain. The vast majority of these operations remain classified to this day. As discussed in chapter two, the government has released some material, however, including U.S. plans to disrupt Soviet control within the USSR, attack the Soviet position in East Germany, and induce key Soviet and satellite leaders to either defect to the United States or establish resistance movements behind the Iron Curtain. The rejection of Kennan's coercive strategy for the much less certain effort to overthrow the Soviet government led in May 1952 to a reassessment of the Packet and U.S. political-warfare capabilities in general.

The development of the Packet was coordinated by the 10/5 panel composed of Robert Joyce of the State Department, Brigadier General Jesmond Balmer of the JCS, John Magruder of the Defense Department, Palmer Putnam of the PSB, and C. Tracy Barnes, who served as its chairman. They were ordered to determine whether proposed operations were consonant with U.S. national security policy.[135]

Despite his suspicions regarding the Strategic Concept Panel, Barnes understood that without an accepted strategic concept the administration could not implement many of the essential elements of the Packet. Therefore, on 8 May he met with the PSB board members to discuss the implementation of the Packet. Barnes reported that the 10/5 panel believed "the 'Packet' should be endorsed" and that it was essential to prepare the manpower, resources, and training facilities required to meet the operational objectives, even without an accepted strategic concept paper.[136] He believed it was critical for the PSB to provide at least partial approval of the Packet so that the CIA and OPC would not lose the trained personnel assembled since 1947.

Barnes was most concerned with the impact of Bohlen's challenge on U.S. operational planning.[137] In order for the Packet to be completed, the 10/5 panel felt that the board must clarify two key points. First:

> Does U.S. policy, as properly interpreted, include or exclude efforts under any circumstances to overthrow or subvert the governments of the satellites or the U.S.S.R.?

Second, Barnes inquired:

> Does U.S. policy, as properly interpreted, contemplate supplying overt physical support to revolutionary factions that might emerge in the wake of Stalin's death, if the situation is offered a reasonable chance of changing a regime to suit U.S. interests without precipitating general war?

On 8 May 1952, the Psychological Strategy Board met to discuss Barnes's paper. General Smith agreed that little progress had been made in rectifying the "magnitude" problems he first raised in May of 1951.[138] Consequently, the CIA had been forced to accept many projects and major operations that Smith "still consider[ed] dangerous to its security" as well as to traditional intelligence-gathering operations. Smith was especially displeased with the state of the Packet. On the one hand, he expressed the concern that the PSB had not expended enough time analyzing the vast number of programs it had proposed. On the other hand, he expressed frustration with his inability to influence the authors of the Packet through his critiques. "I sent that thing back so many times that the people who wrote the explanatory briefs got better and better each time until now the defense is unassailable," he lamented.[139]

Still awaiting the outcome of the NSC debate, Smith did not give Barnes an answer to his questions. Instead, Smith established a new committee, dubbed the "Murder Board," that would dedicate "six to seven months" to analyze the results of projects currently under way and determine which showed promise and which should be abandoned. In addition, he ordered the 10/5 panel to continue to work on the Packet, studying each project "with definitely a jaundiced eye."[140]

The New Psychological Program

Barnes received the first report from the CIA "Murder Board" on 18 August 1952, nearly three weeks after the merger of the OPC and the OSO into the new Directorate of Operations.[141] Although the author remains classified, the document states that he served as "the point of contact" between the review group and the 10/5 panel. The Packet, the report concluded, had lost much of its "currency" during the eight months since its first submission. According to the author of the Review Board report, the United States simply did not have the resources "commensurate with the optimum program that was envisioned in the 'Packet' and which constitute the scope and pace dictated by the provision of NSC 10/5" and as interpreted by the interim strategic concept. Furthermore, it was unlikely that the United States would develop such capabilities in the immediate future. As a result, the Packet was extensively revised by the Review Board with the hope of organizing a strategic concept more in line with U.S. resources. The revision resulted in the "elimination of a considerable number of projects previously contained in the 'Packet,'" with the approval of both General Smith and Frank Wisner. Those projects that remained were reorganized to establish a single program for each country.[142]

The author anticipated that the Review Board would have a new "packet" for consideration by October containing scaled-down programs for the panel's review. The report concluded, "although it is premature to say that the original 'Packet' has been withdrawn, it is my belief that the panel should not devote extensive time and effort on the 'Packet' until it has been revised into the proposed programs."

A New Glimmer of Hope: The Soviet Vulnerabilities Project and the Election of Dwight D. Eisenhower

By August 1952, U.S. national security policy had substantially retreated from its original ambitions. The Truman administration accepted Bohlen's judgment that the cold war would end only with the removal of the Soviet regime, the Strategic Concept Panel concluded that no definitive strategy was possible until the Soviet system deteriorated, and the growing Soviet nuclear capability placed in doubt the hopes for preponderant power.

A new administration was on the verge of coming to power—an administration publicly committed to the liberation of Eastern Europe. Consequently, hope existed that a new approach could be devised to fill the void left by the Truman administration. That August, a new program entitled "The Strategy of the Third Choice" was developed by a team of political-warfare specialists sponsored by the Center for International Studies at MIT (CENIS).[143]

The Soviet Vulnerabilities Project began work in late 1951 under the direction of Walt Rostow and CENIS, in association with McGeorge Bundy of the Russian Research Center at Harvard University and Philip Mosely, director of the Russian Institute at Columbia University. The list of contributors included some of the top Soviet scholars and psychological-warfare specialists in the field, including Clyde Kluckhohn, Adam Ulam, Barrington Moore, Merle Fainsod, Bertram Wolfe, and a young Richard Pipes. The report received significant support from the U.S. government—Charles Bohlen, Admiral Leslie Stevens, Allen Dulles, Loftus Becker, and Richard Bissel served on an advisory panel.

The U.S. government helped organize the Soviet Vulnerabilities Project in order to continue the work begun by Project TROY to develop sophisticated psychological-warfare techniques to attack the Soviet leadership.[144] The project soon took on a much more important meaning as the administration scrutinized the utility of extant political-warfare capabilities to achieve U.S. objectives—particularly the overthrow of the Soviet regime. Responding to these pressures, the program's authors realized that to make a credible contribution they would have to offer a much more nuanced strategy to effectively use the political-warfare capabilities of the United States. While they still urged the use of "spoiling operations" in situations where the United States possessed the necessary assets and where the risk of war remained acceptable, the group concluded that such activities were not as capable of achieving American objectives as their alternative method, "The Strategy of the Third Choice." The foundation of this approach was:

> [to] hold out to those within the society of a hostile power a realistic and attractive alternative to the choices presented them by that power—an alterna-

> tive which will induce them to act in ways conducive to the objectives of the initiating power.[145]

Scholars had long contended that Soviet power rested on the regime's ability to present a terrifying picture of the world to the average Soviet citizen, to the extent that he accepted the tyranny of the state in order to avoid a possibly worse alternative: an American-sponsored global war and fascist German revanchism. The objective of "The Strategy of the Third Choice" was to demonstrate to key sectors of Soviet society that the policy choices presented to them by the ruling elites were not true choices, but were instead rhetorical justifications used by the regime to maintain power. Therefore, it would have to be the objective of America's political-warfare apparatus to indicate that a third choice existed. This choice would demonstrate American affinity with traditional Russian security concerns that no single power would dominate the European continent and that no hostile states should border Russia, while discrediting Soviet expansionist ambitions. Furthermore, this third alternative would hold out to the many dissatisfied with the Stalinist system that it was possible to improve the situation within their country, to challenge Communist Party leadership, and to open the country to the outside world without endangering traditional Russian security interests.

The authors of the report argued that the Soviet military was the "ultimate key to the power and survival" of the Soviet dictatorship and that "no lasting transfer of power can be made without their acquiescence." Therefore, the main focus of the strategy was to convince the Soviet military leadership that a "third choice" existed and that as an institution it should seek the adoption of the "third choice" as Soviet national security policy even if it meant direct opposition to the Communist Party leadership. If the Soviet military high command could be so convinced, it might coerce a post-Stalin government to accept the "third choice" as official Soviet policy.

The authors considered the Soviet military the most opportune target for American political-warfare activities for a number of reasons. Prior to World War II, its officer corps was decimated in Stalin's attempt to ensure the political reliability of the armed forces, and in the postwar period the secret police continued to expend enormous efforts to ensure its conformity to party authority. Information provided by Soviet military defectors indicated widespread resentment and dissatisfaction within the officer corps over the activities of the secret police. Furthermore, these same sources claimed that much of the senior officer corps was deeply skeptical of the Communist Party's claim of a Western military threat and that a number of military officials harbored a great deal of admiration for Western democratic practices—even to the point of supporting the unification of Germany based upon these principles. From these sources the project's authors concluded that the Soviet military could be amenable to "third choice" policy alternatives and might use its power in a succession crisis to force their adoption.

Consequently, the Soviet Vulnerabilities Project determined that the United States must immediately begin to establish covert networks within the USSR to serve as a conduit between the United States and factions within Soviet society who would be most interested in a new government with a new international policy. If successfully carried out, such networks could offer the United States the capability to influence the outcome of a post-Stalin succession struggle.

While the project members intentionally avoided determining specific policies to implement their strategy, they did explore possible opportunities to exploit Stalin's death and further developed Operation Cancellation, the strategy first prepared by Project TROY and the basis for PSB D-24. According to their analysis the Soviet Politburo was roughly divided into two opposing camps. On one side were the Old Bolsheviks, men such as Molotov and Kaganovich, pre-revolutionary party members who had been personally close to Stalin during his reign. They were the true builders of the Soviet Union of the 1950s, who manipulated Bolshevik theory and practice in the Stalinist structure of power. Yet they were also in power during a period of relatively warm U.S.-Soviet relations and consequently had the opportunity to develop many personal contacts with the United States. The Soviet Vulnerabilities Project believed that their adherence to the present Soviet foreign policy was conditioned more by their personal loyalty to Stalin than their adherence to communist principles, and consequently they might not continue such policies after Stalin's death.

Opposing this group were the New Bolsheviks: Beria, Malenkov, Khrushchev, Bulganin, and Kosygin, men who were considered the very "creatures of Stalinism." The roots of their thinking lay not in revolutionary theory but in their experiences in the Stalinist totalitarian bureaucracy. Unlike the Old Bolsheviks, the New Bolsheviks had little experience beyond the confines of the Soviet Union. They did not have the contacts with the West to disabuse them of Stalinist propaganda, and were considered to be much more likely to cling to current Soviet foreign policy.

While it was considered possible that Stalin's death could be followed by an orderly transfer to a successor regime, the nature of the Soviet power structure virtually dictated that eventually a power struggle would erupt within the Politburo. The crucial determinant in the struggle would be the power centers of the Communist Party, secret police, military, and the state bureaucracy. Stalin had successfully combined all these elements into his power base and, concurrently, had prevented any of his subordinates from consolidating their own authority. Thus it was crucial that American political-warfare strategies be ready when Stalin eventually died to "incite or widen a personal split in the Politburo," particularly between the Old and

New Bolsheviks, and to prevent any immediate consolidation of power. Communist Party leader Georgii Malenkov and secret police chief Lavrentii Beria were considered the most likely members of the New Bolsheviks to rise to power. They were also considered the most likely to continue Stalin's foreign-policy line and to remain irreconcilably opposed to any rapprochement with the United States. Consequently, the Soviet Vulnerabilities Project concluded, "U.S. political warfare directed at Bolshevik leadership should aim first of all to destroy the power of Malenkov and Beria," a process that should begin immediately.

In addition to these clandestine activities, the Soviet Vulnerabilities Project recommended that when Stalin did finally die, the president and key foreign-policy advisors would deliver speeches, not to offer condolences, but to express the regret that Stalin never visited the United States and learned the truth about American democracy. The speeches would be directed at the Russian people and aim to demonstrate the yearning of the American people for a normalization of relations between the two countries.

The Soviet Vulnerabilities Project was completed in August 1952, too late to have much influence on Truman administration planning. However, through Walt Rostow's association with C. D. Jackson, we shall see that the report came to heavily influence the Eisenhower administration's response when Stalin did die on 5 March 1953.

On 4 November 1952, Dwight Eisenhower was elected president, and all the Truman administration's decisions regarding U.S. policy toward the Soviet bloc were now inconsequential. The psychological-warfare experts knew that new leaders were coming into office who would have a far different appreciation from their predecessors for the merits of psychological warfare, men like John Foster Dulles, C. D. Jackson, and Eisenhower himself. The disgruntled members of the PSB, such as Gordon Gray and Robert Cutler, would be assuming positions of significance, most prominently as Eisenhower's future special assistants for national security affairs. C. D. Jackson would move to become Eisenhower's advisor on cold war planning. The real coup, many believed, came with the elevation of the Dulles brothers to secretary of state and CIA director, and the ensconcement of two key supporters of psychological warfare as leaders of the two departments which caused so much difficulty in the past. Covert operatives celebrated the passing of the Truman administration and the ascension of the Eisenhower administration as the rebirth of U.S. psychological-warfare efforts.

But it would be a grave error to conclude that the Truman administration was not serious about its efforts to destabilize the Soviet bloc and end the cold war. As we have seen, the period from 1948 to 1952 was one of the most contentious for the evolution of American national security policy. The Truman administration made clear that it saw its mandate to be not the containment of communism, but the elimination of the Soviet threat and the creation of a stable international system. The decisions made by the Truman administration to abandon those efforts were made only after enormous debate and with great reluctance. Its commitment to resolve the cold war will become especially clear as we examine the policies of the Eisenhower administration.

[4]

Liberation, Coexistence, or Annihilation: U.S. Policy in the Era of the Hydrogen Bomb, 1953–1956

Dwight D. Eisenhower's landslide victory in the 1952 presidential election represented for many a new beginning in U.S. national security policy, portending the replacement of containment with a dynamic, aggressive strategy including a public commitment to support the rollback and defeat of Soviet communism. The new president filled many key government positions with supporters of political warfare, men such as C. D. Jackson and Robert Cutler who had experienced the frustrations of the Truman administration's retrenchment and shared the new Republican administration's antipathy toward its Democratic predecessor. They believed that with a president publicly committed to the goal of satellite liberation they would finally be able to employ psychological warfare to its fullest potential.

Events were to prove them wrong. Not only did President Eisenhower not initiate the intensely aggressive campaign many expected, within a year of coming to office the new team concluded that the threat of thermonuclear war precluded any national strategy other than accommodation with the Soviet Union. The Soviet hydrogen bomb detonation convinced many that aggressive psychological warfare was an excessive risk for American policymakers. It also caused the administration to conclude that military preponderance offered little political advantage to the United States. With the advent of thermonuclear weapons even the significantly inferior Soviet stockpile threatened the survival of the United States, forcing the administration to recognize that the security of the country depended upon a stable and secure balance of nuclear power. By 1955 the Eisenhower administration would, in essence, adopt Charles Bohlen's "doctrine of rational hope" and abandon its efforts to foment revolution within Eastern Europe in lieu of an "evolutionary" approach designed to promote minor changes within the communist system without risking war.[1]

Part One: Review of the Truman Administration's National Security Policy

Upon taking office President Eisenhower ordered Robert Cutler to review the Truman administration's national security policy as well as the organizational effectiveness of the NSC. Eisenhower also directed the newly created Special Committee on Information Activities to analyze the results of U.S. psychological-warfare programs since the end of World War II. These studies—written by many of the same PSB specialists reviled by Truman's State Department—were an exercise in revenge. They disparaged the objectives pursued by the Truman administration, criticized efforts at implementation, and condemned the previous administration's attempt to conduct political warfare. By reaffirming the Republican campaign's critique of Truman's foreign policy the Cutler and Jackson committee reports were a calculated attempt to set the stage for the development of a new national security policy, a policy that intended to take full advantage of political warfare.

The Cutler Reports

By mid-March Cutler had completed work on his two studies. In his first report, Cutler expressed his distaste for the Truman administration in a harsh and somewhat misrepresentative analysis of its key national security papers. Cutler belittled NSC 20/4 as merely a policy of "peaceful coexistence . . . with a Russia retracted within its traditional borders and shorn of its control over the international communist movement."[2] He assailed NSC 68 as being "not really different from NSC 20/4," with the objective of the military buildup being merely to "deter the USSR from making war and live with the Soviets until they change their ways." Since Cutler's review was not intended to be an objective analysis it reads largely as a caricature of the Truman administration's policy. Among his many omissions, Cutler failed to mention that the retraction of Soviet power was to be accompanied by efforts to fundamentally change Soviet behavior to end the cold war. Cutler also ignored the early efforts in NSC 68 and 10/5 to intensify psychological warfare to roll back Soviet power in Eastern Europe and destabilize the Soviet regime.

Cutler concluded by raising a number of fundamental questions that the administration would have to address in devising its new strategy. Did the United States still believe that the Soviets shunned war, either because they could gain their ends otherwise or because of U.S. retaliatory power?[3] If the United States continued to contain Soviet power and build the free world's strength, would an unbearable stalemate ensue? Could the United States reduce Soviet power and influence without deliberate subversion behind the Iron Curtain? Should the United States support any government, even though totalitarian, provided only that it remains independent of Soviet control and influence, or should the United States instead work only with democratic groups? Did existing policies weigh or consider the vulnerabilities of the Kremlin regime? Finally, how far could the United States reduce Soviet power and influence without accepting grave risks of general war?

Cutler believed that if the administration was to examine these questions effectively the NSC analysis and decisionmaking structure needed significant improvement. His second report outlined a strategy to revamp the NSC organization, recommending a significantly increased role for the president and council members in the formulation of policy. While President Truman's National Security Council largely rubber-stamped the policy compromises made by the NSC Senior Staff, Cutler envisioned a far more dominant role for the NSC in the Eisenhower administration.

Cutler proposed the creation of a "special assistant for national security affairs" to oversee implementation of NSC policy, act as an executive officer at council meetings, and preside over the NSC Senior Staff—renamed the Planning Board, but retaining the same functions it held in the Truman administration. He further recommended a "special assistant for cold war affairs" to advise the president on the implementation of cold war policy. These two officials were to act as the president's eyes and ears, bringing to his attention any problems with policy implementation and ensuring that the agencies carried out the president's views. Regular attendance at NSC meetings was to be expanded to include not only the statutory members (i.e., the president, vice president, secretaries of state, defense, and treasury, and directors of Mutual Security and Defense Mobilization) but also "participant members" who attended at the discretion of the president; and "advisors" including the chairman of the JCS, director of the CIA, and the newly created special assistant to the president for cold war affairs. Meetings were to be held on a weekly basis with "special" sessions called by the president when necessary. Regular presidential attendance raised the importance of these meetings to levels seldom reached in the Truman administration, where the president met with the council infrequently.

The Jackson Committee Report

On 24 January, Eisenhower ordered a study of the "information policies" of the Truman administration.[4] The chairman of the eight-man committee was William H. Jackson, former deputy director of the CIA in the Truman administration.[5] Other members of the "Jackson committee" included Cutler, Gordon Gray, C. D. Jackson, and Deputy Secretary of Defense Roger Kyes.[6]

The report, issued on 30 June 1953, strongly condemned the misuses of psychological warfare by the Truman administration. This can hardly be considered surprising, since several of its members—William Jackson, Gordon Gray, and Robert Cutler—had intimate knowledge of the policy process within the administration and all left office deeply disgruntled at the administration's failure to develop a coherent strategic concept and national psychological program.[7] Ironically, instead of attacking the retrenchment of the covert program in 1952, the Jackson committee critiqued the excessive zeal of the administration's psychological-warfare planners. Echoing Charles Bohlen's criticisms of the National Committee for a Free Europe during the Princeton meeting of May 1952, the Jackson committee charged that the Truman administration "failed to define its specific goals clearly and precisely" and often announced "unrealizable goals" that had the affect of "arousing excessive hopes in the satellite countries or elsewhere" and were likely to undermine the "world position of the United States." The authors disclosed that some committee witnesses admitted that in formulating their psychological-warfare plans they "had failed to take adequate account of the capabilities of the United States and its allies." The committee warned that future U.S. national security policy must take into account the fact that its success would be judged not only on the things it was able to achieve, "but also on the gap between these and its announced policies."[8] The report concluded that:

> The distinction should be clearly made between policies and objectives with respect to which the United States commits itself to act and those ends to which we, as a nation aspire but regarding which the government is not committed to take action. In the conduct of political warfare it is important that the United States avoid confusion between its specific policy objectives and its aspirations.[9]

It was essential that the new administration improve policy formulation and implementation within the government. The authors condemned the PSB for its inability to coordinate the various agencies in carrying out the administration's psychological-warfare policy and for failing to develop a strategic concept. Consequently, the committee adopted Gordon Gray's solution and called for the creation of an "Operations Coordinating Board" residing in the NSC and serving to oversee the implementation of NSC policy—particularly the psychological aspects of this policy.[10] A board comprising the under secretary of state, the director of central intelligence, the deputy secretary of defense, and the special assistant for national security affairs would oversee the operation of the OCB. The staff would prepare frequent progress reports concerning implementation of NSC projects and report to the NSC if problems arose. Eisenhower approved most of the Jackson committee's recommendations and on 3 September 1953 abolished the Psychological Strategy Board, along with the NSC 10/2–10/5 Consultants

Group which had served to oversee execution of psychological policy since the creation of the Office of Policy Coordination in 1948.

Part Two: Stalin's Death and the Uprisings in Eastern Europe

A Turning Point Appears

On 5 March 1953 Joseph Stalin died. The moment that the United States had awaited since the earliest days of the cold war had arrived, yet there was strong disagreement over the most effective manner to exploit this long-coveted opportunity.[11] Eisenhower was informed during an early-morning meeting with several aides, including Allen Dulles, Robert Cutler, C. D. Jackson, and Press Secretary James Haggerty. The president ordered the group to develop a psychological program that would take full advantage of the possibilities created by Stalin's death.

Ironically, initial euphoria at the prospects offered by this potentially decisive moment gave way to the fear that the United States might instead damage long-range goals if an aggressive response caused the administration to appear callous and undignified in the eyes of the Soviet population. Secretary of Defense Charles Wilson joined John Foster Dulles in suggesting that the tone of any presidential statement should not be perceived as "an appeal to the Soviet people to rise up against their rulers in a period of mourning." The NSC ordered the CIA to prepare a new intelligence estimate of the situation in Eastern Europe and the PSB to prepare an action plan to exploit the psychological ramifications of this event.[12]

Although the death of Stalin had long been considered the single most decisive event in the development of the Soviet system,[13] the only official psychological warplan, PSB D-24, failed to provide any specific courses of action for the administration to follow.[14] Upon reviewing the document, C. D. Jackson exclaimed that it was "worthless" and immediately began assembling a team of political-warfare specialists to prepare a new study. Eisenhower lamented that:

> Ever since 1946, I know that all the so-called experts have been yapping about what would happen when Stalin dies and what we as a nation, should do about it. Well, he's dead. And you can turn the files of our government inside out—in vain—looking for any plans laid. We have no plan. We are not even sure what difference his death makes.[15]

For over a week the government was locked in dispute as the State Department and Psychological Strategy Board debated the most appropriate strategy. Advice trickled in from numerous quarters. Charles Bohlen argued that in the short term Stalin's death was unlikely to undermine the Kremlin's hold on power.[16] He predicted that the Soviet leadership would make every effort to demonstrate the unity and strength of the new regime to the outside world. Over the long run, however, Stalin's death could expose the true nature of Soviet domination and raise nationalist feelings within the satellites. Bohlen counseled that U.S. policy must be prepared to take advantage of all possibilities that might arise and "encourage and support any such indications in the manner best designed to be effective in hastening the disintegration of the Soviet empire." He warned that such possibilities were likely to emerge "only after many years" and that in the meantime American actions should remain as circumspect as possible given the likelihood that aggressive action would aid the new regime's ability to establish its authority. Bohlen concluded that this event represented a seminal moment for American policy in the cold war.[17] He wrote:

> Hanging over all of our plans and actions in regard to this developing situation is the question as to whether this nation has now or will find itself shortly committed to the overthrow of the Kremlin regime as contrasted with a willingness to reach even a temporary *modus vivendi* which would be more satisfactory than the present situation.[18]

Paul Nitze agreed that the immediate aftermath of Stalin's death was not the most propitious moment for the United States to initiate an aggressive campaign, but suggested that opportunities might arise within a few months. A Korean War settlement could become the centerpiece of a new post-Stalin Soviet policy and provide the United States with improved military, strategic, and political flexibility in prosecuting the cold war. It might also create rifts between Chinese leader Mao Tse-tung and Soviet premier Georgii Malenkov, and "possibly within the Soviet regime" itself, and Nitze urged the use of clandestine means to exploit this opportunity.[19] For instance, U.S. officials might drop hints in Moscow or at the UN that a resolution to the Korean War might make serious negotiations on other issues possible. If these overtures failed to draw interest, Nitze recommended that Bohlen visit Soviet foreign minister Molotov to formally initiate negotiations, with the "overtone of really significant military action in the event the negotiations were unsuccessful."[20]

While discussions continued, the national intelligence board drafted Special Estimate 39, the first intelligence assessment since Stalin's death.[21] The estimate concluded that the fate of the Soviet Union depended upon a peaceful transfer of power. If Malenkov could maintain control without a lengthy leadership contest, the power of the Soviet regime over the USSR, the satellite nations, and the international communist movement would remain intact. The greatest danger for the Soviet bloc was for Malenkov's rivals to challenge him and embroil the Soviet Army. This was precisely the conclusion of numerous PSB analyses in 1951–1952, and the centerpiece of both Project TROY and the Soviet Vulnerabilities Project. If psychological warfare could help to trigger a power struggle within the Kremlin, the edifice of Soviet power throughout the world could collapse.

Inciting such action was a significant part of the plan that C. D. Jackson and his working group began to assemble. Jackson received substantial assistance from Walt W. Rostow of the Center for International Studies at MIT.[22] Rostow, who directed the Soviet Vulnerabilities Project, had come to know Jackson through the Princeton meeting the previous May. Both men had argued for an aggressive attack against Soviet control in Eastern Europe using a full range of political-warfare techniques and were deeply disappointed with the Truman administration's disagreement. Despite this setback, Jackson and Rostow continued their collaboration through 1952 as both men assisted the Eisenhower campaign. Rostow had high hopes that the new administration would look to the final report of the Soviet Vulnerabilities Project for guidance, and Stalin's death seemed to afford that opportunity.[23]

Therefore, with Rostow's assistance, Jackson set about to create a plan based in part on the Soviet Vulnerabilities Project and its "Strategy of the Third Choice." The plan was designated PSB D-40 "Psychological Exploitation of Stalin's Death." The principal objective of PSB D-40 was to:

> confront the Communist rulers with difficult choices in a way which does not encourage them to close ranks, but which tends to isolate them and divide their counsels, while uniting humanity, especially the free world, with us.[24]

To achieve this goal the United States would have to "foster divisive forces within the top hierarchy of the Kremlin, between the Kremlin and major power elements in the USSR [particularly the military] and between the Kremlin and the satellites including Communist China."[25] The United States would try to energize the population by "maximizing popular disaffection and foster[ing] internal antagonisms" while confronting the new regime with situations likely to provoke internecine conflict, yet avoiding threats and "saber-rattling."[26] Efforts would be made to "plague the new regime with doubts" as to the loyalty and reliability of key individuals and groups, foment nationalistic feelings within leadership circles, and exploit possible rifts between the Kremlin and communist parties. Jackson considered the Soviet military central to this effort. Therefore, he formulated a specific psychological-war plan entitled PSB D-43, "Plan for the Exploitation of Dissidence in Soviet Bloc and USSR Armed Forces."[27] The plan remains classified; however, it is mentioned in a memorandum from Acting Director of the Office of Public Affairs Joseph Phillips to Under Secretary of State Walter Bedell Smith.[28] According to the memo, the plan's objectives were:

1) To induce the Soviet armed forces to overthrow the Soviet regime at a propitious future time and replace it with a system amenable to international cooperation;
2) To weaken Soviet power by psychological exploitation of the vulnerabilities of the Soviet armed forces.

The key was to coordinate U.S. policy such that the United States could provide inducements to both the Soviet military and civilian agencies to act in accordance with American objectives and replace the communist regime.[29]

The centerpiece of the public effort would be a message from President Eisenhower addressed to the Soviet government and the population—not a message of "pious platitudes," but a message that would have a "bite for the Soviet regime, and the satellites, and Western Europe, and Asia, and this country."[30] Eisenhower would call for a foreign ministers conference attended by the United States, Great Britain, France, and the USSR to negotiate a Korean peace treaty, German and Austrian unification, and serious arms-control negotiations.[31] The U.S. government would stress both in the address itself and follow-up diplomatic activity that this was not a "short-run gesture or propaganda gimmick" but a serious diplomatic initiative the United States would pursue for years if necessary.

The Jackson-Rostow plan received strong support from a surprising source: George Kennan. Kennan was brought to Jackson's attention by Rostow, who met Kennan on 5 March at the home of Max Millikan, where the two men proceeded to discuss the ramifications of Stalin's death.[32] Rostow was stunned at how closely Kennan's analysis reflected the conclusions of the Soviet Vulnerabilities Project and how sharply it differed from the views popularly attributed to Kennan as the "author of containment."[33] Rostow set out to convince Jackson to seek Kennan's advice. Kennan, then in retirement at his Pennsylvania farm, immediately agreed to travel to Washington, D.C.[34]

Kennan and Jackson were in complete agreement that the time had arrived for a decisive psychological-warfare effort designed to lead to the unification of Germany "and the continent," including the withdrawal of Soviet and American forces, leaving behind a "predominantly democratic and unified area."[35] Kennan warned Jackson that his German initiative would, however, require the full support of President Eisenhower and Secretary of State Dulles. If this condition could be met, then there was "no need to worry excessively about other opinions in Washington or about the short period of excitement in the foreign offices of Great Britain, France, and Bonn."[36] Kennan was confident that after an initial period of controversy the allies would come to support the initiative.

Kennan was so commendatory of Jackson's plan that he announced "it will reverse the direction the wheels of diplomacy had been spinning for some years." According to Rostow, Kennan then took Jackson by the arms and declared "you have the weight of the world on your shoulders—Good luck."[37] Kennan's presentation made Jackson acutely aware that his knowledge and experience would be invaluable to the government, and on 10 March Jackson raised the issue of Kennan's future with Secretary of State Dulles. Dulles replied that Kennan had already tendered his resignation to the Foreign Service and that the matter was in the hands of Under Secretary of State Walter Bedell Smith. Smith confirmed that Secretary Dulles was loath to bring Kennan into the State Department for fear of adverse congressional reaction and requested that Jackson drop the matter.[38]

Jackson could have used Kennan's support in the State Department, for he faced a powerful set of opponents, including Charles Bohlen, Paul Nitze, and particularly Under Secretary of State Smith, who again emerged as a strong opponent of aggressive covert action against the Soviet Union. Smith, who was even averse to Nitze's threat of increased military activity in Korea, issued a point-by-point critique of Jackson's plan only a day before a crucial NSC meeting. Smith argued that while Stalin's death may have opened opportunities to influence the Soviet Union, an aggressive policy of heightening cold war pressures "especially in the field of covert propaganda" would assist the new regime to consolidate its power and might even preclude the emergence of opportunities in the future.[39] Smith considered the presidential address envisioned by Jackson counterproduductive since the allies would have to be fully briefed, any proposed settlement required months of analysis, and progress on the European Defense Community would almost certainly be delayed.[40]

Faced with such strong opposition, Jackson appealed to Secretary of State Dulles to intervene on his behalf during the NSC meeting scheduled for 11 March.[41] Dulles observed that "he personally did not endorse all the objections to Mr. Jackson's plan which had been raised in the State Department."[42] He agreed with Jackson that Stalin's death could potentially release powerful undercurrents of nationalism and discontent that pervaded Soviet society. Yet he admitted that he was in accord with those who argued that an aggressive political offensive against the Soviet Union was inappropriate when "the Soviet was now involved in a family funeral."[43] The best time to act was when "the corpse was buried and the mourners gone off to their homes to read the will." Echoing both Bohlen and Smith, Dulles concluded that "if we move precipitately we might very well enhance Soviet family loyalty and disrupt the free world's."[44] Dulles was in emphatic agreement with his department that the type of speech proposed by Jackson "would have disastrous effects on our ties with our allies unless we obtained prior consent to the agenda for such a meeting." Discussion of German unity would indeed damage prospects for the European Defense Community while "inviting the fall of the French, German, and Italian governments."[45]

Dulles did agree with Jackson that a televised presidential address directed to the Soviet population could be useful, but only so long as the speech did not cover the issues Jackson proposed. Eisenhower, who didn't believe that the death of Stalin was as significant as his advisors believed,[46] felt that a speech concentrating on the need to raise world standards of living would be a far more effective means to influence world public opinion than a more expansive presentation.[47] Eisenhower assigned C. D. Jackson the task of writing the new speech, but without his cherished four-power summit.

On 16 April 1953, after nearly six weeks and a dozen drafts, President Eisenhower presented the official U.S. response to Stalin's death in an address entitled "The Chance for Peace."[48] Eisenhower began with a discussion of American policy in the cold war. The United States, he argued, believed that:

> No people on earth can be held, as a people, to be an enemy. . . . No nation's security and well-being can be lastingly achieved in isolation but only in effective cooperation with fellow nations. . . . Any nation's right to form a government and an economic system of its own choosing is inalienable. . . . Any nation's attempt to dictate to other nations their form of government is indefensible. . . . And finally, a nation's hope for lasting peace cannot be firmly based upon any race in armaments but rather upon just relations and honest understanding with all other nations.[49]

Eisenhower examined the enormous cost of the cold war and concluded that the world could significantly raise living standards if governments assigned more resources to "butter" than "guns." "The cost of one modern heavy bomber," he argued, "is this: a modern brick school in more than 30 cities. It is two fine, fully equipped hospitals. It is some 50 miles of concrete highway. . . . A destroyer equaled homes for 8,000 people, a fighter plane cost a half million bushels of wheat." The new leadership in Moscow, he argued, had it in their power to change the fate of the world, to end the East-West confrontation and ensure world peace. They must help end the war in Korea, allow the Eastern European nations to choose their own governments, and engage in serious disarmament negotiations with stringent UN verification procedures.

The Kremlin responded with a powerful campaign intended to derail Western security efforts and to paint the United States as the world's true warmonger. Immediately after Stalin's death the new Soviet leadership pressured the North Koreans into exchanging wounded prisoners of war with the United Nations forces, called for a foreign ministers conference to settle outstanding issues over German unification, sent out diplomatic feelers indicating interest in an Eisenhower-Malenkov summit, requested Soviet-British talks to reduce air incidents in Berlin, and permitted a group of American correspondents to enter the USSR.[50] Although they printed Eisenhower's speech in its entirety, the Soviets criticized its "failure" to offer real solutions to the problem of German unification, neglect of agreements reached at the

Potsdam Conference ending World War II, rejection of Communist China as the rightful representative of the Chinese people, and encouragement of the "restoration of the reactionary regimes overthrown by these [Eastern European] peoples."[51]

These moves surprised the administration, particularly Allen Dulles, who had interpreted them as the start of a new and more potent peace offensive.[52] No one had anticipated that Malenkov would be in a position to initiate a new foreign policy so soon after Stalin's death. Furthermore, Malenkov's "soft policy" demonstrated that he was far from being the "creature of Stalinism" portrayed in the Soviet Vulnerabilities Project. The question remained, however, whether this "soft policy" represented a fundamental change in policy or simply a change in tactics. Bohlen, now ensconced as the U.S. ambassador in Moscow, did not believe that the "soft policy" represented a fundamental break with the Stalinist past. The ambassador reiterated his thesis that the tenor of Soviet foreign policy was determined by the structure of the Soviet state, and while the top leadership seemed to have replaced Stalin's cult of personality with rule by committee the state structure remained totalitarian, with its primary objective to maintain power. As long as the Soviet state retained its totalitarian structure, Soviet foreign policy would continue to depict the world as hostile to the USSR, requiring harsh internal security measures and continued sacrifice on the part of the population. Consequently, while the new Kremlin leadership was eager to reduce world tensions and the likelihood of war as it established its power base, the "menace [they] present to the free nations will remain constant regardless of the particular aspect [they] choose to present to the outside world." Bohlen advised Dulles to continue efforts to strengthen Western military and political power, sustain the tone of confidence exuded by Eisenhower's speech, and remain "receptive to any diplomatic opportunity to settle outstanding issues along acceptable lines." But he advised against the administration attempting any "superficial and temporary" propaganda effort that might result in reversing America's position.[53]

Although C. D. Jackson failed to convince the Eisenhower administration of the importance of the four-power summit, he successfully lobbied for the use of covert action to engender rifts within the Soviet power structure as demonstrated with the approval of PSB D-40. Furthermore, administration strategists recognized that despite the short-term survival of the Soviet regime, significant political struggles lay ahead for the post-Stalin leadership, particularly as they struggled to maintain control of their satellites.[54]

The Impact of the East German Uprising on U.S. Policy: June–July 1953

The combination of mass industrialization and collectivization campaigns initiated in spring 1953 inflicted such added hardship on the East

German population that on 16–17 June 1953 nearly 370,000 people in 274 locations took to the streets, burning Soviet and Communist Party buildings, overturning police cars, and attacking oncoming Soviet tanks.[55] By 18 June, Soviet occupation forces had quelled the uprising. Yet the disturbances clearly demonstrated the level of discontent prevailing in East German society and provided C. D. Jackson with his best opportunity to motivate the administration to initiate the type of political offensive he had been proposing for well over a year. He immediately began to pressure the administration to approve a psychological strategy designed to exploit these growing fissures.

Jackson presented his psychological-warfare plan—entitled PSB D-45 "Interim Strategy for the Exploitation of Soviet and Satellite Vulnerabilities"—during the 22 June meeting of the NSC Planning Board. Although a clear opportunity had seemed to present itself, he was stunned by the amount of resistance his plan received. The State Department asserted that the aggressive plans Jackson presented raised the risk of war by providing the false hope of U.S. intervention to a dissatisfied and angry East German public and threatening to provoke a Soviet military move against Berlin or even Western Europe. Jackson responded that this uprising provided the United States with the first significant opportunity to weaken Soviet control in the region since the end of World War II.[56]

This time Jackson's views prevailed, and on 25 June he submitted for NSC approval a revision of PSB D-45 entitled "Interim U.S. Psychological Strategy Plan for Exploitation of Unrest in Satellite Europe." Jackson assured his critics that the PSB did not approach its work in a "starry-eyed and unrealistic fashion," and accordingly divided its proposed actions into two phases, one covering actions to be taken within the next sixty days and a second exploring long-range operations. President Eisenhower approved the report as NSC 158 on 25 June with only a few changes.[57] While the NSC meeting of 29 June remains classified, NSC 158 was finally released in late 1996.

Jackson designed NSC 158, re-titled "United States Objectives and Actions to Exploit the Unrest in the Satellite States," to meet four objectives.[58]

a. To nourish resistance to communist oppression throughout satellite Europe, short of mass rebellion in areas under Soviet military control, and without compromising its spontaneous nature.
b. To undermine satellite puppet authority.
c. To exploit satellite unrest as demonstrable proof that the Soviet Empire is beginning to crumble.
d. To convince the free world, particularly Western Europe, that love of liberty and hatred of alien oppression are stronger behind the Iron Curtain than it has dared to believe and that resistance to totalitarianism is less hopeless than had been imagined.

The short-term psychological measures included "covertly stimulat[ing]" resistance "short of mass rebellion," encouraging defection of satellite political leaders and military personnel "and Soviet military personnel," "re-emphasizing U.S. support for German unity based on free elections followed by a peace treaty," and immediate implementation of the Volunteer Freedom Corps,[59] while promoting the "elimination of key puppet officials." The United States would encourage passive, but not active, resistance to Soviet and satellite authority.[60]

The five long-range courses of action represented Jackson's psychological-warfare wish list and bears witness to the influence of Rostow's Soviet Vulnerabilities Project. Over an indeterminate period the United States would seek to "organize, train, and equip underground organizations capable of launching large-scale raids or sustained warfare when directed"; push for "free elections in the satellites and association with the Western European Community"; "s[t]imulat[e]" Soviet officer conspiracy to establish honorable peace with the West"; and enhance cooperation "between satellite resistance elements and nationalists within non-Russian Soviet republics."[61] The NSC even considered arming Eastern European revolutionaries should the opportunity arise.[62]

The administration considered NSC 158 and both PSB D-40 and D-45 to be "quickies," i.e., plans designed to exploit a specific set of events rather than provide long-range guidance for the Soviet-satellite region.[63] Therefore, once this initial work was completed, Jackson established a working group, called the D 40-45 group, with the mandate to provide planning for long-term operations and begin the process of consolidating U.S. policy toward Eastern Europe and the Soviet Union.[64] These efforts were overshadowed, however, by the full-scale review of national security policy that dominated the spring and summer of 1953.

Part Three: The Solarium Project and the Development of the New Administration Policy

Project Solarium, named after the White House solarium where the idea was first approved, was the most extensive examination of U.S. national security policy during the early years of the cold war. With three teams of experts examining several different policy alternatives, not even NSC 68 compares in its breadth. Yet Solarium was not an unrestrained exercise as was NSC 68, where President Truman gave a broad mandate to the State-Defense Team to reexamine U.S. policy in light of Soviet atomic capabilities. The Solarium project was under the tight control and supervision of President Eisenhower and a small group of trusted officials including Robert Cutler, Walter Bedell Smith, and Allen Dulles. Eisenhower and Cutler together established the extent of the review, including the very specific lines of argument assigned to each task force. The president did not intend Solarium to be an unfettered intellectual enterprise with the outcome decided by the fertile minds of some two dozen analysts. Indeed, he knew precisely what issues he wanted analyzed and offered little latitude beyond these parameters.[65]

On 9 May, Eisenhower established both the Working Committee of the National Security Council and the Solarium Panel, which were responsible for choosing participants for each of the task forces, establishing each task force's mandate, and providing logistical support. The Working Committee consisted of Walter Bedell Smith, Robert Cutler, and Allen Dulles, while the Solarium Panel members included General James Doolittle, Robert Amory Jr., Lieutenant General Lyman Lemnitzer, Dean Rusk, and Vice Admiral Leslie C. Stevens, formerly chairman of the Strategic Concept Panel in the Truman administration.[66]

The Working Committee directed Task Force A to develop a policy premised upon existing NSC directives and consonant with the new fiscal emphasis of the Eisenhower administration. The task force would devise a strategy that would continue to pursue the retraction and reduction of Soviet power, but without risking general war.[67] Task Force B was responsible for determining the areas of the world that the United States would not permit to fall to communism, "whether by overt or covert aggression, by subversion of indigenous peoples, or otherwise." The United States would "draw a line" around such areas and consider the fall of any country to be grounds for retaliating militarily. The Working Committee authorized Task Force C to prepare a plan for aggressive covert and overt psychological warfare designed to "create a [world wide] climate of victory" and undermine Soviet power and control behind the Iron Curtain. This task force was to assume that time was working against the United States and that U.S. security would be gravely threatened if decisive measures were not taken to achieve victory in the cold war.

The task force directives reflected the conflict at the top level of the Eisenhower administration between those who favored a restrained policy promoting peaceful coexistence and negotiated settlements with the Soviet Union and others who called for a much more aggressive campaign to destroy Soviet power. Task Force B represented the quixotic hope that American nuclear superiority could provide an answer to the continued threat of peripheral aggression.

These policy alternatives also reflected divisions within the State Department itself as debate escalated between Under Secretary of State Smith and his supporters and Secretary of State Dulles, who remained committed to rolling back Soviet power. Although Dulles may have opposed aggressive action in the circumstances surrounding Stalin's death and the uprising in

East Germany, he maintained the belief that the United States needed an assertive policy "to induce the disintegration of the Soviet power."[68] During an NSC meeting held on 8 May, Dulles articulated his support for the premises of Task Force C and stressed the long-term vulnerability of the U.S. position. "Practically everywhere one looks—Africa, Middle East, India, South East Asia, and Far East," Dulles argued, "there is no strong holding point and the danger everywhere of Communist penetration. South America is vulnerable. West Germany might take the Communist bait and block EDC, thus risking a NATO collapse." "In the world chess game," Dulles concluded, "the Reds today have the better position."[69] He warned that the government's "defensive" posture was potentially "fatal" since the United States was "always worrying about what the Soviets will take next." He admonished his colleagues that "unless we change this policy or get some break, we will lose bit by bit the free world and break ourselves financially."[70] Dulles's solution was in essence a combination of strategies proposed by Task Force B and Task Force C. "Either on a grand or lesser scale" the United States could draw a line and declare a *casus belli* if crossed by the Soviets. Simultaneously, the United States would initiate an aggressive campaign against the Soviet bloc to force the Kremlin to "think more of holding what it has, less of gaining additional territory and turning the Soviet bloc into a loose alliance, without aggressive capacities, far different from Stalin's monolith."[71] Although Eisenhower declared that a final decision on a policy of "decisive action" would have to await the completion of the Solarium project, he expressed a clear disinclination toward any policy based upon issuing a *casus belli*.[72]

On 1 June, the Working Committee and the Solarium Panel arrived at the final courses of action for the three task forces. They presented twenty-one specific questions for each task force to analyze, while prohibiting four topics: unilateral disarmament and a retreat into "fortress Europe"; a course of action that relied solely upon U.S. economic and military strength; a course of action that involved a major change in the structure of international organization; and the initiation of a preventive war against the Soviet Union.[73]

Although the administration considered all three analyses "alternatives," only Task Force reports A and C dealt with overall U.S. policy toward the Soviet Union, while Task Force B explored the uses of American atomic superiority in deterring Soviet or satellite military aggression. Eisenhower had restricted alternative A to improving the policy of the Truman administration, taking such measures required to meet U.S. objectives and exploit Soviet weakness "without materially increasing the risk of general war." The mandate provided alternative C, however, was much more aggressive, allowing the task force to propose a strategy that significantly risked global war. The following discussion will focus on the differences between Solarium Task Force A and Task Force C.

Task Force Report A

The driving force behind Task Force A was George Kennan. Since Eisenhower and Cutler confined alternative A to an examination of the existing U.S. policy, they decided that its membership should comprise those with an "intimate understanding of the past policies and actions of the United States, the rest of the free world, and of the Soviet Union."[74] The logical choice as Task Force chairman was Kennan, and the former Policy Planning Staff director took full advantage of this new opportunity to influence once again U.S. grand strategy in the cold war; the final product clearly bears his imprimatur. So dominant was Kennan that the entire section analyzing U.S. objectives was a reprise of NSC 20/1 "U.S. Objectives towards Russia," the 1948 Kennan Policy Planning Staff paper that led directly to NSC 20/4.[75]

Although Report A is widely considered the containment option of the Solarium project, a full reading of the report suggests instead that Task Force A appealed for policies and measures that it hoped would eventually cause the liberation of the satellite nations and fundamentally change Soviet international behavior.[76] The crucial limitation was that it not propose actions that would greatly increase the risk of war, a stark contrast to the parameters issued Task Force C.[77] Regardless, Task Force A determined that significant improvements could be made to existing U.S. policy and considered itself "at liberty to examine not only what has been and is being done under its directive but also what could be done within the framework of its provisions."[78]

Report A resolved that a successful U.S. policy must reduce Soviet power to a level that would not threaten the international community while it strengthened the free-world coalition. It summarized its policy objective as follows:

> With the assistance of Allies to achieve through progressive steps and without undue risk of war, but recognizing that the threat of war must not inhibit our unfolding courses of action, a stop to Soviet expansion; the diminution and progressive retraction of Soviet control over its east European Satellites and Red China; the discrediting of Soviet power and Communist ideology as effective instruments of Soviet foreign policy; and a maximum contribution to the increase in internal stresses and conflicts within the Soviet system; to the end that the Soviet rulers will be forced to accept the necessity of adjusting their objectives to those of peaceful co-existence with the Free World.[79]

While Stalin's death and the East German uprising indicated that it was a propitious moment for the United States to move against the Soviet Union, the task force felt that much work was needed to repair U.S. relations with its allies and avowed neutrals among the recently decolonized nations. It considered the "marked decline in the confidence with which the U.S. is viewed in a great many parts of the non-Communist world" the primary threat to U.S. policy in the cold war. It warned that if left unchecked "this trend can well undo a great deal of what has been achieved in the way of unity within the non-Communist world."[80] The death of Stalin and the growing dissension throughout the Soviet bloc resulted, however, in a "comparable effect in weakening Moscow's range of influence." Given the nearly analogous situation facing both cold war adversaries the task force concluded that as long as the United States maintained the integrity of the free-world coalition, the overall position of the United States and the "free world" would remain "basically sounder and more powerful than that of the Soviet-Communist Orbit."[81]

To retain its superior position the United States needed to avoid "pursuing in time of peace aims which have essentially a wartime objective."[82] U.S. foreign policy must create the impression of "steadiness and reliability" in its implementation while avoiding any abrupt or erratic behavior that could undermine allied confidence in American leadership. In negotiating with the Soviet Union the United States must appear "sincere and reasonable" in its approach, taking positions that attested to U.S. desires for a fair settlement of East-West issues. Task Force A established as its own goal the development of a foreign-policy position that could both nurture the free-world coalition and lead to the reduction of Soviet power and change in the fundamental behavior of Soviet foreign policy. It believed that events in 1953 meant that the time had arrived for the United States to "assume the strategic offensive in its conflicts with Soviet-Communism." Yet to achieve both objectives the strategic offensive must exhibit greater flexibility, cohesion, and integration. "If such steps are taken, this revised strategy will give the greatest assurance as against other possible alternatives for the successful disintegration of the Soviet threat without recourse to general war."[83]

The task force argued that the Soviet system suffered from numerous weaknesses that the West could both aggravate and exploit. It depended heavily upon both a highly centralized command and control structure and "the elaborate facade of political and economic progress at home, of high-minded policies abroad, of invincible economic and military power, and of the infallibility of Communist doctrine and Soviet leadership."[84] By attacking this control machinery and discrediting Soviet ideology, the West might damage Soviet political capabilities abroad and weaken the Soviet system even within the USSR.[85]

Task Force A supported the use of psychological and covert means to weaken Soviet power. Its members warned, however, that the successful use of political warfare might require many years of organization and preparation. Seldom did "one-shot" covert operations result in major successes, and if attempted too hastily they could lead to the "dissipation of resources, the forewarning of our adversaries, and the alarming of our allies."[86] Use of émigré organizations ran the risk of security breaches or the pursuit of headstrong ventures that could damage U.S. prestige or involve U.S. interests in explosive situations.

The task force believed it essential that U.S. efforts provide both the leaders of the satellite nations and their people with the hope that if they could break away from the Soviet orbit "they can find a secure and respected place in the Free World community."[87] In certain circumstances, political warfare might cause the liberation of some of the satellites from the Soviet bloc. It had the potential to place severe burdens on the communist government in China as well as contribute to a straining of relations between the Soviet Union and Communist China.

The report considered resolution of the German issue the linchpin of any Western strategy to reduce Soviet power in Europe. The authors wrote that "a new approach to the problem of German reunification can" if effectively handled "exploit and intensify present Soviet internal stresses and achieve, in due time, the first major roll back of Soviet hegemony over Eastern Europe."[88] The arrest of Beria on 26 June 1953, the East German uprising, and the apparent dissension that existed throughout the Soviet bloc demonstrated that it was appropriate for the United States to take the initiative. A successful reunification of Germany and the withdrawal of Soviet occupation forces would remove the last shred of legality to Soviet force deployments in Poland, providing the Poles with the opportunity to negotiate the end of the Soviet military presence. The completion of an Austrian State Treaty could likewise lead to the removal of Soviet military forces from Hungary and Romania.[89] German reunification offered the West a unique opportunity to remove Soviet military power from five Central and Eastern European states: East Germany, Austria, Poland, Hungary, and Romania, resulting in the most significant shift in the balance of power in Europe since the Nazi surrender.

The authors cautioned, however, that while the withdrawal of Soviet power from Eastern Europe was important, it "should not be pursued without regard for the more remote, but ultimately the more important, objective of bringing about an alteration in basic Soviet aims."[90] The key to altering Soviet aims was not only attacking the Soviet system, but also discrediting Soviet-communist theories of international relations, particularly the oft-stated prediction that capitalism faced impending collapse. The West "must try and make them [the Soviets] realize that in seeking to undermine and destroy the Free World, they are in fact steadily incurring burdens and risks which sooner or later will undermine and destroy Soviet Communism." They concluded that "we must try to stimulate within their minds a growing and gnawing awareness that the theories which have enslaved them are not only morally evil, but are historically outmoded, scientifically unsound, and practically unworkable."[91] In doing so, however, the West must make clear to the Soviets that "it is not too late to turn back from their present course."[92]

Task Force A stressed that if the Soviets adopted policies consistent with "an international system based upon freedom and justice" they would be accepted as a "respected member of the international community."[93]

Task Force A supported a policy that went well beyond traditional conceptions of containment. It supported covert and psychological activities that it hoped would lead eventually to the liberation of the satellite nations. It encouraged the U.S. government to take the initiative toward German unification, not as a way of ending the cold war, but as a first step to the retraction of Soviet power from Eastern Europe. The task force members further stressed that liberation of the satellites was not the sine qua non of policy, but part of the overall U.S. objective of fundamentally altering Soviet international behavior. The task force was fully confident that adoption of its policy would result in the disintegration of the Soviet threat. Thus, the objectives of Task Force A were consistent with the "rollback" policies espoused by Dulles during the 1952 campaign and usually attributed to Task Force C.

What most differentiated Task Force A from the other task forces was the limitation that its proposed policy actions not raise the risk of war and not harm U.S. relations with the allies, restrictions that did not apply to Task Force C. Consequently, Task Force A restricted itself to proposing largely diplomatic and covert measures that it believed would simultaneously reduce Soviet power, change Soviet behavior, and strengthen the free-world coalition. Task Force A was in all but one significant aspect very similar to Task Force C.

Task Force Report C

While the deeply conceptual analysis of Task Force A reflected the keen academic mind of George Kennan, alternative C was written in a strong, aggressive, and curt fashion, reflecting its predominantly military membership.[94] While Report A offered a theoretical treatise on U.S. policy in the cold war, Task Force C presented a warplan organized in great detail, including a point-by-point list of actions designed to achieve its objectives.

The problem facing Task Force C, as outlined by Eisenhower on 9 May, was to devise a strategy that would "increase efforts to disturb and weaken the Soviet bloc and to accelerate the consolidation and strengthening of the free world to enable it to assume the greater risks involved; and to create the maximum disruption and popular resistance throughout the Soviet bloc."[95] Task Force C organized these objectives into three time periods: phase one, 1953–1958; phase two, 1958–1965; and phase three, extending past 1965 indefinitely. The majority of the report focused on phase one activities, while limiting discussion of phases two and three to general courses of action.

The general objective of Task Force C during phase one would be to:

> Force the Soviets to shift their efforts to holding what they already have rather than concentrating on gaining control of additional territories and peoples and, at the same time, to produce a climate of victory encouraging to the free world. While this policy is not designed to provoke war with the Soviet Union, it involves a substantial risk of general war which will vary according to the nature and timing of the steps taken to implement it.[96]

Task Force C considered the development of Soviet nuclear capabilities the most critical factor in determining the scope and pace of U.S. actions. It argued that "the basic problem has been to correlate the timing of actions (political, military and economic) by the United States against the time when the Soviet Union will be capable of dealing a destructive blow to the United States." The task force concluded that within five years (by 1958) the Soviet Union would have an extensive nuclear stockpile and would be capable of devastating the continental United States.[97] In an argument nearly identical to that made by Paul Nitze and the State-Defense Team three years before, the task force concluded that the objectives outlined for phase one must be completed while the United States still possessed nuclear superiority. Furthermore, a military buildup (approximately sixty-five billion dollars a year over five years) would be necessary to continue the aggressive action into later phases.[98]

While Task Force A and Task Force C agreed on the goal of rolling back Soviet power from Eastern Europe and both accepted the need to utilize covert operations, the ultimate goal of Task Force A was peaceful coexistence with a fundamentally transformed Soviet Union.[99] The ultimate objective of Task Force C was the overthrow of the Soviet government itself. This aim is not apparent in the sanitized version of the task force reports declassified in 1991, but has now surfaced in a synopsis of the three Solarium reports declassified in January 1995. According to this synopsis, U.S. policy toward the Soviet Union would include "ending the Iron Curtain, cutting down the strength of any communist elements left in the USSR, and overthrowing the Soviet leadership."[100]

Phase one objectives were to develop the military posture of the United States and its allies, develop a worldwide covert apparatus, attack the communist apparatus outside the Iron Curtain, and penetrate "by all means" the Soviet bloc.[101] Assuming adoption of these policies, Task Force C estimated that by 1958 the global balance of power would have shifted in favor of the United States. Although the Korean War would still rage, the United States would have "administered a sound military defeat" to the Chinese, including "the destruction of some of their industrial centers," with the intention of fostering severe strains in the Chinese-Soviet relationship as the Soviets recoiled from the heavy expenditures required to reequip the Chinese military.[102]

The European allies would present a "united front" against the Soviets. Germany would either be unified and neutral, although clearly oriented toward the capitalist states, or divided, with West Germany a rearmed member of NATO. Soviet military forces would be withdrawn to the borders of the Soviet Union, though continuing to threaten the satellite states. The administration would intensify covert and propaganda activities within the satellites in order to reduce living conditions and incite unrest.

During phase two, from 1958 to 1965, the task force proposed an increasingly aggressive effort, but expressed a willingness to discuss a settlement with the Soviet bloc "since we will be negotiating from a position of strength." The West would initiate an all-out political offensive "to overthrow the Satellite governments and bring them into the family of free nations."[103] The United States would continue to tighten its military encirclement of the Soviet Union while not initiating an overt military attack. By 1965, either the satellites would be freed or "in such a state of disaffection with the USSR as to constitute a serious weakness rather than strength in the Soviet Bloc."[104] Additionally, relations between Communist China and the USSR were expected to have reached a point "where prospects are favorable for driving a final wedge between them."[105] Finally, the long-term (post-1965) objectives of Task Force C were "the reduction of Soviet power and militancy and the elimination of the Communist conspiracy; and, the overthrow of the Communist regime in China" and ultimately the Soviet government itself.[106]

Task Force C was aggressive in both tone and content. However, if one focuses attention on phase one and ignores phases two and three, then it differed little from Task Force A. Both stressed the primary importance of rebuilding free-world strength. Both believed that German unification could decisively tilt the balance of power in Europe while providing an important step in the eventual liberation of the satellites. If unification attempts failed, both called for continued West German rearmament and integration into Western military structures. Most important, both believed that U.S. policy must encourage the eventual liberation of the satellite nations, though Task Force C presented a far more detailed plan. Even so, Task Force C envisioned the possible liberation of the satellites no earlier than 1965, a full twelve years hence.[107]

The Soviet nuclear threat represented one of the most significant areas of disagreement between the two task forces. Though they acknowledged the danger of atomic war rising from crisis miscalculation, Task Force A did not consider the growing Soviet nuclear capabilities a danger to continued American efforts to roll back Soviet power. Furthermore, a firm commitment to improving U.S. continental defenses would reduce even this limited threat.[108]

The policy recommendations of Task Force C, however, demanded that the United States take actions greatly increasing the risk of war. This distinction was clearly demonstrated during an exchange between George Kennan and Task Force C chairman Admiral R. L. Conolly as he presented the report for Task Force C. Kennan remarked that "[Task Force report] A has the right to do all these things," to which Conolly responded that Task Force "C would assume the risk of general war much more than A."[109] So important was the growth of Soviet nuclear power that Task Force C determined the scheduling of its goals in accordance with projections of the escalating Soviet nuclear threat. Consequently, the question of whether the United States could pursue its objectives without risking war remained the crucial factor in the future development of U.S. policy.

Reconciling the Task Force Reports

On 16 July, the three task forces presented their strategies. Upon completion, Eisenhower ordered the three to prepare a common policy. Despite a clear overlap in their overall objectives, Task Force A and Task Force C found too many tactical differences to arrive at a common policy. The most significant obstacle was Eisenhower's own decision to provide both sides with distinctly different working premises, namely that Task Force A would assume a favorable international environment whereas Task Force C would assume an increasingly hostile atmosphere. Additionally, Eisenhower staffed each task force with members who strongly believed in the policy option they were examining. Not surprisingly the task force members were unable to settle their differences.[110]

Task Force A did not view the Soviet threat in as apocalyptic a manner as Task Force C. As long as the United States could maintain its alliances, its economy, a robust defense posture, and prevent Soviet expansion, the threat of global war would be too great a risk for Soviet aggression. Time would then remain on "the side of the United States" in the cold war conflict. Task Force A was not nearly as sanguine, however, that the militantly aggressive covert operations proposed by Task Force C would succeed. The members rejected the claim that such a campaign was worth the substantially increased risks, since it might "lead the Soviet leaders to choose war as an alternative to accepting further risks to their security." Task Force A contended that if the administration chose to enact Task Force C's program the Europeans would resist to the point that a "neutral third force grouping of nations would be created in the place of the present U.S. allies." The Soviet Union might then subvert this neutralist group, possibly resulting in the reduction of U.S. power and banishment of U.S. military forces from the Eurasian periphery.[111]

Not surprisingly, Task Force C condemned Task Force A for not appreciating the gravity of the world situation. They declared that coexistence with the Soviet Union remained impossible until Soviet capabilities were significantly reduced; even then the USSR would continue to be a threat as long as a communist regime retained power. In addition, the United States needed to accomplish this objective before the Soviet Union achieved "atomic plenty," when the Soviet nuclear stockpile could defeat the United States in a first strike. The very survival of the United States depended upon the administration taking action to eliminate the Soviet threat.[112]

Task Force C explicitly rejected two of Task Force A's criticisms. Though recognizing that its strategy risked war with the Soviet Union to a much greater extent than the alternatives, Task Force C believed the Soviet threshold to be so great that its program, if implemented, would not in fact trigger global war with the Soviet Union as predicted by Task Force A. Second, the task force was much more confident that the United States could overcome allied opposition to an aggressive U.S. policy once victories began to appear and a climate of success was created. Consequently, the report's authors dismissed the contention that their policies might be detrimental to U.S. national security.[113]

On 30 July, the National Security Council began deliberations on the Solarium task force reports. Eisenhower, angered over the inability of the three task forces to arrive at a common policy framework, established the Special Committee for Project Solarium to prepare a consolidated statement according to a set of guidelines prepared by the National Security Council.[114] These guidelines—demonstrating initial support for Task Force C—included taking "selected aggressive actions of a limited scope, involving moderately increased risks of general war, to eliminate Soviet-dominated areas within the free world, and to reduce Soviet power in the satellite periphery" and "to take action, other than military, to reduce indigenous Communist power in the nations of the free world."[115] The Special Committee would in general follow—but not be bound by—the policy described in a memorandum written by Robert Cutler entitled "Points for Consideration in Drafting New Policy."[116] The NSC determined that the new policy would:

(1) Estimate the risk of general war resulting from aggressive action directed at the Soviet Bloc as less grave at the present time than did Task Force 'A';
(2) Accept moderately increased risks of general war by taking *some* of the aggressive actions against the satellites proposed by Task Force 'C'; [emphasis in original]; and
(3) Aim during the near future to create a 'climate of victory' to bolster the morale and strength of the free world while forcing the Soviet bloc on the defensive.[117]

Throughout August and early September the Solarium Special Committee prepared a series of draft studies as the first step in arriving at a new national security policy. These studies were consolidated into one forty-two-page report transmitted to the Planning Board for review. While most of the Special Committee's work remains classified, it is apparent that by the end of September the Eisenhower administration policy had shifted to reject the overall approach argued in Task Force C and to pursue instead a policy of "peaceful coexistence" rather than "the destruction of Soviet power."[118] After reviewing the Special Committee's work, Robert Cutler concluded that the policy paper "may be characterized as not a new policy at all" but instead only a "lavish Harriman policy" that would not exceed the policy position of the late Truman administration.[119] It was Cutler's judgment that "in view of the H-bomb this is the only solution short of initiating aggressive war."[120] The Solarium Special Committee concluded that while the "more aggressive" actions of Task Force C should be incorporated into the policy statement, the objectives of that policy would center on accommodation and negotiation with the Soviet Union.

On 18 September, the Special Committee presented the NSC Planning Board with the group's final report for consideration at the Planning Board meeting scheduled for 22 September. NSC executive secretary James Lay circulated the draft paper for comments to be submitted to Director of the Policy Planning Staff Robert Bowie. Bowie attempted to synthesize the various remarks into a revised paper that he resubmitted to the Planning Board, Under Secretary of State Smith, and various State Department bureau chiefs.

The commentary demonstrated that most officials realized that the United States could resolve the cold war only through moderating Soviet behavior; how the administration could achieve this process—solely through aggressive psychological warfare or through a combination of psychological warfare and negotiation—remained a matter of contention. Repeated attempts by Bowie failed to fashion a consensus, resulting in the Planning Board's decision to submit the paper to the NSC with the differences explicitly stated.[121] These disagreements were far too important to ignore and could only be resolved by President Eisenhower and the NSC.

The Establishment of Policy: The NSC 162 Series

On 30 September 1953, the National Security Council received NSC 162 "Review of Basic National Security Policy," the final paper of the Solarium review process. Cutler disguised the authorship of the staff paper's conflicting elements under the rubric of sides "A" and "B."

Both sides agreed that the Soviet regime "does not appear to have been impaired by the events since Stalin's death, or be likely to be appreciably weakened during the next few years."[122] Although the East German uprisings pointed to the continued resistance against Soviet domination, the Kremlin's ability to exploit the satellites' resources "remain[ed] intact" so long as the Soviet military occupation continued.[123] The NSC Planning Board concluded unanimously that the "detachment of any major European satellite from the Soviet bloc does not now appear feasible except by Soviet acquiescence or by war."[124] Although the Planning Board estimated that the Soviets would not deliberately attack the United States between 1953 and 1955, it warned that they "would not be deterred by fear of general war from taking measures they consider necessary to counter Western actions which they view as a serious threat to their security."[125] Agreement broke down over what actions the United States should take to reduce the Soviet threat. Side A contended that this could be achieved only through "mutually advantageous negotiations of outstanding difficulties," and that any pressures imposed upon the Soviets should be "designed primarily to create . . . conditions which will induce the Soviet leadership to be more receptive to acceptable negotiated settlements."[126] Side A also insisted that such actions not include the use of force against Soviet bloc territory since it would not alleviate the Soviet threat even if successful, might threaten the integrity of the free-world coalition, and might "destroy chances for agreement with the U.S.S.R. [while] materially increase[ing] the risk of general war."[127] They argued that the best method to induce a possible settlement was to "forego pressures at least against the USSR itself; to attempt to reduce tensions on secondary issues; and try to convince the Soviet leaders that if they renounce aggression and domination of other peoples the United States has no intention of interfering with the internal organization or the territorial integrity of the USSR."[128]

Side B considered the possibility of such negotiated settlements remote since the Soviet Union would not negotiate with the West unless coerced by aggressive actions. Emulating the position taken by Task Force C, Side B argued to the contrary that some aggressive measures were necessary to create conditions within the Soviet bloc obliging negotiation with the West.[129]

Despite deep disagreement over tactics, both sides concluded that the nuclear balance of power was the deciding factor in the long-term U.S. ability to reduce Soviet power. They both supported the statement that "the broad aim of U.S. security policy must be to create, prior to the achievement of mutual atomic plenty, conditions under which the United States and the free world coalition are prepared to meet the Soviet-Communist threat." They further warned that:

> The foregoing conclusions are valid only so long as the United States maintains a retaliatory capability that cannot be neutralized by a surprise Soviet attack. Whenever there is substantial evidence that the USSR is likely to develop the capability to knock out our atomic striking power, the entire policy of the United States toward the USSR will have to be radically reexamined.[130]

The National Security Council met on 7 October to debate the proposed policy. This NSC meeting represented a turning point in the development of

U.S. national security policy, as Dulles's earlier belief that aggressive U.S. action could lead to the disintegration of the Soviet bloc had now shifted to a concern that the United States must accept serious negotiations with the Soviet Union if it were to resolve important cold war disputes.

At the NSC meeting of 7 October Dulles played the key role in advocating the position of side A: that the United States should take no actions against the Soviet bloc that could impair the possibility of a negotiated settlement. Dulles was strongly challenged by C. D. Jackson, and, to some extent, by Eisenhower himself. After Robert Cutler completed his presentation, Jackson responded that side A was so passive that if their position had been policy a few months earlier "we could not have gone through with the food program in East Germany."[131] Budget director Joseph Dodge agreed, adding that Side 'A' suggested to him "continuous concessions to the USSR which the record of the past has shown to be very unsuccessful."[132] After confirming with Policy Planning Staff director Robert Bowie that side A was the State Department's position, Dulles retorted that "it might be possible to reach general agreement with the Soviets, for example, on reduction of armaments, but that we were certainly not in a position to impose such settlements on them." This did not mean that the United States could not take action to improve unilaterally its "power position" vis-à-vis the Soviet Union, nor work with its allies "to push our power position forward against the USSR." It did mean, however, that the United States must be willing to "grant a *quid pro quo* if we wish to achieve a final settlement towards Korea or possibly even East Germany."[133] Dulles was particularly concerned by side B's argument that the United States should build a superior power position even at the cost of negotiating settlements with the Soviet Union. "If you subordinate the achievement of mutually acceptable settlements to improving the power position of the United States as against the USSR," warned the secretary, "you will eliminate all hope of settlements in Korea, Austria, Germany, etc." When, after further deliberations, it began to appear that momentum for side B was growing, Dulles interjected a warning that:

> In his view we could not reduce tensions with the USSR if in each case we expected to gain all the advantage and the Soviets none. Such settlements must be mutually acceptable, and what was being proposed appeared to be reversing this Administration's whole policy—a fact that was all the more dangerous in view of Soviet possession of the H-bomb.[134]

While Eisenhower accepted Dulles's opinion that the United States must be ready to negotiate a final settlement, he strongly disagreed that he should limit psychological-warfare pressures to inducing the Soviets to the negotiating table and "at once stated his preference for the views expressed by Side "B" on this issue."[135] With that decision, "there was no further discussion" on the issue.

On 29 October the NSC Planning Board presented the revised version of the new U.S. national security policy as NSC 162/2, which Eisenhower approved the following day. Although elements of both sides A and B are found in NSC 162/2, the document completed the Eisenhower administration's shift away from its earlier aspirations of "inducing the disintegration of Soviet power" to accepting negotiation as the most effective method of reducing the Soviet threat.[136]

This draft omitted the early administration belief that "if we keep our pressures on . . . we may force a collapse of the Kremlin regime."[137] Instead, NSC 162/2 accepted that the death of Stalin had not threatened the Communist Party's control of the Soviet Union. Nor did Stalin's passing increase the prospects for the liberation of a major European satellite except by Soviet acquiescence or global war. Indeed, the Planning Board had even come to question the military rationale for rollback itself. Since 1948 Soviet military forces in Eastern Europe had posed the most immediate threat to Western Europe. Since Western Europe could suffer devastating nuclear attacks from aircraft launched from Soviet soil, the members now felt that withdrawal of Soviet forces from Eastern Europe would no longer enhance the security of Western Europe, which seriously undermined the continued wisdom of an aggressive campaign behind the Iron Curtain.

Breaking with past policy, the administration no longer considered a fundamental change in the Soviet structure of power a prerequisite for negotiated settlements with the Soviet Union. Unlike NSC 20/4, which argued that a significant change in Soviet behavior was mandatory for a world settlement, the new Eisenhower administration policy concluded instead that as long as the free world maintained sufficient nuclear retaliatory power and continued to prosper economically the Soviet leadership might accept negotiations "without necessarily abandoning hostility to the non-Soviet world." It called for the United States to take "such feasible political, economic, propaganda and covert measures designed to create and exploit troublesome problems for the USSR" so as to induce the Soviet leadership "to be more receptive to acceptable negotiated settlements."[138] The document declared:

> In the face of the developing Soviet threat, the broad aim of U.S. security policies must be to create, prior to the achievement of mutual atomic plenty, conditions under which the United States and the free world coalition are prepared to meet the Soviet-Communist threat with resolution and to negotiate for its alleviation under proper safeguards.[139]

The document closed with the warning that the foregoing policy conclusions "are valid only so long as the United States maintains a retaliatory capability that cannot be neutralized by a surprise Soviet attack."[140]

Growing Calls for a Cold War Settlement

The growing threat of nuclear annihilation, strong State Department opposition, and the increasing concern that an aggressive political-warfare campaign might lead to war inspired Dulles's conversion from hard-line cold warrior to a supporter of a negotiated settlement with the Kremlin. Changes within the Soviet Union, moreover, also seemed to indicate that some limited negotiations might be fruitful.

Charles Bohlen expressed this opinion to Secretary of State Dulles while Dulles was attending the North Atlantic Council ministerial session in Paris.[141] Bohlen concluded that the shift from Stalin's personal dictatorship to rule by committee, coupled with the new Soviet leadership's need to present the appearance of normality, might provide the basis for a limited détente with the West. Yet Bohlen warned that a limited agreement would represent only a tactical—not a fundamental—shift in Soviet foreign policy. So long as the Soviet Union remained a totalitarian police state, concentrating its resources on economic and military development, it was highly unlikely to adopt a policy of accommodation with the West and negotiate comprehensive settlements over outstanding cold war issues. Any détente would fall within the very limited range imposed by the nature of a Soviet system that required a hostile West in order to secure its power base at home. The Soviets would continue to try to divide the West and undermine efforts at improving Western strength, particularly the European Defense Community and German rearmament. Therefore, while some relaxation of tensions was possible, a definitive East-West settlement remained improbable.

The intelligence community corroborated Bohlen's views in Special Estimate-42.[142] While it might be possible for the United States to reach an armistice in Korea, the analysts warned that Soviet policy toward Europe would remain similar to that under Stalin—only shrewder. Soviet proposals for German unification were unlikely to contain anything that would undermine Soviet control over East Germany and were certain to contain elements unacceptable to the West, split the allies, preclude development of the EDC, and derail German rearmament.[143]

Still, many within the State Department contended that, however difficult, the United States had no alternative but to seek a negotiated settlement to the cold war. The debate became especially intense during the final stages of the Solarium review process when the Special Committee circulated its draft policy statement throughout the government. The responses Bowie received were nearly unanimous that significant attempts must be made to arrive at a settlement with the Soviets. Jacob Beam, former chargé d'affaires in the U.S. embassy in Moscow, argued that two obstacles stood in the way of a settlement: the Kremlin's reluctance to assume the political loss of Germany through free elections and the U.S. military presence in Europe and along the Soviet periphery. Beam believed that any negotiation needed to address how to unify German without threatening Soviet security, how the United States could withdraw from Western Europe without leaving a tremendous military imbalance on the continent, and, finally, how to arrive at a balanced arms-limitation treaty as a prerequisite for the removal of American military bases along the Soviet periphery.[144]

Others argued that the Soviet concept of security was so expansive that it was nearly impossible to accommodate without completely stripping the defenses of America's allies. Yet confidence was expressed that a period of progressive détente might lessen—or "mellow"—the "Soviet security neurosis" so that some accommodation could be reached in Europe.[145]

Analysts considered such settlements, however difficult they might be to engender, the most realistic method to end the cold war and secure Europe. Henry Owen of the State Department's Office of Intelligence Research argued that the worldwide campaign called for by Task Force C, and initially favored by the administration, would backfire: it would increase global tensions and undermine efforts to oust the Soviet Union from Eastern Europe peacefully.[146] Owen concluded that the United States had failed to achieve a level of predominant Western political, economic, and military strength that would permit it to retract Soviet power without undue risk of war. The buildup in allied ground forces in Europe was not sufficient, he believed, to defend Europe in the face of a full-scale Soviet attack, and the Middle East and Japan were also at risk. Moreover, the growing Soviet nuclear arsenal would soon be capable of striking a devastating blow at the United States.[147]

Since predominant military strength was no longer a possibility, Owen concluded that an offensive policy as prescribed by Task Force C would undermine American security by heightening tensions at a time when the military posture of the United States was not properly prepared. Although psychological-warfare efforts might succeed in stimulating some disturbances in vulnerable satellite nations, he did not believe they would contribute to the reduction of Soviet power throughout Eastern Europe. The use of military force might reduce Soviet power in certain extraneous positions, such as Albania or Hainan Island, without leading to general war. Yet, Owen asked, what would the United States gain by wresting Albania and Hainan from the Soviets and Chinese? U.S. intelligence estimates agreed that such actions would frighten and divide the European allies without undermining Soviet control over the remaining bloc members.[148] The only possible option, Owen concluded, was a defensive policy designed to improve Western European security, maintain control of the periphery, and rely on "the essential superiority of our political, social, and economic system [which] would make itself felt in a prolonged non-military contest."[149]

Most interesting was an exchange between Dulles and Eisenhower during the final stage of the Solarium project. In the aftermath of the Soviet detonation of the hydrogen bomb, Dulles began to express significant concerns over the long-term nature and potentially enormous cost of the cold war. In a memo dated 6 September 1953, Dulles declared that recent developments had convinced him of the need for a radical revision in U.S. national security policy.[150] First, he contended that the combination of Soviet nuclear weapons and the growing indigenous opposition to U.S. overseas bases threatened the long-term viability of many U.S. military commitments. Second, Dulles reasoned that the "NATO concept was losing its grip" among the Europeans precisely because a defense against Soviet nuclear attack was impossible, and if the Europeans escaped the initial attack they "might prefer to stay out" altogether. Finally, Dulles expressed great concern that the significant military cutbacks soon to be announced would be interpreted as "final proof of an isolationist trend" and the adoption of the "fortress America concept" for American national security policy. Dulles proposed that the United States "explore the possibility of taking this occasion to make a spectacular effort to relax world tensions on a global basis and execute the mutual withdrawals of Red Army forces and of U.S. forces abroad." Now was the time for such action: the world situation remained stable and with the armistice in Korea, the overthrow of Mossadeq in Iran, and the victory of Christian Democratic leader Konrad Adenauer in West Germany, the United States could still negotiate from a position of strength.

Dulles called for the withdrawal of the Soviet Union from the satellite nations and the United States from Europe. Second, Soviet-satellite relations would mirror Soviet-Finnish relations, i.e., the satellite nations would be politically free but oriented toward the USSR. Third, the United States and Soviet Union would place atomic and hydrogen weapons and guided missiles under international control. Fourth, the Soviets would abandon attempts to foment a "world revolution" while, fifth, the United States would "open up East-West trade." With the central elements of the conflict settled, Dulles reasoned that other issues could be resolved without a great deal of effort.

Two days later Eisenhower responded that he was in "emphatic agreement that renewed efforts should be made to relax world tensions on a global basis."[151] He felt, however, that a relaxation of tensions was only one possible solution to Dulles's national-security quandary. Eisenhower even wondered whether growing Soviet nuclear capabilities might inevitably force the United States to "initiate war at the most propitious moment" to fulfill our "duties to future generations."[152] Despite Eisenhower's eagerness to explore other options, we have already seen his adoption of a national security policy founded largely upon a negotiated settlement with the Soviet Union. The only question was how the possibility of a negotiated settlement would affect U.S. policy toward Eastern Europe.

Part Four: The New Administration Policy toward Eastern Europe

The Bowie-Jackson Studies

Central to the national security debates of 1953 was the issue of U.S. policy toward Eastern Europe. If, on the one hand, the United States continued a policy of aggressive covert and psychological warfare against the Soviet bloc, Eastern Europe would be the main target. On the other hand, if the United States chose to negotiate a resolution to the cold war, the future of Eastern Europe would again be of central importance. C. D. Jackson was certainly aware of this fact and focused the attention of the PSB D 40-45 working group on developing a coherent policy.

Robert Bowie also understood the significance of this issue and in the spring of 1953 assumed control of a separate review of the Truman administration's policy toward the region.[153] Although overshadowed by NSC 68 and NSC 10/5, NSC 58/2 "United States Policy toward the Soviet Satellite States in Eastern Europe" had remained official policy guidance for the region. Written in the aftermath of the 1948 Yugoslav-Soviet break, NSC 58/2 committed the United States to promote Titoist tendencies among the remaining Soviet satellite states. The document's authors understood the uniqueness of the Yugoslav-Soviet break, yet believed that there was more likelihood of nationalistic communists coming to power in Eastern Europe than democratic governments. The relentless purging of these nationalists from the ruling leadership of the East bloc nations led the Truman administration to question the wisdom of this policy, however. Consequently, with the approval of NSC 68 and NSC 10/5, the administration shelved these efforts in lieu of supporting democratic resistance movements behind the Iron Curtain. By 1952 many officials, including Charles Bohlen and Under Secretary of State James Webb, considered the analysis in NSC 58/2 so irrelevant that they called for the drafting of an altogether new policy paper.[154]

Bowie and the rest of his Policy Planning Staff team agreed that the U.S. government needed a new policy statement and presented a revised draft based upon the work begun by Bohlen.[155] This first attempt did not meet with success, however. A critique of this still-classified draft chastised the new version for failing to break new ground and for not distinguishing between the various possibilities of disrupting Soviet power in the satellite area.[156]

Before the Planning Board could complete its analysis, however, the East German uprising demanded the administration's immediate attention. Furthermore, it shifted the focus of decisionmaking away from the NSC Planning Board to the PSB and C. D. Jackson. Under Jackson's guidance, PSB D-45 emerged as the principal policy statement. Jackson contended that the

United States needed an integrated assessment of its capabilities and opportunities if it were to exploit Soviet bloc instabilities to their fullest. He convinced the leadership of the new Operations Coordinating Board (OCB) to order the D 40-45 working group to prepare a consolidated plan.[157]

On 3 September 1953, the Eisenhower administration dissolved the PSB and incorporated its various projects and responsibilities into the OCB. One of the most important outcomes of the Jackson committee report, the OCB was responsible for coordinating the implementation of NSC policy papers among the various agencies. It was headed by a five-member board chaired by Walter Bedell Smith and included Deputy Secretary of Defense Roger Kyes, Director of the Foreign Operations Administration Harold Stassen,[158] Allen Dulles, and C. D. Jackson.[159] Although ostensibly an interdepartmental agency, the OCB was officially located within the NSC.

On 13 November, Jackson's D 40-45 working group submitted to OCB executive director Elmer Staats a draft plan entitled OCB 16 "National Operations Plan—USSR and European Satellites," superseding PSB D-40 and D-45. Much of the document remains classified, and the parts that have been declassified merely repeat the conventional analysis regarding Soviet vulnerabilities and the assets the United States possessed to exploit them. The plan was sharply criticized, however, for not conforming to national policy as it had developed by November of 1953. In a memo to Walter Bedell Smith, Robert Cutler argued that the document contained many items that were "in conflict with policy . . . were unclear as to whether or not they conformed to existing policy . . . or which seemed to venture into fields where there was no existing policy."[160] He concluded that these confusions resulted from trying to combine different studies that the PSB had formulated months previously. Cutler recommended that the OCB desist from trying to combine approaches to Eastern Europe and the Soviet Union and instead proceed with assembling a paper that separated the two regions. As PSB D-40 remained the only guidance for the Soviet Union, Cutler urged the OCB to provide the NSC with a policy paper specifically geared to exploiting Soviet vulnerabilities, since NSC 162/2 was too broad in scope while PSB D-40 and NSC 158 were considered "quickies." The national security advisor informed Smith that the council would be interested in developing an NSC paper providing guidance regarding such problems as "whether the U.S. should pursue a policy of non-predetermination or a policy to support in some form the independence of the nationalities of the Soviet Union. This issue was raised by the 'Plan' and is intimately related to basic U.S. policy towards the Soviet Union." On 25 November the OCB initiated an analysis of Soviet vulnerabilities to succeed PSB D-40.[161] Meanwhile, Robert Bowie and the Planning Board continued work on their version of a new paper on U.S. policy toward Eastern Europe, NSC 174, which was submitted to the NSC on 11 December.

NSC 174 reconfirmed the conclusions of NSC 162/2 that Soviet control over Eastern Europe remained secure despite the death of Stalin and widespread unrest and discontent among the populace. Yet the paper's basic policy objectives still reflected the belief that aggressive U.S. actions could reduce Soviet control and eventually cause the liberation of the satellites, a position that seemed at variance with negotiating an equitable settlement to the cold war.

NSC 174 defined long-range U.S. objectives as "the eventual fulfillment of the rights of the peoples of the Soviet satellites to enjoy governments of their own choosing, free of Soviet domination and participating as peaceful members in the world community." U.S. policy would attempt:

a. To disrupt the Soviet-satellite relationship, minimize satellite contributions to Soviet power, and deter aggressive world policies by the USSR by diverting Soviet attention and energies to problems and difficulties within the Soviet bloc.
b. To undermine the satellite regimes and promote conditions favorable to the eventual liberation of the satellite peoples.
c. To conserve and strengthen the assets within the satellites and among their nationals outside, which may contribute to U.S. interests in peace and war, and to the ultimate freedom of the satellites.
d. To lay the groundwork, as feasible with reasonable risk, for resistance to the Soviet in the event of war.[162]

The United States would use all means short of war to reach these objectives, including fostering nationalism within the satellite nations, stimulating and exploiting conflicts within the ruling circles of the satellite states and between the satellites and the Kremlin, and fostering disaffection in satellite military forces in order to reduce their ability to suppress revolt and diminish their wartime military potential. Additional efforts would encourage democratic, anti-communist forces while remaining prepared to exploit Titoist tendencies, entice the defection of key satellite personnel, and continue VOA, RFE, and RL broadcasts. NSC 174 warned, however, that in pursuing liberation the United States must avoid either committing itself to specific courses of action or inciting the peoples of Eastern Europe into a premature revolt that might result in Soviet reprisals and a significant loss of clandestine U.S. capabilities.[163]

NSC 174 demonstrated that the Eisenhower administration retained a somewhat incompatible hope that proper exploitation of Soviet vulnerabilities in Eastern Europe could eventually lead to the liberation of the satellites, while simultaneously realizing that:

> The chances are negligible at the present time that any existing satellite communist regime would or could break away from Moscow under its own power

> or . . . that any anti-Soviet faction could seize or hold power in a satellite and bring about its detachment from the Soviet bloc.[164]

NSC 174 represented a consolidation of the Bowie and Jackson variants, and therefore was both internally inconsistent and—at least regarding those sections influenced by Jackson—conflicted with the new national security policy in NSC 162/2, which stressed a negotiated end to the cold war over aggressive psychological-warfare efforts to roll back Soviet power. Within a year, the Eisenhower administration would come to recognize this dilemma; in the meantime NSC 174 would supplant all other work done on Eastern Europe. The new NSC 174 working group assumed all the responsibilities undertaken by Jackson's D 40-45 working group, resolving the division between C. D. Jackson's PSB studies and the Planning Board work completed under Bowie.[165] One may suspect that Eisenhower and his key national security advisors were reluctant to abandon an objective—rollback—that they considered quite dear, and to accept a policy—containment and a negotiated settlement to the cold war—that they had maligned both in private and in public for two years. Their uncertainty over the implications of the Soviet thermonuclear capability may also have contributed to this confusion.

Part Five: The Soviet Hydrogen Bomb and the Intensified Nuclear Threat

Ever since the explosion of the first Soviet atomic bomb on 29 August 1949, the willingness of the United States to pursue its objectives vis-à-vis the Soviet Union and Eastern Europe was balanced against the risk that the Soviets might respond to these actions with a nuclear attack against the continental United States. The Truman administration believed that a massive military buildup and development of the hydrogen bomb would provide sufficient cover for the United States to intensify the political offensive needed to achieve American objectives.

During its first months in power the Eisenhower administration viewed the strategic balance in a similar manner, with the key exception that President Eisenhower recognized that the nuclear balance so favored the United States that a significant political offensive to retract Soviet power was possible even though the administration sought to reduce its defense spending. This viewpoint was substantiated in part by the Special Evaluation Subcommittee report submitted to the NSC on 15 May 1953.[166]

Eisenhower had ordered the committee to evaluate the impact of a surprise Soviet attack on the continental United States on two dates: 1 July 1953 and 1 July 1955. The document assumed that the Soviets would possess no deliverable thermonuclear weapon at either time and would achieve total surprise against the U.S. forces. The committee concluded that a Soviet attack could destroy 24 percent of the U.S. bomber force in 1953—increasing to 30 percent in 1955—reducing the monthly sortie rate of SAC bombers by about 50 percent. A Soviet attack on industrial centers would initially paralyze one-third of total U.S. production in 1953—increasing to two-thirds by 1955—while casualty figures would total 9 million in 1953 and 12.5 million in 1955.[167] While these numbers clearly demonstrated that the United States would suffer significant destruction in a surprise attack, the damage would not preclude the United States from responding with a devastating nuclear attack upon the Soviet Union and mobilizing American capabilities for a successful prosecution of the war. American resiliency coupled with enormous U.S. nuclear superiority led committee chairman Lieutenant General Idwal H. Edwards to conclude that "any attack upon the United States by the Soviets during this period would be an act of desperation and not an exercise of military judgment."[168]

The Soviet boosted-fission detonation on 12 August 1953 (designated "Joe-4") fundamentally transformed General Edwards's judgment. Although not a true thermonuclear explosion, the exponential increase in Soviet nuclear power in only three years—"Joe-4" yielded four hundred kilotons, ten times that of previous tests[169]—stunned the administration and portended a future when the USSR would possess the capability to "annihilate Western civilization" altogether.[170]

The inevitable development of multi-megaton weapons by the Soviet Union changed the character of the nuclear balance of power well beyond the effect of simple atomic weapons.[171] Due to the NSC 68 mobilization officials had believed that the United States was no longer susceptible to a decisive atomic first strike.[172] Estimates provided by the newly created Net Capabilities Evaluation Subcommittee, however, demonstrated that the deployment of multi-megaton thermonuclear weapons in the Soviet arsenal would dramatically alter this conclusion. While reiterating that the Soviets could not deliver a "knockout" blow to America solely through the delivery of even a substantial number of atomic weapons, the subcommittee demonstrated that the delivery of only a handful of thermonuclear weapons could devastate the United States. The subcommittee concluded that:

> In the postulated high altitude attack 85% of the casualties resulted from the *two* 10 megaton bombs detonated on target, and only 15% of the casualties from the other *70* bombs detonated on target. . . . In the postulated low altitude attack, approximately 45% of the casualties resulted from only *one* 10 megaton bomb detonated on target, with the remaining 55% of the casualties resulting from the *170* 60 kt [kiloton] bombs which landed on target.[173] (Emphasis in original)

These figures demonstrated that the effect of the hydrogen bomb was dramatically out of proportion to the original impact of Soviet atomic capabilities.[174] While the latter could disarm the United States during the outset of war, the former could completely destroy American society. Realizing that the survival of the United States was now at stake, Eisenhower began to openly discuss the possibility of a preemptive nuclear strike to destroy Soviet capabilities.

One of the most compelling pieces of evidence of Eisenhower's concerns comes from the 24 September 1953 NSC meeting concerning the "Joe-4" test. Upon receiving the report of CIA director Allen Dulles, Eisenhower declared:

> It was plain . . . that we can no longer ignore the fact that the Russians know how to make fusion weapons. Accordingly, if the United States Government were to present to the Soviet Union a large-scale reasonable program for a negotiated settlement, and such a program was rejected by the Soviets, what were we then to do? It looked to him . . . as though the hour of decision were at hand, and that we should presently have to really face the question of whether or not we would have to throw everything at once against the enemy.[175]

These remarks echo his 8 September response to John Foster Dulles's request for a grand initiative to resolve the cold war. While agreeing that some significant efforts should be made to ease cold war tensions, Eisenhower warned that the growing Soviet nuclear threat was of such a magnitude that it might compel his administration to "consider whether or not our duty to future generations did not require us to *initiate* war at the most propitious moment that we could designate."[176] Conversely, Eisenhower also cautioned that the administration might have to abandon aggressive aspects of U.S. policy due to his "doubts about how much we should poke at the animal through the bars of the cage."[177]

Eisenhower's conflicting responses were not uncommon for that period. The development of multi-megaton weapons so threatened national survival that it made the cost of suffering a nuclear first strike intolerable, particularly in an era absent secure second-strike nuclear capabilities. In addition, with the deployment of its own thermonuclear weapons and the introduction of the B-52 bomber the United States was quickly developing the ability to launch its own first strike capable of resolving the Soviet threat altogether. According to NSC consultant Robert Sprague, America's lead in thermonuclear weapons would give it the ability to launch a decisive (i.e., war-winning) first strike by 1956, with that capability continuing into the indefinite future.[178] By contrast, the report estimated that the Soviet Union would develop a decisive first-strike capability by 1958, giving the United States a two-year window of opportunity either to eliminate the Soviet Union or to reach an accommodation capable of resolving the cold war. Most ominously, the report warned that by 1960 both sides would have first-strike capabilities, presaging a future in which the world lived on a hair trigger and survival depended on the successful management of crisis between the two powers. As will be discussed later, an increasing number of the president's advisors would contend that the United States should use its nuclear superiority to arrive at an accommodation with the Kremlin.

Fear of surprise attack continued to predominate strategic thought in the mid-1950s while mutual deterrence was considered but one less likely outcome. In a reprise of the Bohlen-Nitze debates of 1951–1952 the argument focused on the extent of Soviet risk-taking. As with Bohlen and Nitze, the ability of the United States to retaliate against a Soviet first strike with sufficient force to destroy the Soviet regime was the subject of the debate. Would the Soviet Union remain fearful of America's retaliation as its nuclear capability improved, or would the Soviets strike at the first opportunity? The answer to this question lay in resolving another dilemma: did the Kremlin see the U.S.-Soviet strategic relationship in the same manner as the United States? Did they fear nuclear attack as much as the United States? What precise level of nuclear devastation would be sufficient to deter the Soviet Union from initiating global war? These questions would plague American strategic thinkers for decades; however, the preliminary assessments were less than sanguine. Four of the most important studies of the period, NSC 68, Project Solarium, Albert Wohlstetter's study of the vulnerability of SAC bombers (RAND report 266), and the Killian commission report, warned that the United States was in ever increasing danger of being defeated by a Soviet first strike.[179] While these studies did not convince Eisenhower to build a multi-billion-dollar continental defense system, they undermined confidence in a national security policy premised upon deterrence.[180]

The Implications of a Thermonuclear Arms Race for United States Policy

By March of 1954, the administration realized the full ramifications of the nuclear arms race. The horror of thermonuclear weapons led Eisenhower to conclude that a third world war must be avoided. While war with atomic weapons would severely damage the United States, particularly its ability to prosecute a global war, a war with thermonuclear weapons threatened the nation's very survival. Eisenhower believed that a war involving hydrogen weapons would be so devastating that in its aftermath all nations would need dictatorships to rebuild. Most estimates concluded that if war erupted in 1954 the United States would emerge better off than the Soviets. This military success, however, would be achieved only at the cost of a postwar dictatorship and the loss of the American way of life, an outcome Eisenhower considered unacceptable.

The growing realization of the costs of thermonuclear war dominated the NSC revisions to U.S. war objectives. Army Chief of Staff General Matthew Ridgeway and Chief of Naval Operations Robert B. Carney argued that U.S.

strategic planning must account for postwar objectives. They maintained that "full exploitation of our nuclear capability might inflict such chaos and destruction and suffering in the Soviet Union . . . [that] it was impossible to visualize how the United States could cope with the victory it might achieve."[181] Eisenhower attacked the JCS position, stating that it was his belief that with the terrible nature of thermonuclear warfare, "everything in a future war with the Soviet bloc would have to be subordinated to winning that war."[182] The president denounced attempts to establish political goals in the aftermath of a third world war as "impossible and impractical." "We can't tell what we will do after we achieve a victory in what will be total and not in any sense limited warfare," he stated.[183] He concluded that U.S. war objectives should be nothing more than victory and that there should be no limitations or restrictions as General Ridgeway and Admiral Carney suggested. The United States would be "applying a force so terrible" that it would not be possible to limit the damage of such an attack, nor would Eisenhower even seek to do so. The president reasoned that since the United States would enter the war only in "retaliation against a heavy Soviet atomic attack" he could take no other course of action than to strike the Soviets with the most devastating force.[184]

The political implications of thermonuclear war resulted in further significant revisions to the administration's basic national security policy paper. Whereas NSC 162/2 spoke of the "probable capacity to inflict critical damage on the other," eight months later the Planning Board concluded that "the strategic use by both sides of nuclear weapons would bring such extensive destruction as to threaten the survival of Western civilization and the Soviet regime."[185] One consequence was that Eisenhower relented slightly on his resistance to planning a continental defense program, if for no other reason than to try to reassure the U.S. public that all steps were being taken to respond to the new danger.[186]

According to a National Intelligence Estimate presented on 28 April 1954 the American public was not the only group that needed reassuring. NIE-100-54 "Probable Effects of Increasing Nuclear Capabilities on the Policies of US Allies" determined that the possible responses of the U.S. allies to the threat of thermonuclear war might include "seek[ing] to obtain greater influence over US policy, in order to ensure a cautious and non-provocative attitude toward the Communist states."[187] By November, the threat of thermonuclear war encouraged the State Department to support the adoption of a non-provocative national security policy. A State Department report prepared for the NSC and endorsed by Secretary Dulles declared that "U.S. policy should take full account of the fact that total war would be an incalculable disaster." The report continued that "the primary aim [of U.S. policy] must be to deter any Communist armed aggression and to avoid the danger that such aggression would develop into a general nuclear war. . . . The U.S., however, should forego actions which would generally be regarded as provocative."[188] Even Joint Chiefs of Staff chairman Admiral Arthur W. Radford expressed the concern that once the USSR had attained nuclear parity "the relative power position of the United States would have so changed that the U.S. could no longer count on the Russians being afraid of starting general war." Consequently, he warned that "the United States had only a limited time with which to reach accommodation with the Communists."[189]

While Eisenhower debated Admiral Radford over the type of policy to achieve such an accommodation, he clearly agonized over the emerging strategic dilemma, so much in fact that he established the Net Evaluations Subcommittee to provide estimates as to when the Soviet nuclear threat would reach critical dimensions. According to Eisenhower's directive the group would prepare a report on "what series or group of possible Soviet actions should leave no doubt in the President's mind to the need of taking immediate military actions to save the United States from the consequences of enemy attack or to ameliorate the existing hostile situation."[190]

Consequently, while Eisenhower never came close to ordering a preventive war and in the end would decide to reduce provocative policies that might incite war, he certainly contemplated its possibility and so agonized over the growing security dilemma posed by two first-strike capabilities that he would contemplate preventive action until the end of his administration.[191]

The implications of thermonuclear war pushed the debate over U.S. national security policy to a climax: could the United States continue to risk world war by taking the aggressive measures necessary to roll back Soviet power in Eastern Europe? As it became apparent that successful U.S. covert operations would have to take much greater risks of war than previously anticipated, this issue came to the forefront of the debate. Numerous officials had already taken contrary positions on this issue, forcing a reconsideration of U.S. policy.

Part Six: Review of U.S. Policy toward the Soviet Bloc

The OCB Reports: June–December 1954

In January of 1954, Robert Cutler approached Walter Bedell Smith, Allen Dulles, and C. D. Jackson about the need to formulate a specific NSC position regarding the exploitation of Soviet vulnerabilities beyond that espoused by PSB D-40. Unlike Eastern Europe, which had historically received far greater attention, no single NSC paper directed U.S. psychological-warfare efforts against the USSR alone. Cutler had been arguing since November that a single separate NSC statement of policy was needed in order to bridge the gap between the highly generalized nature of NSC 162/2 and specific operational instructions needed by the departments. Smith, Dulles, and Jackson agreed with Cutler that such a paper was needed but they decided to review past U.S. efforts to exploit Soviet vulnerabilities as well. Cutler established a committee under the direction of Horace Craig, chief of the OCB Special Staff, Paul Comstock, and T. B. Koons of the NSC Staff with the responsibility to ascertain whether the NSC needed to develop a new policy statement specifically for the Soviet Union. The committee received access to all pertinent NSC, PSB, OCB, CIA, and State Department records, and was allowed to submit questions to both the CIA and State Department concerning their respective interpretations of current NSC mandates.

The study, completed on 8 June 1954, highlighted the incongruity of pursuing a negotiated solution to the cold war while continuing to exploit Soviet vulnerabilities in Eastern Europe through aggressive covert action. The authors wrote that:

> As it has been formulated, NSC policy towards the USSR has not provided a 'strategic concept' adequate for operational guidance in the exploitation of Soviet vulnerabilities. . . . There is no clear guidance in NSC policies for determining the balance and relationship between measures taken within the context of a policy of co-existence and measures to be taken within a context which postulates the destruction of the Soviet system and regime.[192]

The report recommended that the NSC devise a new "strategic concept" to resolve the dichotomy between efforts to encourage "peaceful coexistence" and attempts to exploit Soviet vulnerabilities.[193] Additionally, it called for the OCB to study the possibilities of detaching a major Soviet satellite (i.e., a satellite other than Albania), to determine the attainability of NSC 174.[194]

The OCB received part of that proposed study—entitled "The Vulnerabilities of the European Satellites"—on 21 September.[195] Its authors concluded that Soviet control over the satellites remained "virtually complete and is unlikely to diminish or to be successfully challenged from within."[196] Although they continued to expect the "passive resistance" of the satellite populations "to the Sovietization of Eastern Europe," no active and organized opposition existed to impair "Soviet control or threaten the stability of the Satellite governments." Furthermore, the report forewarned that over the next two years (1954–1956) the Soviet Union would concentrate on strengthening controls on the satellite nations.

The document concluded that the Soviets had successfully subjugated all elements of power within the satellite nations, including party organs, the armed forces, and the security apparatus. It recognized that the satellite leadership rose to positions of power only with the approval of Moscow, and constituted the principal instrument of satellite control. The Kremlin routinely called these leaders to Moscow for consultations, and purged any official expressing nationalist sentiments. The USSR further enhanced its control by placing Soviet nationals in key administrative positions within the satellite states. Soviet Field Marshal Konstantin Rokossovskii commanded the Polish Army, while the MVD (predecessor to the KGB) directly administered the satellite internal police forces, extensively purging all "unreliable" elements. The document estimated Soviet military forces in the satellite countries at 531,000 army troops and 24,000 security troops, constituting a crucial deterrent to any satellite defection.

Six weeks later the NSC 174 Working Group presented a report that concurred that the Sovietization of Eastern Europe was nearly complete, but maintaining that two slight opportunities for exploitation continued to exist. This recently declassified report stressed that the Soviet position in both East Germany and Czechoslovakia remained unstable and, given both satellites' proximity to the West, offered long-term opportunities for continued American action. East Germany in particular represented the weak link of Soviet control in Eastern Europe, given its strong resistance to Soviet domination and extensive exposure to West Germany. The Working Group contended that American psychological-warfare efforts could exploit the Soviet position as part of a strategy leading toward unification on Western terms. German unification, the group argued, might "set in motion a chain reaction throughout Eastern Europe," with Czechoslovakia one of the more promising opportunities. Nevertheless, both operations would entail an extensive commitment of U.S. resources and remained remote possibilities.[197]

These conclusions heavily influenced the final OCB study entitled "Analysis of the Situation with Respect to Possible Detachment of a Major Soviet Satellite," presented to the board on 10 December 1954.[198] The implications of this study for U.S. national security policy were unmistakable:

a. At present, given the strength of the Soviet position, no major Soviet satellite presents vulnerabilities of such extent that their exploitation can be expected to result in its detachment from the Soviet bloc.
b. U.S. capabilities under present conditions are not sufficient to accomplish the detachment of any major Soviet satellite by means short of war.
c. Unless the power balance between the United States and the Soviet Union changes drastically in our favor, there is little likelihood of detaching a major satellite at any time without grave risk of war except by negotiation. The only satellite which now lends itself to possible detachment by this means is East Germany [by way of reunification with West Germany].

The conclusion that peaceful retraction of Soviet power from Eastern Europe could not take place unless the balance of power shifted decisively in the United States's favor spelled the end of America's efforts to liberate Eastern Europe, since nuclear weapons no longer made such a shift possible. By mid-1954, the U.S. national security establishment had come to believe that the Soviets would eventually build a stockpile of nuclear weapons capable of destroying North America, even though the United States would maintain a significant numerical superiority. This factor—termed "enoughness" by Allen Dulles—meant that development of clear-cut nuclear superiority by the United States since NSC 68 would not reduce the threat posed by the significantly inferior Soviet nuclear force. Consequently, it was impossible for the United States to build the preponderant military power required to shield the aggressive level of political warfare needed to attack the Soviet bloc.[199] This conclusion—coupled with a determination made by the NSC 174 Working Group that an effective covert offensive to undermine Soviet power in Eastern Europe would "probably [be] the equivalent of war"—ended the belief that the peaceful liberation of the satellite states was possible through covert means, auguring a new era in U.S. policy toward Eastern Europe.[200]

Accommodation and Coexistence: The New National Security Policy Is Decided

The dilemma presented by the conclusion of the OCB's staff studies set the stage for the significant revision in policy debated by the NSC Planning Board during November and December of 1954. The State Department believed that Soviet "atomic plenty" required that the United States abandon "aggressive" measures which entailed a significant risk of war and search for negotiated solutions to the world's major trouble spots. The department's Planning Board representatives argued, much as Charles Bohlen had two years before, that U.S. policy must focus instead on the development of a healthy international system and resign itself to a long struggle against the Soviet bloc. America had either to reduce to a non-threatening level or abandon altogether its efforts to weaken Soviet power in Eastern Europe. The Joint Chiefs, on the other hand, believed that the impending Soviet capability to destroy the United States (now estimated for 1960) required a robust American policy that would force the Soviet Union into accommodation with the United States prior to that time.

As with the debates over NSC 162, both arguments were presented in NSC 5440, the draft basic national security policy statement, and were extensively discussed by the NSC, culminating with the NSC meeting of 21 December 1954. This session represented a crossroads in the development of the administration's national security policy. The key participants concurred that the principal Soviet threat was no longer its ideology but instead its growing nuclear capacity to devastate the continental united States. They agreed that because of this new capacity, aggressive anti-Soviet measures called for by the JCS were too hazardous and had to be abandoned. Finally, the council members admitted that the only viable cold war policy was to continue efforts to strengthen the international system, to resist Soviet encroachment, and to negotiate a reduction of world tensions and armaments—a policy identical to that proposed by Charles Bohlen in the spring and summer of 1952, and a policy that many within the Eisenhower administration had once held in contempt.

The meeting was originally intended to review the new U.S. national security policy statement, NSC 5440, which was submitted for NSC approval on 13 December 1954. The session soon took on greater significance, however, when Secretary of State Dulles decided to speak broadly about U.S. policy. Soon all the participants joined Dulles in expanding their comments beyond the original scope of the session.[201]

Dulles sympathized with the JCS call for greater dynamism in U.S. policy toward the communist world, since "after all, during the 1952 campaign he had himself called for a more dynamic U.S. policy vis-à-vis Communism." "However," he intoned, "experience indicated that it was not easy to go very much beyond the point that this administration had reached in translating dynamic policy into courses of action."[202]

Dulles turned his attention to the various opportunities available to the United States. He emphatically rejected preventive war as an option, then questioned the prospect that aggressive measures could "change the basic character of the Soviet system" while the United States retained its atomic superiority over the enemy. Dulles contended that "this would call, in effect, for an effort to overthrow the Communist regimes in China and in the European satellites and to detach these countries from the USSR." He stated that "such a course of action would involve the United States in general war." Even if it did not result in war, Dulles felt that if the United States did succeed in detaching Communist China and the satellite nations from the USSR, "this in itself would not touch the heart of the problem: Soviet atomic plenty." He continued that "even if we split the Soviet bloc, in other words, we would still have to face the terrible problem and threat of an unimpaired nuclear capability in the USSR itself." Dulles concluded that a more dynamic and aggressive policy would not achieve the basic U.S. goal of eliminating the threat from the Soviet Union, unless these aggressive measures led to a world war that the United States could win. Furthermore, while these more aggressive policies might result in the collapse of the Soviet bloc, "they would almost certainly cause the disintegration of the free world bloc . . . for our allies in the free world would never go along with such courses of action as these." Therefore, Dulles concluded that "this kind of aggressive policy was not in the best interests of the United States."[203]

In addition, Dulles rejected the suggestion that the United States present the Soviet Union with an ultimatum stating that if it continued efforts to subdue other free-world countries "such as Finland or Vietnam" the United

States would regard such an attempt as a *casus belli*. Dulles argued that "even if it did succeed, it would not touch the heart of the problem of Soviet atomic capabilities, and would likewise prove disastrous to the unity of the free world coalition." Furthermore, except for the Middle East, the remaining areas open to Soviet expansion "were not areas whose acquisition . . . would notably increase the actual power of the Soviet bloc." Consequently, present national security policies "were pretty generally adequate." NATO had succeeded in stabilizing Western Europe, while the Caracas Pact had "the same effect in the Western Hemisphere." The principal concern in the Pacific was Indonesia, which, he argued, was of "very great importance to us and to certain of our allies, especially Japan."[204] Though Southeast Asia, particularly Vietnam, Cambodia, and Laos, was vulnerable, "these countries were not really of great significance to us, other than from the point of view of prestige, except that they must be regarded as staging grounds for further forward thrusts by the Communist powers."

Dulles concluded that satellite nationalism might lead to some disintegration of the communist bloc so that at least "no single nation can decide upon and take sudden action without considering the views of its allies." Otherwise, "the overall U.S. position in the world was quite satisfactory except for the Middle East where the loss of oil resources would be a grievous blow to the West. Furthermore, he could see no clear substitute for existing policies except in Indonesia, Vietnam, and the Middle East."[205]

Secretary of the Treasury George Humphrey strongly supported Dulles's position. Humphrey confirmed that preventive war and "an aggressive course of action to roll back Communism" were not acceptable policy options since "we would lose our allies, and such a course of action was not worth the risks it entailed." Humphrey concluded that the United States would now "in effect [be] practicing a policy of co-existence," suggesting that "the United States must, in other words, now learn to live the way many of the other nations of the world have lived for many centuries—that is by co-existence based on the maintenance of the balance of power." America, he argued, "must participate in a world division of power so carefully balanced that neither side dares to 'jump' the other." For these reasons "we should avoid provocative actions vis-à-vis the USSR and not get ourselves into positions which are untenable from the point of view of their defense."[206] Humphrey concluded that "he was not the least bit afraid of coexistence. Our American system was sufficiently strong to undertake such a policy, and in competition with the Soviet Union we certainly could beat them."

Secretary of Defense Charles Wilson agreed with both Dulles and Humphrey that aggressive policies did not enhance U.S. national security. He stated that "he was—for lack of a better word—in favor of containment." Wilson argued that, "plainly, we must live for the time being with Communism." While we ourselves "can't do much externally to destroy it," he was sure that "ultimately it would destroy itself." Wilson concluded that:

> Our policy should be strong, but that we could no more bully the Soviet Union than we could bully the labor unions. We should, accordingly, deal with the Soviet Union from strength and in the confidence that our own system was much the better, instead of adopting courses of action in imitation of Soviet methods.[207]

The National Security Council continued discussion of NSC 5440 on 5 January 1955, formally approving the document on 7 January as NSC 5501 "Basic National Security Policy," superseding NSC 162/2 and NSC 5422/2 as official U.S. policy.[208] NSC 5501 defined two possible U.S. responses to the growing Soviet challenge: first, "destroying the power of the Soviet-Communist bloc," and second, "modifying the policies of the Soviet-Communist bloc along lines more compatible with U.S. security interests." The document concluded that there was little prospect of impeding the growth of Soviet nuclear capabilities "except by mutually acceptable agreements with the Soviets." It warned that within five years the Soviet Union "will almost certainly develop the *net* capability to strike a crippling blow at the United States." Therefore, NSC 5501 concluded that the only viable strategy to reduce the Soviet threat was a U.S. policy designed to modify Soviet conduct in ways that furthered U.S. national interests by:

a. Deterring further Communist aggression and preventing the occurrence of total war so far as compatible with U.S. security.
b. Maintaining and developing in the free world the mutuality of interest and common purpose, and the necessary will, strength and stability, to face the Soviet-Communist threat and to provide constructive and attractive alternatives to Communism, which sustain the hope and confidence of free peoples.

The United States would restrain Soviet conduct by: "(1) influencing them and their peoples toward the choice of those alternative lines of action which, while in their national interest, do not conflict with the security interests of the U.S.; and (2) exploiting differences between such regimes, and their other vulnerabilities, in ways consistent with this general strategy."[209]

Because it acknowledged the existence of legitimate Soviet national security interests, this statement represented a paradigm shift in U.S. national security policy. Previously analysts had considered Soviet hostility illegitimate, a manifestation of that regime's desire to maintain its power base in the USSR—a position best expressed by George Kennan in NSC 20/1. Kennan wrote:

> Our difficulty with the Soviet Government lies basically in the fact that its leaders are animated by concepts of the theory and practice of international relations which are not only radically opposed to our own but are clearly inconsistent with any peaceful and mutually profitable development of relations between that government and other members of the international community, individually and collectively.[210]

No middle ground existed between U.S. and Soviet national security interests. Resolution of the cold war required a fundamental change in Soviet behavior that could be accomplished only by American pressure.[211]

Within weeks, NSC 5501 altered U.S. policy toward Eastern Europe. On 31 January 1955, President Eisenhower approved NSC 5505/1 "Exploitation of Soviet and European Satellite Vulnerabilities" as the basic guide for exploiting discontent behind the Iron Curtain. Although it did not supersede NSC 174 and still committed U.S. policy to "weakening the ties that bind the satellites to the USSR," the document clearly stressed that this policy meant the modification of internal satellite conditions and not the detachment of the satellite states.[212] The United States would convey to the Eastern Europeans that while the Soviet system was obviously flawed, "many of the discontents and other problems are . . . not . . . inherent conditions reparable only by revolution but conditions susceptible to correction by the regime if it chooses to take the necessary action." Evolutionary measures were fully capable of improving living conditions within these nations; thus U.S. propaganda efforts would stress the need to avoid revolution.

The policy statement warned that modification of USSR and satellite security policy was possible "only if further communist expansion is prevented," as the USSR and its satellites "are not likely to experiment with alternatives more consistent with U.S. interests as long as the accustomed Communist techniques of military and political pressure on and in the free world show signs of achieving success."[213]

It was very difficult for the administration to accept an evolutionary approach to reducing Soviet power in Eastern Europe. On 27 January the NSC met to discuss the implications of NSC 5505. Despite supporting the new position, both Allen and John Foster Dulles and Vice President Richard Nixon stated that the United States must remain prepared to incite revolution behind the Iron Curtain.[214] Nixon pointedly asked Cutler whether the strategy set forth in the document "would not rule out resort to revolutionary methods if they seemed likely to be successful." Cutler assured him that the new policy did not rule out such possibilities. To emphasize the point, the Dulles brothers stated firmly that:

> They did not wish the guidance provided by NSC 5505, on the exploitation of Soviet vulnerabilities along evolutionary rather than revolutionary lines, to

destroy all possibility of seizing opportunities for exploiting a different type of strategy if such opportunities clearly presented themselves.[215]

President Eisenhower, however, was no longer convinced that a revolutionary approach remained practicable. Eisenhower contended that he could see nothing wrong with taking an evolutionary approach to change in the Soviet bloc and that "it was, in general, following the right line." He made clear his belief that the United States was "not in a position to state that it would promote revolution in the Soviet Union." "What we must do," he intoned, "was win 'these guys' over." Therefore, he ordered Nelson Rockefeller (who replaced C. D. Jackson as special assistant for cold war affairs in March) to assemble a working group to begin to enact a new plan.[216]

While NSC 5505/1 (the approved version of the document) did not supersede the objectives of NSC 174—the ultimate intention of U.S. policy remained the independence of the satellite states—it did establish a new approach to achieving this goal. Furthermore, even though both Nixon and the Dulles brothers insisted that the United States retain the option of resorting to revolutionary methods to liberate the satellite states, it was clear that NSC 5505/1 represented a significant change of approach. The Rockefeller group quickly realized in their attempts to formulate a strategy that the new NSC policy did reflect "a somewhat subtler strategy and different emphasis than the policy conclusions underlying NSC 174."[217]

Another casualty in the continuing American retrenchment was U.S. covert policy behind the Iron Curtain. On 15 March 1954, NSC 5412 replaced NSC 10/2 and NSC 10/5 as guidance for covert operations against the Soviet bloc. Final approval of NSC 5412 would not come for another sixteen months, or until the administration had settled its debate over the nature of American policy behind the Iron Curtain. The administration completed the final version of the document on 28 December 1955, and approved as NSC 5412/2 "National Security Council Directive on Covert Operations."[218] Though NSC 5412/2 committed the United States to continue to engage in covert activities that would exploit differences in the communist world, it represented a substantial retreat from the ambitious policies of NSC 10/5.[219] NSC 10/5 committed U.S. covert policy to:

> place the maximum strain on the Soviet structure of power, including the relationships between the USSR, its satellites, and Communist China; and when and where appropriate in the light of U.S. and Soviet capabilities and the risk of war, contribute to the retraction and reduction of Soviet power and influence to limits which no longer constitute a threat to U.S. security.

NSC 5412/2 committed the United States to:

> create and exploit troublesome problems for International Communism, impair relations between the USSR and Communist China and between

> them and their satellites, complicate control within the USSR, Communist China and their satellites, and retard the growth of the military and economic potential of the Soviet bloc.

NSC 5412/2 limited covert action to creating "troublesome problems" for the USSR and China and retarding the growth of their economic and military potential. Covert action, however, was not the principal tool to reduce Soviet power—only mutually acceptable negotiated solutions would achieve that. Furthermore, the retraction of Soviet power, while remaining a long-range goal, was no longer an immediate objective of American policy.

PART SEVEN: NUCLEAR SUPERIORITY AND DE-STALINIZATION: 1955–1957

The Quantico Vulnerabilities Report

Ironically, as the Soviet nuclear threat forced the United States to shift its national security strategy away from aggressive covert activities, the United States had acquired the numerical position of decisive nuclear superiority.[220] A group of stalwart cold warriors seized upon this fact as they tried to convince the administration that it was still possible to fashion an aggressive policy to win the cold war. Nelson Rockefeller invited a panel of experts to Quantico, Virginia, in June 1955 to explore new methods of exploiting Soviet vulnerabilities. Walter W. Rostow chaired the panel, which included fellow MIT colleagues Frederick Dunn, Max Millikan, Ellis Johnson, and George Pettee. They were joined by C. D. Jackson, now working for Time-Life, Paul Linebarger of the Johns Hopkins School of Advanced International Studies, Philip Mosely of the Russian Institute at Columbia University, Stefan Possony, intelligence specialist for the Air Force, Charles A. H. Thompson of the Brookings Institution, and Hans Speier of the RAND Corporation. They concluded that as of 1955 the United States had achieved a position of "decisive nuclear superiority" over the Soviet Union and that the time had come for the United States to use this advantage to begin a series of negotiations with the Soviet Union "presenting [them] with heavy demands for major concessions on their part at a price that is tolerable to us."[221] In essence the panel argued for a policy of nuclear coercion to achieve victory in the cold war. The goal of American strategy was not to ease world tensions, but to force the Soviets to retreat from their present positions, to unify the European continent "from Turkey to Norway, from Poland to Spain," to strain relations between the Soviets and Communist China, to unify Germany and tie it to NATO, and to force the Soviets into accepting arms-control provisions with intrusive verification measures which would insure a continuation of American preponderance.[222]

Because the window of opportunity was closing rapidly, these scholars urged American officials to move quickly. They estimated that the United States had approximately two years to achieve these objectives because Soviet capabilities would grow to rough parity within five years. In addition, the Eisenhower administration had to avoid being sidetracked by the Soviet peace offensives and their efforts to appear willing to negotiate key cold war issues. The Soviets feared their present strategic inferiority, the panel asserted, and were interested in easing tensions only to avoid a crisis with the United States before they had resolved some of their social and economic problems and developed their strategic nuclear capability.

By mid-1955 however, the focus of the Eisenhower administration had shifted from the opportunities created by strategic superiority to coming to grips with a heavily armed Soviet state that possessed a growing capacity to launch a surprise nuclear attack against the continental United States. Beginning in 1950, U.S. calculations determined the strategic balance of power based on the ratio of the number of warheads plus delivery vehicles to the number of the enemy's key targets. Consequently, JIC 502, NSC 135/3, and the Disarmament Panel Report concurred that while the United States might possess strategic superiority in absolute terms, the Soviets were quickly approaching the point that their much inferior nuclear arsenal could successfully destroy the American warfighting capacity in a surprise attack. Therefore, short of an actual willingness on the part of the United States to employ its nuclear capabilities to destroy Soviet power, nuclear superiority did not offer the opportunities suggested by the Quantico Panel.

Furthermore, even though the United States would soon possess decisive nuclear superiority over the Soviet Union it could not risk war with impunity. Only a few months before receiving the Quantico Vulnerabilities Report, the Killian Commission briefed Eisenhower on its report "Meeting the Threat of Surprise Attack," which challenged the notion that the United States could manipulate strategic superiority without fear of retaliation. The commission agreed that the United States would move into a position of strategic superiority vis-à-vis the Soviet Union by 1956 and that intensive study should be given to the type of political and diplomatic policies the United States could develop to exploit the situation. The authors warned, however, that these "policies should recognize that any war which might occur would result in severe damage to the U.S. despite our great relative strength" and urged that the United States undertake an extensive expansion of its continental defense capabilities to reduce this threat.[223]

This growing sense of vulnerability was further strengthened by RAND report R-266, *Selection and Use of Strategic Air Bases*, better known as the Wohlstetter Basing Study after its principal author, Albert Wohlstetter. The report demonstrated that the U.S. strategic bomber forces were highly exposed to surprise attack and unless significant defensive measures were taken growing Soviet nuclear capabilities threatened preemption.[224]

The approach of the Quantico Panel was not accepted because of the uncertainty of using nuclear coercion against a nuclear-armed adversary. The Quantico Panel assumed that the diplomatic initiatives of the post-Stalin Soviet government resulted from fear over the grave strategic predicament they faced. Because it might result in the defeat of the Soviet Union and the death of the world communist movement, the Soviets had to avoid war with the United States until the development of parity. The panel concluded that a concentrated effort by the Eisenhower administration could result in significant diplomatic gains sufficient even to win the cold war.

The question remained, however, what would the Eisenhower administration do if the Soviets resisted their demands? Furthermore, since American strategic predominance would last for only a few years, what would motivate the Soviets to accept American objectives instead of resisting until the development of rough strategic equality? The Quantico Panel's approach could work only under two conditions: first, if the Soviets fully believed that the United States would initiate a surprise attack, and second, if the period of Soviet inferiority would last for many years. Over a greater period of time, a significantly inferior Soviet Union might be intimidated into concessions by American threats since the possibility of crisis and escalation to war would be much greater. It was clear that the American advantage would not last that long, however, undermining the whole point of the report.

These views were solidified during the Geneva Conference held in July of 1955. It was the hope of the Quantico Panel that if the appropriate measures were applied the United States could score a significant political victory and commence the liberation of Eastern Europe. As C. D. Jackson explained to Henry Luce, "this is the first time I have ever smelled victory."[225] Instead, the Eisenhower administration chose to follow the advice of the British and French, who argued that the possibilities for an agreement on Germany superseded concerns over Eastern Europe. Any discussions about Eastern Europe, they counseled, should be restricted to private conversations and not made an official part of the conference. Following this advice, both Eisenhower and Dulles met privately with Soviet premier Nikolai Bulganin, stressing that full normalization of relations with the Soviet Union could take place only if the two nations could resolve the situation in Eastern Europe. Dulles emphasized that the United States had no "desire that the Soviet Union should be ringed by a group of hostile states" and suggested that a relationship based upon the Soviet-Finnish model would be acceptable to the Eisenhower administration. Bulganin refused to discuss the issue and warned that "it was a subject which it would do no good to pursue at this conference."[226]

De-Stalinization, Revolution, and Repression: The End of Liberation

The failure of the Geneva Conference would have represented the denouement of the administration's satellite policy had it not been for a momentous decision by Soviet Communist Party general secretary Nikita Khrushchev to denounce Stalin and begin the liberalization of Soviet and Eastern European societies.[227] At the Twentieth Congress of the Communist Party of the Soviet Union in February 1956, Khrushchev attempted to destroy Stalin's legend, denouncing him as "a supreme egotist and sadist, capable of sacrificing everything and anybody for the sake of his own power and glory" and blaming him for the USSR's total lack of preparation on the eve of World War II and near catastrophic defeat.[228]

Khrushchev's address caused shock and dismay within Moscow and amazement within Washington. Allen Dulles reviewed the speech for the NSC at its 22 March meeting. Clearly recognizing its significance, Dulles declared that Khrushchev had "deliberately sought to destroy Stalin . . . and afforded the United States a great opportunity, both covertly and overtly, to exploit the situation to its advantage," a view that quickly achieved consensus among the rest of the NSC.[229] Khrushchev's speech and the de-Stalinization program that followed seemed to represent the long-awaited weakening of the Soviet system, and offered the best prospect for a renewed American effort to reshape the Soviet bloc.

By mid-1956 the Eisenhower administration realized that NSC 174 and NSC 5505/1 required reexamination in the light of the new Soviet policies. On the one hand, the Soviet leadership was pursuing a policy of de-Stalinization that included the rehabilitation of many victims of Stalin's purges, reestablishment of relations with Tito, and withdrawal of its forces from Austria in 1955 in accordance with the Austrian State Treaty. On the other hand, the Soviets strengthened their military domination of the region by creating the Warsaw Pact Alliance in 1955 as well. Therefore, on 18 July Eisenhower approved NSC 5608/1 "U.S. Policy toward the Soviet Satellites in Eastern Europe" as the new statement of U.S. objectives, superseding NSC 174.[230] NSC 5608/1 reiterated NSC 174's contention that Soviet control in Eastern Europe would remain firm as long as the satellite nations were dominated by governments subservient to Moscow and the Soviet army remained poised to intervene. However, it stressed that the changes brought about since 1953—particularly Khrushchev's speech, Soviet acceptance of the "many roads to socialism" thesis, and the rise of nationalist communist opposition within the satellite leadership—raised the possibility for renewed American efforts for the:

> encouragement of evolutionary change resulting in the weakening of Soviet controls and the attainment of national independence by the countries concerned, even though there may be no immediate change in their internal political structure.[231]

Courses of action described in NSC 5608/1 included encouraging passive resistance of the satellite populations, developing democratic, anti-communist elements, exploiting the Western institutions such as the European Common Market as a "force of attraction for the satellites," and being prepared to negotiate issues between the United States and the individual satellite regimes though always emphasizing the right of the Eastern European peoples to independent governments of their own choosing. Most of all, the document stressed that the residents of the East bloc could improve the condition of the satellite states by non-revolutionary methods.

Events throughout Eastern Europe during the spring and summer of 1956 confirmed that a policy stressing evolutionary change was capable of success. Student demonstrations in Czechoslovakia during May, followed by large-scale riots at Poznań, Poland, and a steelworkers' strike in Hungary proved that Khrushchev's liberalization program was beginning to undermine the power of the Eastern European satellites.[232]

Events in Poland during October of 1956 were both the most surprising and promising outcome that year. The workers' riots resulted in a political crisis as Stalinist and nationalist forces within the Polish Communist Party leadership struggled for power. The nationalist forces triumphed over the Stalinist communist faction at the Eighth Session of the Polish Communist Party and took over most of the key positions within the Politburo.[233] The "Polish October" resulted in the rehabilitation of many figures purged during Stalin's last years—including the new Communist Party leader Wladislaw Gomulka—a substantial easing of the mass industrialization program, a slowdown of the hated collectivization campaign, and most important, the removal of Soviet Marshal Konstantin Rokossovskii from his position as Polish defense minister.

Khrushchev immediately traveled to Warsaw with defense minister Marshal Georgii Zhukov and Warsaw Pact commander Ivan Konev to discuss matters with the new leadership. Additionally, Soviet forces began maneuvers near the Polish border, an ominous reminder of the Kremlin's intervention in East Germany three years earlier. Yet, after a heated session with Gomulka, Khrushchev realized the extent of Polish resistance, accepted the new government, suspended the troop movements, and returned to Moscow. Gomulka also realized that he had walked a very fine line in asserting Poland's sovereignty and understood that he could go no further without risking a bloodbath.

The Warsaw agreement might have represented a turning point in Eastern European and Soviet relations, as the Stalinist era of total domination would have given way to a semiautonomous existence, perhaps even the Finlandization of Eastern Europe. As Adam Ulam has remarked, "had the Hungarian drama not taken place one might have well believed at the end of 1956 that the new spirit in the Kremlin was amenable to the eventual development of a genuine Communist commonwealth of nations, and that 'proletariat internationalism' . . . might indeed have come into its own."[234]

The chances for liberalization within the East bloc seemed brighter than at any time since the 1948 Tito-Stalin crisis.

The Eisenhower administration interpreted the Polish October as a confirmation of the success of U.S. efforts to promote peaceful evolution behind the Iron Curtain and as a model for the development of Eastern European–Soviet relations. The Polish October was precisely the outcome John Foster Dulles had longed for since late 1954 and the course of action he urged the Soviets to follow at Geneva. Dulles requested Under Secretary of State Herbert Hoover Jr. to prepare a statement "expressing hope that Poland was achieving the independence promised by the UN Charter" and on 20 October the NSC formed a special committee chaired by Jacob Beam to prepare American policy for this new opportunity. Yet Dulles also understood that Poland had reached the limits of its liberalization and that further moves, particularly mass uprisings and a complete collapse of communist power, could result in Soviet military intervention. Directives were sent to Munich warning Radio Free Europe operators against inciting civil disorder and limiting its news programs to straight factual reporting.[235]

World attention quickly shifted from the stabilization of the Polish crisis to one of the greatest disasters of the cold war: the Hungarian revolution. On 22 October a series of public meetings involving students and intellectuals took place in Budapest to show support for Warsaw's recent moves toward independence. Joined later by thousands of workers, these protesters marched on the parliament building demanding the reinstatement of Prime Minister Imre Nagy, while others went to the government radio building to have their demands aired on Hungarian National Radio. After a few tense hours the government secret police attacked the protesters, turning the peaceful protests into a violent uprising. Army troops called in to quell the protesters refused to fire and, in many incidences, joined their ranks. On 24 October Soviet forces entered Budapest and for the next five days battled the insurgents. Hostilities ended on the 28th only after the Hungarian government made numerous concessions and Soviet forces withdrew from the city.

Washington reacted to the news with shock and excitement. A successful revolution had taken place in Eastern Europe. The American embassy in Budapest reported that the "Hungarian uprising is now a fact of history" and explained that the Soviets were intimidated by the strength of the rebel movement and were most likely planning to withdraw from Hungary altogether.[236] In addition, *Pravda*, the official mouthpiece of the Soviet Communist Party, declared on 30 October that the Soviet Union and its Eastern European allies could "build their mutual relations only on the principle of complete equality . . . and non-interference in one another's affairs."

On 3 November this success turned into disaster as Soviet forces launched an all-out attack against Budapest and toppled the Nagy regime. The Hungarian capital was the scene of some of the fiercest fighting since the end of World War II as protesters battled Soviet tanks with rifles and Molotov cocktails. The result was the collapse of the Hungarian revolution with thousands of dead protesters and hundreds of thousands of refugees.

Many nations denounced the United States, particularly the Eisenhower administration's public support for liberation, as the true reason for the Hungarian disaster. The crushing of the Hungarian revolution devastated American efforts to influence the Soviet bloc. It showed that even evolutionary change required such significant control on the part of the satellite regime and resistance leaders that it might be too difficult to execute in most circumstances. More ominously, it proved that despite the years of public support for satellite liberation the United States would take no overt action to support an independent Eastern Europe.

The proceedings of November 1956 bore an eerie similarity to the predictions made by Charles Bohlen in his unpublished response to John Foster Dulles's article "A Policy of Boldness."[237] By publicly associating American policy with liberation efforts behind the Iron Curtain, the Eisenhower administration turned a covert policy originally designed to disassociate the United States from its clandestine activities into an overt policy which clearly placed the administration at the focal point for Eastern European resistance. This undermined potential resistance forces by making them seem to be acting on behalf of the United States and placed the United States in the position of assuming responsibility for the events that transpired. Such a policy only made sense if the Eisenhower administration was willing to support militarily Eastern European revolution; otherwise it was needless and damaging to American national security. The covert policy of the Truman administration would have been far more applicable during the tumult of 1956 and might have avoided the bloodshed in the streets of Budapest since the protesters would not have had the words of support from both Eisenhower and John Foster Dulles from which to draw inspiration. It is quite likely that Hungarian officials would have followed the line of Gomulka if they assumed that no chance existed for American intervention. Even though the Eisenhower administration began in 1955 to stress to the satellite populations that their plight could be improved by working with the existing regimes, the public calls for liberation provided room for the type of misinterpretation that normally occurs during crisis. There was no misinterpreting the public pronouncements of the Truman administration since the debates over public policy had centered almost solely upon containment of Soviet expansion and not rollback. The citizens of Eastern Europe would never have had the speeches of Harry S. Truman and Dean Acheson to cling to had they decided to revolt during the Truman administration. Furthermore, the administration would still have been able to pursue action behind the Iron Curtain. The crushing of the Hungarian revolution ended any effective role for American policy behind the Iron Curtain. Although efforts continued to support the Gomulka regime in Poland and to urge other nations to follow that course, American prestige was shattered.

The Soviet Union halted its de-Stalinization program in Eastern Europe, increased pressures on the satellite regimes to conform to the Soviet line, and began to establish greater and greater control over the satellite armies to avoid a repeat of the Hungarian situation, when an estimated 80 percent of the Hungarian national army sided with the protesters. The Soviets crushed attempts by nationalist communist leaders in other satellite states to emulate the Gomulka line. In its last policy statement regarding Eastern Europe, NSC 5811/1 "U.S. Policy toward the Soviet-Dominated Nations in Eastern Europe," the Eisenhower administration recognized this outcome.[238] It had become apparent that the Soviet Union was making an enormous effort to enforce party discipline among the satellites. Although America would continue to support the idea of an independent Eastern Europe, it no longer had the same legitimacy in the eyes of both the Soviet Union and the satellite populations to effectively influence them toward that end. As the Eisenhower period came to a close it had become painfully clear that American policy to eliminate the threat from the Soviet Union, end its control over Eastern Europe, and bring the Soviet bloc into the U.S.-led international system had failed.

Conclusion: America's Cold War Objectives

Much has been made of the new cold war history emerging from the Soviet and Eastern European archives that seems to confirm the view that the immediate postwar goals of the Soviet Union included expansion throughout all of Eurasia. We now know that the war scares of 1946 and 1948 were indeed real and not manufactured by the Truman administration, and that the Soviet Union provided significant aid to the Italian and French communist parties prior to the 1948 elections, approved the North Korean attack on South Korea, convinced the Chinese to enter that war, and demanded that both nations continue its prosecution well after both desired an end to the conflict.[1]

Yet newly declassified documents released from the American archives paint a much more aggressive picture of American activities as well. We now know that for eight years it was the basic objective of national security planners not merely to contain Soviet expansion but to destroy communist power and end the Soviet threat to the liberal international order without resorting to military conflict. Although this objective was never attained, the attempt itself demonstrates that the cold war policies of the United States were far more complex than scholars have generally understood and can no longer be considered merely an extension of containment.

America's offensive strategy emerged not from a desire to establish world economic hegemony, however, but from two interrelated fears: that the continued presence of a hostile bloc under Soviet domination could lead to economic chaos and global war and—even if neither of those two events occurred—that a long cold war deadlock might either bankrupt the American economy or force the United States to abandon its most cherished democratic institutions.

From the vantage point of nearly fifty years we can conclude that none of these fears was well founded. Despite the existence of the Soviet Union until 1991, the United States successfully averted global war, developed a prosperous international economic system, and avoided becoming a garrison state. Instead, it was the Soviet Union and its economic system that failed miserably and collapsed into fifteen new countries on Christmas Day, 1991. Nevertheless, the eight-year effort to devise the best strategy to destroy the Soviet Union attests to American planners' lack of faith in the long-term survival of the American way of life in the face of a totalitarian enemy and, conversely, to their belief in the utility of psychological warfare and covert action to end the danger posed by Soviet communism.[2]

This assertiveness in American policy significantly modifies the traditional picture of U.S.-Soviet relations in the immediate aftermath of World War II. In analyzing the origins of the cold war historical scholarship has long focused on the diplomatic wrangling over Eastern Europe, Germany, the Middle East, and Southeast Asia. This book describes a very different relationship between the two countries, one where the goal of the United States was not merely to negotiate with the USSR as it would Great Britain or France, but to employ psychological warfare and covert action to undermine the Soviet government and either compel it to abandon its expansionist ambitions or cause the collapse of the communist bloc altogether. Consequently, covert action and psychological warfare emerge as important components of American foreign policy and an integral element of strategic planning at the highest levels. While many studies have demonstrated the utility of these instruments, none has been able to show how thoroughly integrated they were into American national security planning. One exception is Ann Karalekas's study of the CIA prepared for the Senate Select Committee on Intelligence (Church Committee) hearings in the early 1970s.[3]

Nor have many studies recognized the importance of the strategic balance of power to American national security ambitions. The seminal works of Marc Trachtenberg and Melvyn Leffler have explored how the balance of power influenced U.S. efforts to defend Western Europe, the Middle East, and Asia, arguing that American planners believed preponderant power necessary to support the aggressive policies required to ensure U.S. vital interests.[4] Yet the rollback of Soviet power itself was one of the most dangerous of U.S. attempts during the early cold war and was affected to an even greater extent by the shifting U.S.-Soviet balance of power, with the nuclear equation itself the most important aspect.

Therefore, in this conclusion I explore the importance of these revelations in assessing the objectives of American policy, the utilization of covert action, and the influence of nuclear weapons on American policy.

America's Cold War Objectives

Scholars have debated the nature of America's cold war objectives for decades. Were the policies pursued by the United States intended solely to prevent Soviet domination of the Eurasian continent, or were they instead determined by America's own desire to establish global hegemony? In other words, who was the aggressor in the cold war and who bears ultimate responsibility for its inception? The scholarly debates inspired by these questions plunged cold war historiography into its most severe crisis, as traditionalists contended that the cold war was a consequence of America's legitimate need to stop Soviet expansion while New Left revisionism claimed instead that it arose from the efforts of the United States to secure the Soviet Union and Eastern Europe for its international markets.[5] Spearheaded by the work of John Lewis Gaddis, a post-revisionist synthesis emerged that ameliorated the intensity of the decades-long struggle that had engulfed cold war studies. The post-revisionist synthesis acknowledged that while American actions certainly played a role in heightening U.S.-Soviet tensions and that therefore the United States bears some responsibility for the intensity and duration of the cold war, American objectives were motivated not by economics but instead by a complex interaction of domestic politics and international strategic concerns. Therefore, while post-revisionism succeeded in reducing the Manichaean character of cold war historiography, it added a whole new set of factors for scholarly consideration and legitimated the notion that American policy was not solely defensive.

While it is not the purpose of this book to explore the origins of the cold war, its contention that America's cold war objectives included the destabilization of the Soviet bloc bears significantly on the historiographic debate. The recently declassified documents from America's archives attest to the offensive ambitions of American national security policy and seem to substantiate many of the New Left's charges. My contention, however, is that these materials do not demonstrate that American efforts to subvert the Soviet bloc were part of a broader effort to establish global hegemony. Rather, the United States was motivated by the desire to promote global stability and prevent the recurrence of economic collapse and world war.[6]

Recognition that America's cold war objectives exceeded traditional notions of containment began with the first release of U.S. government documents. Beginning in the late 1970s key national security papers were declassified, providing for the first time a more accurate picture of American strategies and ambitions. These papers, like NSC 20/4 and NSC 68, demonstrated that American objectives aimed to modify Soviet behavior in an attempt to resolve the cold war. While almost no details were available to explain how the government planned to accomplish this goal, these papers forced scholars to consider the implications of an offensive American policy.

Given the ambiguity surrounding these policy directives, it was still possible in the late 1970s and early 1980s to argue that American efforts to moderate Soviet behavior were an outgrowth of U.S. containment policy. In *Strategies of Containment*, published in 1982, Gaddis identified three stages of American strategy: restoration of the European balance of power, reduction of Soviet influence beyond its borders, and a modification of Soviet behavior in order to resolve the cold war.[7] Based on the available evidence, Gaddis argued that American planners hoped to alter Soviet behavior through a combination of inducements and restraints that he referred to as "counter-pressures." American policy would make clear to the Kremlin what policies would be in its best interest and convince it to follow those policies.[8] Thus over the course of many years the United States could influence Soviet action to the point that both powers could resolve outstanding cold war issues.

Benefiting from the release of millions of new documents from the national archives, Melvyn Leffler demonstrated in *A Preponderance of Power* (1992) that American objectives were not only offensive in nature, but were much more aggressive than Gaddis could have recognized. According to Leffler, American planners wanted to "redraw Russia's borders to its pre-1939 status, destroy the Cominform, retract the influence of the Soviet Union, and eventually cause the Soviet system to weaken and decay." He concluded that: "if the free world [could] gather sufficient strength" then "successful containment would evolve into rollback."[9] Yet, while positing a much more ambitious and aggressive effort, Leffler ultimately concurs with Gaddis that American efforts to roll back Soviet power had to await the successful containment of the Soviet Union and establishment of the international system.

By taking advantage of the numerous documents declassified since the publication of *A Preponderance of Power*, it is the argument of this book that the United States initiated offensive action against the Soviet bloc independently of and simultaneously with the inauguration of containment. With the approval of both NSC 20/4 and NSC 10/2 at a time when Marshall Plan aid had only just begun to flow into Western Europe, the Truman administration embarked on an effort to "compel" the Soviet regime to abandon its international ambitions. There would be no delay: containment and a "compellent" strategy would be pursued in parallel, not in sequence.

Yet does the fact that the United States tried to subvert Soviet power prove the thesis of the New Left revisionists that American foreign policy was a manifestation of Open Door economic imperialism? In particular, did America aim to turn the Soviet Union into a raw-material-exporting region as Joyce and Gabriel Kolko contend? I believe that the desire for international political and economic stability and not the need for economic markets determined American policy. While the New Left is correct that U.S. officials feared a recurrence of economic depression after the end of World War II, this was due not to the potential loss of Eastern European and Soviet markets but the prevailing belief that the presence of competing autarkic economic systems inevitably leads to economic and political instability.[10]

Nevertheless, while I reject the notion that American national security elites intentionally planned global economic hegemony, the desire to create a world without competing blocs, coupled with Soviet policies in Eastern Europe, required that the cold war be a struggle for world supremacy with one system ultimately emerging as the victor. As Paul Nitze acknowledged: "We believe that this goal [containment] is inadequate and also unrealistic. We do not believe that the situation can remain indefinitely static. One side will gain and the other will decline as a factor in world affairs. It must be our objective to be the one which gains."[11] Thus, the cold war struggle, particularly from 1948 to 1956, began as a true war between the two camps with one side destined to emerge victorious over the other, as indeed has happened. It was a war fought, however, by non-military methods—psychological warfare and covert action—yet highly influenced by the military balance of power, which ultimately determined its fate.

Covert Action and Psychological Warfare As Instruments of Policy, 1948–1956

During World War II two key U.S. agencies, the Office of Strategic Services and the Office of War Information, had built a staff of specialists committed to the art of psychological warfare, men like Walt Rostow, C. D. Jackson, Robert Joyce, Allen Dulles, Frank Wisner, C. Tracy Barnes, James J. Angleton, and many others. These alumni pervaded academia and government and were determined to use their wartime skills to America's advantage in the cold war. Based on their World War II experiences in Europe, Asia, and Latin America, they were convinced that political warfare was potentially one of the most important instruments in battling international communism. The first postwar tests were the French and Italian elections of 1948, where the significant successes achieved provided great encouragement. From these efforts, it was only logical to extend the role of political warfare to the liberation of the satellite states.

Unlike the World War II experience and the elections of 1948, conditions for pursuing political warfare in Eastern Europe were substantially more adverse. Psychological-warfare campaigns during World War II had the enormous advantage of being one part of a larger, ultimately successful, military mission. Many of the most successful operations, such as Allen Dulles securing the surrender of the German Army in Italy, would have been impossible to achieve without the reality of total defeat hanging over the heads of the Germans. So, too, with the administration's peacetime operations in Latin America and Western Europe. In these circumstances, the United States prevented the rise to power of adversarial governments, both fascist and communist, and possessed the freedom of movement to inundate these nations with a blanket of propaganda through locally controlled radio stations and newspapers. Both situations ultimately proved successful because the United States could directly contact individual citizens within each country in order to influence their political viewpoints.

U.S. planners did not have such opportunities behind the Iron Curtain. Soviet and satellite regimes maintained complete control over access to news and radio, drastically limiting the exposure of their citizens to Western information. The United States had to rely on leaflets dropped from balloons and shortwave radio broadcasts that were subject to jamming as the primary means to contact the citizens of Eastern Europe. Covert activities were even more haphazard, as seen in the failure of the operations in Albania and the apparent failures of the psychological-war plans designed to destabilize other East bloc regimes.

Nevertheless, administration planners believed in psychological warfare and made significant efforts to employ these instruments. By 1948, psychological warfare had become an integral component of the U.S. cold war inventory and became especially important in the aftermath of the Soviet atomic bomb detonation and NSC 68. According to Ann Karalekas the physical expansion of the Office of Policy Coordination from 1949 to 1952 was substantial. In 1949 OPC personnel totaled 302 while by 1952 the number had grown to 2,812 with an additional 3,142 operatives under contract. During that same period, the OPC expanded the number of its overseas stations from seven to forty-seven while its budget exploded from 4.7 million dollars in 1949 to 82 million dollars by 1952.[12]

While Karalekas attributes this expansion to the Korean War, in fact the Policy Planning Staff demanded that the OPC prepare an expanded program immediately after the State-Defense Team completed its work on NSC 68, months before the war erupted. On 19 April, Robert Joyce informed the OPC that it needed to prepare a new covert program to meet the expanded requirements of NSC 68, which called for an "intensification of affirmative and timely measures and *operations by covert* means in the fields of economic warfare and political and psychological warfare with a view to fomenting and supporting unrest and revolt in selected strategic satellite countries."[13] This action would be done in such a way that the United States could "reduce the power and influence of the Kremlin *inside* the Soviet Union and other areas under its control. The objective would be the establishment of friendly regimes not under Kremlin domination."[14] Joyce informed Wisner that the National Security Council expected the OPC to prepare a budget anticipating a "major effort in the field of covert operations" over the course of the next six years. One observer later remarked that this effort "would be a task similar in concept, magnitude, and complexity to the creation of widely deployed military forces together with the logistical support required to conduct manifold, complex, and delicate operations in a wide variety of overseas locations."[15]

After much bickering regarding resource allocation, the NSC repeated its endorsement of this escalation with the approval of NSC 10/5 on 23 October 1951 and gave the responsibility of coordinating this expansion to the newly created Psychological Strategy Board. What emerged was a program referred to as the "Packet," a collection of operations designed to defeat Soviet power worldwide. Unfortunately, the vast majority of these plans remain classified, but from what the government has released we know that the Truman administration aimed first to disrupt the power structures of the communist states and only after that was achieved to incite the public into revolution. Administration planners considered the disruption of these power structures an essential first step in the liberation of the satellite states and the destabilization of the USSR. It was clear that citizens of communists states have, as Charles Bohlen emphasized, "no power of action unless and until [the] state apparatus of control is near collapse."[16] Truman administration officials did not wish to incite to revolution the populations of Eastern Europe and the Soviet Union before schisms emerged within their governments. In striking contrast to their successors in the Eisenhower administration, the Truman administration—and Bohlen in particular—contended that such a policy would be both "useless" and morally indefensible since it would lead to the kind of brutal suppression for which Stalin was notorious. Instead, U.S. political warfare would engage in "spoiling operations" designed to weaken the central organs of power by exploiting the chief weakness of these regimes: the "jealousy and paranoiac suspicion [with]in the ruling groups." The goal was to instigate conflicts between the party and the secret police, the army and the secret police, and the army and the party, using "disinformation and deception" and by "compromis[ing] important officials." Only a covert strategy could succeed since any public declaration would formally commit the U.S. government to the liberation of the satellite states, offer false hopes to the peoples of the Soviet bloc, and provide the Soviets with the "justification for more extreme measures of control."[17]

We have seen how the Truman administration planners identified four possible methods to undermine Soviet power.[18] First, the United States would seek to incapacitate the administrative structure of the Communist Party and state offices. The Stalinist structure of authority itself was the target under this scheme. A second strategy was to increase the incidence of defection to the West. The goal was to incite a significant number of defections from both the military and the security apparatus and shake the party's faith in their allegiance, resulting, analysts hoped, in a new round of purges and a reduction in the party's ability to suppress dissent. A third method was to use disinformation against high-level Soviet leaders, particularly Politburo members, in order to intensify their mutual distrust and induce a power struggle at the apex of the Communist Party. Officials considered this strategy a potentially effective means of disrupting Soviet control in the days immediately following Stalin's death, when the feelings of mutual insecurity within the Politburo would be at their maximum.[19] Lastly, experts planned strategies to accentuate the unreliability of both the Eastern European satellites and Chinese military and political organizations. Analysts devised schemes to reduce the Soviets' confidence in the East German communist party and the reliability of the Soviet armed forces stationed close to the border with the West. Meanwhile, operations continued to detach Albania from the Soviet bloc and to spread disinformation to the Soviet leadership regarding the possible Titoist intentions of the Chinese communists in order to prompt another schism within international communism.

The vast majority of the documentation regarding these operations remains classified; however, the government has released some material—discussed in chapter two—that confirms that specific covert operations were launched in order to achieve the objectives discussed above. Operation Overload and Delay aimed to disrupt Kremlin decisionmaking, Operation Engross attempted to lure and settle high-level Soviet and satellite defectors, and Operation Cancellation intended to incite power struggles within the Kremlin in the aftermath of Stalin's death. From the sources available to us, it is apparent that both the Truman and Eisenhower administrations made significant effort to support these operations, demonstrating the seriousness with which they were viewed.

While administration officials were painfully aware of the difficulties inherent in their psychological-warfare operations, they maintained confidence in their utility and attributed setbacks to poor technique rather than the unreliability of these instruments. The government continuously initiated reviews of the psychological-warfare programs, many of which were harshly critical of America's effort. The Project TROY group convened originally to improve radio transmission into Eastern Europe and the Soviet Union produced one of the most important evaluations. They concluded that the most significant problem facing U.S. political warfare was the lack of centralized planning and the incessant and harmful competition between the State Department, Defense Department, and CIA. Their findings were echoed in NSC 59, which called for the creation of one organization to better coordinate U.S. activities, resulting in the Psychological Strategy Board.

The creation of the PSB not only failed to offer the necessary coordination, it exacerbated the problem. The debate over the extent of the PSB's mandate set back psychological-warfare development nearly a year. Even though broad agreement existed over the objectives of American policy and the methods required to achieve them, the State Department's determination to control all aspects of U.S. foreign policy placed it in direct opposition to the new organization, which it viewed with the greatest disdain. Consequently, more attention was paid to preventing PSB from usurping State Department prerogatives than to carrying out the intensified political-warfare campaign called for in NSC 68. By the time the Truman administration adopted the new political-warfare program, Charles Bohlen had already begun to challenge the premises of NSC 68.

A major reason for this problem was the complete lack of leadership from President Harry S. Truman. Although many cold war histories and biographies portray Truman as a strong and determined president,[20] the evidence clearly shows that he played little—if any—role in determining national security policy, particularly American efforts to disrupt the Soviet bloc. While it is clear that Truman was aware of his administration's policies—he personally approved such key NSC documents as NSC 10/2, NSC 20/4, NSC 68, and NSC 10/5—little documentation exists to show what role Truman actually played in their development. It seems quite possible that Truman merely signed these documents in accordance with the wishes of his NSC advisors and offered little input. This accentuated the importance of the power struggle between the State Department, Defense Department, and PSB, further weakening the effort.

This is in stark contrast to the leadership provided by Dwight Eisenhower and John Foster Dulles, both of whom dominated American national security planning during their tenures. Eisenhower in particular played a crucial role in developing American national security strategy and was a commanding presence in every NSC meeting. He sought to prevent the type of bureaucratic infighting that undermined effective policy implementation, and while he was only partially successful his strong support for psychological warfare created a much more receptive atmosphere within his administration. The presence of John Foster Dulles as secretary of state also improved the climate for psychological warfare, but not to the extent that many hoped. While Dulles strongly supported psychological warfare in general, on several occasions he failed to support the aggressive strategies proposed by C. D. Jackson.

Even with the improved leadership and greater general support, psychological-warfare activities fared little better in the Eisenhower administration than they did in the Truman administration, in large part because the administration failed to develop a coherent strategy before the Soviet hydrogen bomb detonation forced the adoption of a policy of coexistence. Nearly all NSC policy reviews concluded that despite U.S. efforts the Soviets had been able to strengthen their control over Eastern Europe. While the Voice of America, Radio Free Europe, and beginning in 1953 Radio Liberty successfully kept the "spirit of resistance alive" in Eastern Europe, available evidence suggests that covert operations designed to undermine the strength of the satellite regimes and sow dissension within the Soviet political leadership failed to achieve their objectives.[21] Consequently, the conditions that might have allowed for a successful uprising did not develop. The Eisenhower administration recognized this and in 1955 decided to shift its policy to an "evolutionary" strategy, encouraging the peoples of the satellite states that their situation could be improved by working within the system rather than trying to destroy it. The success of the Polish October of 1956 seemed to confirm the validity of this strategy, yet the disastrous Hungarian uprising exposed the policy's clearest weakness: the difficulty in switching to an evolutionary strategy after three years of public support for liberation.

The Influence of Nuclear Weapons

The primary motivation behind the Eisenhower administration's transition from a revolutionary strategy to an evolutionary strategy came, however, from the Soviet nuclear developments. Nuclear weapons were the single greatest influence on the evolution of U.S. national security policy, fundamentally reshaping American strategic thought and playing a direct role in the policy shifts discussed in this book. The first dramatic change occurred with the test of the first Soviet atomic weapon on 12 August 1949. George Kennan had premised his strategy upon the long-term stability of the U.S.-Soviet balance of power, arguing persuasively that as long as the Soviets were not capable of destroying America's war mobilization potential in a decisive strike at the outset of World War III it was highly unlikely that they would launch a military assault against Western Europe. To do so would only involve the USSR in a long and destructive war against the most powerful economy in the world. American mobilization strength backed by its atomic monopoly was sufficient to deter the Soviets while American psychological-warfare efforts weakened the Kremlin's hold on Eastern Europe, encouraged Titoism, and pressured the Soviet leadership to abandon its aggressive ideological goals. Planners hoped that with the death of Stalin, a new leadership would arise and build a foreign policy stripped of the ideological baggage of the Stalin era.

The development of the Soviet atomic bomb dramatically challenged this policy. Military intelligence concluded in JIC 502, released on 20 January 1950, that with an arsenal of two hundred atomic bombs the Soviet Union could destroy the U.S. industrial base and preempt its atomic retaliatory force. Until the preparation of that estimate, administration planners had not looked at Soviet nuclear capabilities with much trepidation. In showing that the American industrial base was vulnerable to attack and destruction, the JIC estimate demonstrated that the United States was susceptible to surprise attack and defeat at the outset of war. American military plans, premised on the enormous strength of the industrial base, could no longer depend on the several years required by the mobilization efforts to build the forces necessary to fight a world war. These new circumstances forced the administration to reconsider the validity of its objectives in the cold war—the task undertaken by NSC 68.

As discussed in chapter two, the State-Defense Team reconfirmed the objectives of American policy as established in NSC 20/4. The crucial difference between Kennan's document and the work of the State-Defense Team lay in the likelihood of global war. NSC 68 argued that the immediacy of that threat was far greater than anticipated in NSC 20/4 and that the United States might have to adopt the strategic policy of Secretary of Defense James V. Forrestal—that is, preparation for war by a particular date. According to the State-Defense Team that date was 1954, when the Joint Intelligence Committee estimated that the Soviet Union would possess a potential surprise attack capability. Unless the United States restored a stable military balance, it would not be able to reduce Soviet power and fundamentally reshape Soviet behavior.

NSC 68 recommended a twofold response: an intensification of the political offensive against the Soviet bloc, discussed above, and a quadrupling of the U.S. military budget. The State-Defense Team called for the initiation of a massive military buildup in order to achieve preponderant power, i.e., military superiority over the Soviet Union. This buildup represented a significant shift in American national security policy away from reliance on mobilization potential to actual forces-in-being. For decades scholars have lamented the so-called "militarization of containment," arguing that the fallacious analysis of NSC 68 transformed the cold war into a military contest, unnecessarily intensifying the superpower rivalry and greatly enhancing the risks of global war.[22] Instead, the militarization of containment was a consequence of the new strategic reality created by the Soviet Union's development of atomic weapons. With the nuclear threat to America's mobilization base, deterrence of Soviet aggression now required real—not potential—military capabilities.

Yet the creation of military superiority was far more problematic than it first appeared. Not only did the Korean War drain the U.S. military buildup, but the Soviet buildup continued unabated. According to the first review of NSC 68 concluded in late 1951, the U.S. military posture had not progressed sufficiently relative to the Soviets. Even more critical, analysts questioned whether nuclear superiority had any meaning in the nuclear age. Throughout the 1950s, the United States possessed unquestioned nuclear superiority in terms of delivery vehicles and warheads, yet it did not possess secure second-strike retaliatory forces and had the majority of its warfighting capabilities concentrated in relatively few targets—only fifty-four targets according to NSC 114.[23] The Soviets, by contrast, suffered from significantly inferior capabilities, yet American planners feared they might possess enough deliverable nuclear warheads to destroy a sufficient portion of America's warfighting capability in a war-winning first strike. Consequently, military superiority—defined in terms of the number of warheads in stockpiles—was irrelevant. Once the Soviet arsenal reached a certain level—what Allen

Dulles termed "enoughness"—the Soviet Union could threaten the United States with a war-winning strike despite the latter's possessing vast nuclear superiority.[24]

While not the basis of Charles Bohlen's challenge to NSC 68, this new strategic relationship served to undermine opposition from the Policy Planning Staff to Bohlen's new national security policy, the "doctrine of rational hope." By late 1952, Bohlen convinced the Truman administration that the objectives of NSC 20/4 could be achieved only through the overthrow of the Soviet regime, a capability the United States did not possess and probably would not possess for an indeterminate length of time. While Bohlen's strategy encouraged the administration to continue to build the capabilities to assist revolution in the future, the best the United States could hope to do in the meantime was to secure the periphery around the Soviet Union, continue building the liberal international economic order, and pursue limited agreements on very specific issues with the Soviet Union—in other words, coexistence. Yet Bohlen did not believe that coexistence with the Soviet Union would necessarily lead to accommodation: that would have to await a fundamental restructuring of the Soviet system.

The final shift to a policy of accommodation took place in the aftermath of the detonation of the first Soviet thermonuclear device on 12 August 1953. While atomic weapons threatened defeat in war, thermonuclear weapons threatened to completely destroy civilization, making the kind of aggressive actions the Eisenhower administration first contemplated potentially disastrous. The new administration recognized these new circumstances almost immediately, as is evident when one compares the strategies and policies first proposed during the spring and summer of 1953 with the final product of policy NSC 162/2 adopted in November of 1953. It is also apparent in the thinking of John Foster Dulles, who in March and April articulated a policy position in support of the aggressive strategies proposed by Solarium Task Force C, yet by the fall had switched his support to a policy more benign than that proposed by Solarium Task Force A.

Largely because of the new Soviet thermonuclear capability, Dulles and the rest of the administration realized that the only way to ease the dangers of the cold war was through negotiations that took into account Soviet security interests. In other words, they hoped to find accommodation with the Soviet Union. It was the search for a mutually acceptable solution to the cold war that distinguished this stage from the policy proposed by Bohlen a year earlier, as Bohlen did not believe that the cold war could be resolved with the communist government of the USSR. The Eisenhower administration, it would seem, had come to hope that the devastating consequences of thermonuclear war would override the ideological fervor of the Soviet leadership and create the conditions necessary for a settlement.

Such an arrangement seemed to be in the offing with the dramatic changes that took place in the aftermath of Stalin's death. The Austrian State Treaty gave some hope for a settlement of the German issue, while the de-Stalinization campaign and the Polish October gave a measure of real optimism that a fundamental change in Soviet-satellite relations was about to take place. Such a change would have been consonant with the evolutionary approach of the Eisenhower administration's Eastern Europe policy and would have allowed the administration to claim that it had fulfilled its campaign pledges toward Eastern Europe. However, the crushing of the Hungarian uprising and the condemnations that rained down upon the administration for publicly advocating liberation—but being unwilling to support it—effectively discredited Eisenhower's policy throughout Eastern Europe, ending America's role in the region. Nevertheless, the administration continued on its course to promote a general accommodation between the United States and the Soviet Union.

By this time the existence of the Soviet Union and an autarkic economic bloc were no longer the central threats to American national security—now it was the growing Soviet nuclear capability that could destroy the liberal international economic order. Therefore the liberation of Eastern Europe and even the overthrow of the Soviet government itself would no longer automatically eliminate the threat to the West, not unless a post-Soviet government was willing to accept what we would today call a significant arms-reduction regime. Yet American planners realized that nuclear weapons, while threatening the world with annihilation, also offered the basis for a stable international system even in a world dominated by two rival political-economic blocs, consequently making irrelevant America's driving postwar fear that the existence of two rival blocs would lead inevitably to global war. Thus with the end of America's efforts to topple Soviet power came the birth of the modern cold war era, an epoch that would last until the emergence of the cancers predicted by Charles Bohlen compelled the USSR's last president Mikhail Gorbachev to begin the process that led to the long-awaited dissolution of the Soviet communist system and an end to the cold war.

Notes

Introduction

1. The most recent example is Robert Bowie and Richard Immerman, *Waging Peace: How Eisenhower Shaped an Enduring Cold War Strategy* (New York: Oxford University Press, 1998).

2. See Robert Pollard, *Economic Security and the Origins of the Cold War, 1945–1950* (New York: Columbia University Press, 1985). See also Melvyn Leffler, *A Preponderance of Power: National Security Policy, the Truman Administration, and the Cold War* (Stanford: Stanford University Press, 1992), 1–24.

3. This phrase comes from the title of George Kennan's first National War College Lecture. See *Measures Short of War: The George F. Kennan Lectures at the National War College 1946–1947*, ed. Giles D. Harlow and George C. Maerz (Washington, D.C.: National Defense University Press, 1991), 3–21.

4. As will be discussed later in this introduction, psychological warfare is a difficult concept to define and, consequently, definitions varied greatly. However, it is important to remember that psychological warfare was considered synonymous with political warfare.

5. Since the transformation of the Soviet regime was the ultimate American objective, application of the term "rollback" is not completely accurate as it connotes only the removal of Soviet power from Eastern Europe.

6. The seminal work on this topic remains Marc Trachtenberg's "'A Wasting Asset': American Strategy and the Shifting Nuclear Balance, 1949–1954," *International Security* 13, no. 3 (Winter 1988/89): 5–49.

7. See Marc Trachtenberg's *A Constructed Peace: The Making of the European Settlement, 1945–1963* (Princeton: Princeton University Press, 1999). Walter Hixson's *Parting the Curtain: Propaganda, Culture, and the Cold War, 1945–1961* (New York: St. Martin's Press, 1997) offers the best analysis of U.S. efforts to use Western culture to reform Soviet society during the cold war.

8. See *We Now Know: Rethinking Cold War History* (New York: Oxford University Press, 1997).

9. See Leffler, *Preponderance of Power*, 20–24.

10. David Foglesong, "The Roots of Liberation: American Images of the Future of Russia in the Early Cold War," *The International History Review* 21, 1 (March 1999): 57–79.

11. Leffler, *Preponderance of Power*, 8, 20–24.

12. Pollard, *Economic Security and the Origins of the Cold War*, 13.

13. As quoted in ibid., 14.

14. See Kennan's "long telegram" in Thomas Etzold and John Lewis Gaddis, eds., *Containment: Documents on American Policy and Strategy, 1945–1950* (New York: Columbia University Press, 1978), 57. See also Gaddis, *We Now Know*, 189–198.

15. See Leffler, *Preponderance of Power*, 1–24.

16. Kennan, the "long telegram," 22 February 1946, in Etzold and Gaddis, eds., *Containment*, 63. In "The Roots of Liberation" historian David Foglesong shows that Kennan's interest in reshaping Russia long preceded the "long telegram" and "The Sources of Soviet Conduct."

17. 163rd Meeting of the NSC, 24 September 1953, in *FRUS*: vol. I, 1952–1954, 469.

18. For "The Sources of Soviet Conduct" see Etzold and Gaddis, *Containment*, 84–90.

19. The phrase "normal dimensions" comes from Kennan's study "U.S. Objectives towards Russia," 20 August 1948, File Folder NSC Meeting 8-19-48, President's Secretary File (PSF) NSC Meetings, 14-27, Box 204, Harry S. Truman Library [hereafter HSTL].

20. On the famine and purges see Robert Conquest's *The Harvest of Sorrow: Soviet Collectivization and the Terror-Famine* (New York: Oxford University Press, 1986) and *The Great Terror: A Reassessment* (New York: Oxford University Press, 1990).

21. "Long telegram," in Etzold and Gaddis, *Containment*, 62.

22. The following chapters will demonstrate that Kennan was not alone in stressing the importance of these generational changes in defining American strategies to exploit Soviet vulnerabilities.

23. Charles Bohlen, "The Possibilities of External Action Against Soviet-Type States," n.d., in file "General Collection 1952–1955," Box 9, RG 59, Records of the Department of State, Records of Charles E. Bohlen, National Archives II.

24. Etzold and Gaddis, *Containment*, 62.

25. As quoted in Walter L. Hixson, *George Kennan: Cold War Iconoclast* (New York: Columbia University Press, 1989), 26. See also Kennan's National War College lecture "The Structure of Internal Power in the USSR," 10 October 1946, in *Measures Short of War*, 21–47.

26. Walter Lippmann offered Kennan his most significant intellectual challenge over "The Sources of Soviet Conduct." See Ronald Steel, *Walter Lippmann and the American Century* (Boston: Little, Brown & Co., 1980), 443–445.

27. As quoted in Christopher Simpson, *Science of Coercion: Communication Research and Psychological Warfare, 1945–1960* (New York: Oxford University Press, 1994), 13.

28. See "The Vulnerability of the Soviet Union and Its European Satellites to Political Warfare," in File Russia (2), Box 62, White House Central Files, Confidential File, Dwight D. Eisenhower Library [hereafter DDEL].

29. NSC 10/2 "Office of Special Projects," in Etzold and Gaddis, *Containment*, 125–128.

30. See Nicholas Bethel, *The Great Betrayal: The Untold Story of Kim Philby's Biggest Coup* (London: Hodder and Stoughton, 1984).

31. This phrase comes from Charles Bohlen's study "The Possibilities of External Action Against Soviet-Type States," n.d., in file "General Collection 1952–1955," Box 9, RG 59, Records of the Department of State, Records of Charles E. Bohlen, National Archives II. These activities will be discussed in chapter two.

32. As will be discussed in chapter two, Director of Central Intelligence Walter Bedell Smith would emerge as the Truman administration's most severe critic of psychological warfare.

33. See Stephen Ambrose, *Ike's Spies: Eisenhower and the Espionage Establishment* (New York: Doubleday, 1981).

34. Memo Omar Bradley to George Marshall 1/15/51, in NSC 68 File, Jan–June 1951, Box 55, RG 59, Records of the Department of State, Records of the Policy Planning Staff, 1947–1953, National Archives II.

35. "U.S. Objectives towards Russia," 20 August 1948, File Folder NSC Meeting 8-19-48, President's Secretary File (PSF) NSC Meetings, 14-27, Box 204, HSTL.

36. Memorandum Nitze to Matthews in *FRUS*: vol. II, "National Security 1952–1954," 59.

37. Leffler, *Preponderance of Power*, 2.

38. Ibid., 221–226.

39. Memo to Secretary of State Dean Acheson, August 8, 1950, in *FRUS*: vol. I, 1950, "National Security," 361–367, quote p. 365.

40. The continental United States was not completely free from threat. The CIA warned that U.S. industry was susceptible to sabotage as well as limited bombing from one-way missions. See CIA 1 "Review of the World Situation as it Relates to the Security of the United States," File Folder NSC Meeting #7, 9-26-47, Box 203, PSF-NSC Meetings, HSTL.

41. *Forestall Diaries*, Walter Millis and E.S. Duffield, eds. (New York: The Viking Press, 1951), 350–351.

42. See *FRUS*: "Emergence of the Intelligence Establishment, 1945–1950," United States Government Printing Office, 1996, 615.

43. Executive Order 12958 can be located on the CIA's web page at http://www.foia.ucia.gov/eofulltext.txt. Implementation efforts are discussed in two articles by George Lardner Jr.: "Defense Bill Provision Could Curb Declassification," *Washington Post*, 31 July 1998, p. A23; and "Automatic Declassification Halted; Defense Bill Calls On Clinton to Protect Nuclear Secrets in Old Files," *Washington Post*, 16 October 1998, p. A25.

44. Tenet's statement can be located on the CIA web page at http://www.cia.gov/cia/public_affairs/press_release/archives/1998/ps071598.html. On CIA stonewalling regarding the release of documents concerning other operations see "Trying to Revisit the 1953 Coup in Iran: The CIA's Response to a Freedom of Information Act Request," by Mark J. Gasiorowski in *SHAFR Newsletter* 29, no. 3 (September 1998): 11–14.

45. Lardner, "Defense Bill Provision Could Curb Declassification."

46. See Eduard Mark's article "The War Scare of 1946 and Its Consequences," *Diplomatic History* 21, no. 3 (Summer 1997): 383–414, particularly footnote 6. Mark, who commented on a draft of this book, believes that significant numbers of extremely important documents will remain classified for years to come.

Chapter One

1. See Thomas W. Wolfe, *Soviet Power and Europe: 1945–1970* (Baltimore: Johns Hopkins University Press, 1970), 32–49. Wolfe cites 1949 as the commencement of the Soviet military buildup; however, Department of Air Force historian Eduard Mark has informed me that according to his research the buildup described by Wolfe began in 1948 (correspondence with author, 17 November 1997).

2. According to Walter Hixson, Kennan believed that the Soviet Union might collapse within ten years. See *George Kennan: Cold War Iconoclast* (New York: Columbia University Press, 1989), 26.

3. This policy was defined by George Kennan in Policy Planning Staff document 33, "Factors Affecting U.S. Defense Arrangements in the Light of Soviet Policies," in Anna Kasten Nelson, ed., *The State Department Policy Planning Staff Papers*, vol. II, 1948 (New York: Garland Press, 1983), 281–292.

4. See Melvyn Leffler, *A Preponderance of Power: National Security, the Truman Administration, and the Cold War* (Stanford: Stanford University Press, 1992), 190, for the classic view of the Cominform's creation. A new document discovered in the Hungarian Communist Party archives indicates that planning for the Cominform began in 1946 and was accelerated by the growing East-West tensions. See "Soviet Plans to Establish the COMINFORM in 1946: New Evidence from the Hungarian Archives," *Cold War International History Project Bulletin*, Issue 10, March 1998.

5. See Dr. Edward P. Lilly, "The Development of American Psychological Operations, 1945–1951," in Box 14, NSC Registry Series White House Office-NSC Staff Papers, 1948–1961,

Dwight D. Eisenhower Library (DDEL). Lilly was a historian of psychological warfare for both the Joint Chiefs of Staff during World War II and the Psychological Strategy Board. This important document is also located on microfiche in the *Declassified Documents Catalogue*, vol. XVII, No. 4, July–Aug. 1991, document 2302, and fiche 213.

6. Ibid.

7. See Christopher Simpson, *Science of Coercion: Communications Research and Psychological Warfare, 1945–1960* (New York: Oxford University Press, 1994), 38. The first NSC document—NSC 1/1—pertained to U.S. policy toward Italy.

8. Ibid.

9. Ibid.

10. See "Activation of Special Procedures Group," 29 March 1948, in *FRUS*: "Establishment of the Intelligence Community," 655–661.

11. Simpson, *Science of Coercion*, 38–41. See also Leffler, *Preponderance of Power*, 203–206.

12. Wilson Miscamble, *George F. Kennan and the Making of American Foreign Policy, 1947–1950* (Princeton: Princeton University Press, 1992), 103. See also Leffler, *Preponderance of Power*, 205.

13. Leffler, *Preponderance of Power*, 213–214.

14. Newly declassified documents from East bloc archives have demonstrated the accuracy of these reports. According to John Lewis Gaddis some two million rapes occurred within the Soviet zone of Germany alone. See Gaddis, *We Now Know: Rethinking Cold War History* (New York: Oxford University Press, 1997), 287.

15. See Ludwell Lee Montague, *General Walter Bedell Smith As Director of Central Intelligence, Oct. 1950–February 1953, Vol. I—The Essential Beginnings, 1945–1950*, in Box 1, RG 263, Records of the Central Intelligence Agency, Office of the Director of Central Intelligence Historical Staff, DCI Historical Series, National Archives II; Thomas Powers, *The Man Who Kept the Secrets* (New York: Knopf, 1997), 35–37; and Miscamble, *George F. Kennan and the Making of American Foreign Policy*, 102–106.

16. Minutes of S/P meeting, 3 May 1948, in file "Meetings 1948," in Box 32, RG 59, Records of the Department of State, Records of the Policy Planning Staff, 1947–1953, S/P Meetings, National Archives II. The document is located in *FRUS*: "The Emergence of the Intelligence Establishment, 1945–1950," 668–672.

17. Kennan memo, "Inauguration of organized political warfare," ibid.

18. Ibid.

19. See Lilly, "Development of American Psychological Operations."

20. Ibid.

21. Ibid.

22. Kennan to Lovett, 8 June 1948, in file "Political and Psychological Warfare," Box 11A, RG 59, Records of the Department of State, Records of the Policy Planning Staff, 1947–1953, Subject Files, National Archives II.

23. Lilly, "Development of American Psychological Operations."

24. Ibid.

25. NSC 10/2 "NSC Directive on Office of Special Projects" in Thomas Etzold and John Lewis Gaddis, eds., *Containment: Documents on American Policy and Strategy, 1945–1950* (New York: Columbia University Press, 1977), 125–128.

26. NSC 5412/2 "National Security Council Directive on Covert Operations," File Folder 1955 (1), WHO-OSANSA, Records 1952–1961, Special Assistants Series-Presidential Subseries, Box 2, DDEL.

27. See Memorandum of Conversation and Understanding, 6 August 1948, in *FRUS*: "Emergence of the Intelligence Establishment," 719–722.

28. Ibid., 720.

29. Ibid.

30. See Lilly, "Development of American Psychological Operations."

31. See Dulles's memorandum to Sidney Souers of the NSC, 13 May 1948, in file "Political and Psychological Warfare," Box 11A, RG 59, Records of the Department of State, Records of the Policy Planning Staff, 1947–1953, Subject Files, National Archives II.

32. This information comes from a newly released CIA analysis entitled "Office of Policy Coordination: 1948–1952." Declassified on 22 July 1997, this report provides no author nor a date for its completion; however, a reference to Radio Liberty activities in 1971 and a comment regarding hindsight of twenty years leads me to conclude that it was written in or around 1971. According to Michael Warner, deputy chief of staff of the CIA's history staff, CIA historian Gerald Miller wrote this article. See "The CIA's Office of Policy Coordination: From NSC 10/2 to NSC 68," in *Intelligence and Counterintelligence* 11, no. 2 (Summer 1998): 211–219. The document can be accessed on the CIA's web page at http://www.foia.ucia.gov (search FOIA requests: covert operations).

33. Ibid.

34. Ibid.

35. "NSC 10/2," in Etzold and Gaddis, *Containment*, 125–128.

36. The best study of U.S. radio warfare is Walter Hixson's *Parting the Curtain: Propaganda, Culture and the Cold War, 1945–1961* (New York: St. Martin's Press, 1997).

37. See Lilly, "Development of American Psychological Operations." See also the Jackson Committee report, which discusses the prejudices within the U.S. government regarding propaganda. The Jackson Committee was established by the Eisenhower administration in January 1953 to review the performance of the American psychological-warfare program during the Truman administration. See *FRUS*: vol. II, "National Security, 1952–1954," 1824–1859.

38. See Miscamble, *George F. Kennan and the Making of American Foreign Policy*, 203.

39. See Sig Mickelson, *America's Other Voice: The Story of Radio Free Europe and Radio Liberty* (New York: Praeger Publishers, 1983), 19.

40. In addition to the secondary sources cited see "Memorandum on Organization and Operations," published by the National Committee for a Free Europe, Inc., 7/25/49, located in file "Office of Policy Coordination" Box 194, PSF: Subject File, NSC Memos and Reports (1) Harry S. Truman Library (HSTL). This document discusses the organization, membership, some elements of financing, and the kind of operations engaged in by the committee during this period.

41. See Mickelson, *America's Other Voice*; see Cord Meyer, *Facing Reality: From World Federalism to the CIA* (New York: Praeger Publishers, 1980). Meyer was a CIA official who worked in both Radio Free Europe and Radio Liberty from 1954 through the 1970s, while Mickelson was RFE/RL president from 1975 to 1976.

42. Despite Secretary Marshall's unease, the S/P strongly supported the use of defectors. See PPS 54 "Policy Relating to Defection and Defectors from Soviet Power," in Nelson, *State Department Policy Planning Staff Papers*, vol. III, 1949, 75–82.

43. According to Mickelson, it was not uncommon for Eastern European representatives to be seated next to exiles of the same country while waiting for an audience with the same State Department official. See Mickelson, *America's Other Voice*.

44. Ibid., 17; Powers, *The Man Who Kept the Secrets*, 34.

45. See Miscamble, *George F. Kennan and the Making of American Foreign Policy*, 204; See Meyer, *Facing Reality*, 110–112. On the role of academic institutions in American psychological warfare see Simpson's *Science of Coercion*.

46. Mickelson, *America's Other Voice*, 25–27.

47. Ibid., 30. By the end of the 1950s, the RFE/RL would deploy 250-kilowatt transmitters.

48. George Kennan, *Memoirs, 1925–1950* (New York: Pantheon Books, 1967), 327.

49. The administration established the NSC staff to facilitate the preparation of documents for NSC perusal. It consisted largely of military officers with the rank of lieutenant colonel and colonel. Most State Department officials, particularly Kennan, deeply resented their independent intrusions into policy. In July 1950 the NSC Staff was replaced with a far more substantial NSC Senior Staff comprised of high-level representatives from all related departments.

50. See NSC 7 "Report by the National Security Council on the Position of the United States with Respect to Soviet-Directed World Communism," in *FRUS*: vol. I, 1948, "National Security," 546.

51. Ibid.

52. Ibid., 547.
53. Ibid., 549.
54. Assistant Secretary of State Willard Thorpe contended that the document paid no attention to the root causes of communism, in particular the economic difficulties of the post–World War II world. See memo to Secretary of State, 7 April 1948, in *FRUS*: vol. I, 1948, 557–560. Under Secretary of State Robert Lovett considered the paper "inadequate" and believed that it "will give a false impression if not revised," although as an "initial study it may have value." For Lovett's opinion see source footnote in *FRUS*: vol. I, 1948, 561. Charles Bohlen, Loy Henderson, Dean Rusk, John Hickerson, and W. Walton Butterworth, in addition to Kennan, also opposed NSC 7. See ibid.
55. Memo, Under Secretary of State Robert Lovett to Secretary of Defense Forrestal, n.d., in NSC 20 file, Box 54, Records Group 59, General Records of the Department of State, Records of the Policy Planning Staff, 1947–1953, National Archives II, College Park, Maryland.
56. Memo, Kennan to Marshall, 27 May 1948, in ibid.
57. Bohlen was counselor to Secretary of State Marshall while Stevens was chief of the State Department's Russia Division. Neither Bohlen's nor Stevens's remarks could be located.
58. See *State Department Policy Planning Staff Papers*, vol. II, 1948, ed. Anna Kasten Nelson, 282.
59. A host of intelligence estimates supported Kennan's reasoning. See in particular CIA "Reviews of the World Situation" dated 27 September 1947, 12 January, 10 March, and 8 April 1948, as well as ORE report 22–48 "The Possibility of Direct Soviet Military Action During 1948," 2 April 1948. All are located in the PSF-Intelligence Files at the Truman Presidential Library.
60. PPS 33 "Factors Affecting the Nature of the U.S. Defense Arrangements in the Light of Soviet Policies." This view reflected the enormous importance of geopolitical and geostrategic factors in the formulation of American national security policy. See in particular Leffler's *Preponderance of Power*. See also Gaddis, *Strategies of Containment* (New York: Oxford University Press, 1982).
61. In a memo to Acheson, Kennan wrote that "In particular, they [the Soviets] are not attracted by the prospect . . . of occupying all of Western Europe before they are able to crush U.S. industrial and military power; for they would thereby only place themselves in a position analogous to that of the Germans in 1942, and incur heavy responsibilities to which there would be no calculable satisfactory termination at any early date." August 8, 1950, in *FRUS*: vol. I, 1950, "National Security," 361–367, quote p. 365.
62. See David Mayers, *George Kennan and the Dilemmas of U.S. Foreign Policy* (New York: Oxford University Press, 1988), 114–116; Miscamble, *George F. Kennan and the Making of American Foreign Policy*, 65–68; Hixson, *George F. Kennan: Cold War Iconoclast*, 73–78; and John Lewis Gaddis, "The Strategy of Containment," in Gaddis and Etzold, *Containment*, 35.
63. See Gaddis, *Strategies of Containment*, 98–106.
64. See memo, Nitze to Executive Secretary McWilliams, 10/1/48, in NSC 20 file, Box 54, RG 59, General Records of the Department of State, Records of the Policy Planning Staff 1947–1953, National Archives II.
65. See memo from Hugh Farley to Sidney Souers, 13 July 1948, in file "NSC Chronological File: 1948-June–July," in Box 9, Records of the NSC, Chronological file: 1947–1948, HSTL.
66. Memo, Butler to Kennan, 13 July 1948, in NSC 20 File, Box 54, RG 59, General Records of the Department of State, Records of the Policy Planning Staff, 1947–1953, National Archives II.
67. See "NSC 20 (Objectives and Implementation)," NSC 20 File, Box 54, RG 59, General Records of the Department of State, Records of the Policy Planning Staff, 1947–1953, National Archives II.
68. Memo to Lovett and Marshall, 8-5-48, NSC 20 File, Box 54, RG 59, General Records of the Department of State, Records of the Policy Planning Staff 1947–1953, National Archives II.
69. NSC 20 (Objectives and Implementation).
70. See Gaddis, *Strategies of Containment*, 30.

71. See Leffler, *Preponderance of Power*, 21.

72. As Wilson Miscamble astutely observed, "the temptation to characterize Kennan as a Moses-type figure descending to give the law of containment over to a disoriented group of American policymakers should be resisted." See *George F. Kennan and the Making of American Foreign Policy*, 32.

73. "U.S. Objectives towards Russia," 20 August 1948, File Folder NSC Meeting 8-19-48, President's Secretary File (PSF) NSC Meetings, 14-27, Box 204, Harry S. Truman Library (HSTL).

74. Ibid., i–ii.

75. Ibid.

76. See Kennan's memorandum to Dean Rusk, 7 September 1949 in *FRUS*: vol. I, 1949, "National Security," 381.

77. Kennan felt that "within five or ten years" Russia would be "overwhelmed by clouds of civil disintegration." See Hixson, *George Kennan: Cold War Iconoclast*, 26.

78. PPS 38, 21.

79. Ibid., 16–20. Charles Bohlen had discussed the nature of a legitimate Soviet sphere of influence in Eastern Europe as early as 1945. See his memorandum of 18 October 1945, in file "Spheres of Influence," Box 8, RG 59, Records of the Department of State, Records of Charles E. Bohlen, 1942–1952, National Archives II. On this point see Eduard Mark, "Charles E. Bohlen and the Acceptable Limits of Soviet Hegemony in Eastern Europe: A Memorandum of 18 October 1945," *Diplomatic History* 3 (Spring 1979): 201–214; and "American Policy Towards Eastern Europe and the Origins of the Cold War, 1941–46: An Alternative Explanation," *Journal of American History* 68 (September 1981): 313–336. See also Ronald Kreb, "Liberation à la Finland: Reexamining Eisenhower Administration Objectives in Eastern Europe," *Journal of Strategic Studies* 20, no. 3 (September 1997): 1–26.

80. PS 38, 18.

81. Ibid., 17.

82. Memo, Kennan to Lovett, 8 June 1948, in file "Political and Psychological Warfare," Box 11A, RG 59, Records of the Department of State, Records of the Policy Planning Staff, 1947–1953, Subject Files, National Archives II.

83. For the role of academia in psychological warfare see Christopher Simpson, *Science of Coercion*. Walter Rostow was deeply involved in psychological warfare at the Center for International Studies at MIT, where he would take part in several major psychological-warfare studies including Project TROY and the Soviet Vulnerabilities Project. McGeorge Bundy, then at Harvard's Russian Research Center, collaborated with Rostow on the Soviet Vulnerabilities Project. Henry Kissinger consulted with the U.S. government regarding psychological efforts in Germany and would take part in the 1955 report entitled "Psychological Aspects of United States Policy" located in Box 10, White House Office of the Special Assistant for National Security Affairs, NSC Series, Subject Subseries, DDEL.

84. PPS 38, 18.

85. S/P meeting, 18 October 1949, in file "Meetings 1949," in Box 32, RG 59, Records of the Department of State, Records of the Policy Planning Staff, 1947–1953, S/P Meetings, NA II. Tufts served with Kennan on the Policy Planning Staff.

86. Ibid.

87. See Miscamble, *George F. Kennan and the Making of American Foreign Policy*, 197–198.

88. PPS 38, 24.

89. Ibid., 25.

90. Ibid., 26.

91. Ibid.

92. Ibid., 12–15.

93. Ibid., 13–14.

94. See "NSC 20 (Objectives and Implementation)" in NSC 20 File, Box 54, RG 59, General Records of the Department of State, Records of the Policy Planning Staff 1947–1953, National Archives II. The document provides an outline of development of the NSC 20 series. Max

Bishop was a career foreign service officer who in 1948–1949 served as coordinator for the National Security Council.

95. Ibid.

96. Ibid.

97. Memo, Kennan to Lovett, 10-20-48, in NSC 20 file, Box 54, ibid.

98. Despite an extensive search, no comments from Charles Bohlen were located in the archival records. According to the available information, Bohlen presented his views to the Policy Planning Staff on 15 July; unfortunately, S/P member Carlton Savage failed to elaborate (in his minutes of the meeting). This item is located in file "Minutes 1948," in Box 32, RG 59, Records of the Department of State, Records of the Policy Planning Staff, 1947–1953, National Archives II.

99. Memo, Nitze to Executive Secretary McWilliams, 10/1/48, in NSC 20 file, Box 54, RG 59, General Records of the Department of State, Records of the Policy Planning Staff 1947–1953, National Archives II.

100. "NSC 20 (Objectives and Implementation)," in ibid.

101. Memo, Hickerson to McWilliams, 10/4/48, in ibid.

102. Bohlen's critique is the subject of chapter three.

103. Memo, George Butler to Kennan, 10/11/48, in NSC 20 file, Box 54, RG 59, Records of the Department of State, Records of the Policy Planning Staff, 1947–1953, National Archives II.

104. Memo, Max Bishop to Kennan, 10/29/48, in ibid.

105. Ibid.

106. Humelsine to Kennan, 4/25/49, in ibid.

107. See Miscamble, *George F. Kennan and the Making of American Foreign Policy*, 199; Etzold and Gaddis, *Containment*, 203, 383–385; Robert Bowie and Richard Immerman, *Waging Peace: How Eisenhower Shaped an Enduring Cold War Strategy* (New York: Oxford University Press, 1998), 17–18.

108. The common view that NSC 68 represented a fundamental shift in American policy replacing NSC 20/4 as the definitive statement of U.S. policy is best articulated by John Lewis Gaddis in *Strategies of Containment*, 84–117. See also Bowie and Immerman, *Waging Peace.*

109. See "Review of Basic National Security Policies," 6 February 1953, in *FRUS*: vol. II, "National Security," 1952–1954, 223–231.

110. NSC 20/4 "U.S. Objectives with Respect to the USSR to Counter Soviet Threats to U.S. Security," File Folder: NSC Meetings #27, 11-23-48, PSF-NSC Meetings 14-27, Box 204, HSTL.

111. Ibid., 10–11.

112. Address, 22 October 1946, Kennan Papers, Box 16, as quoted in Anders Stephanson, *Kennan and the Art of Foreign Policy* (Cambridge: Harvard University Press, 1989), 89.

113. Memo, Cabot to Marshall, 7 June 1947, in *FRUS*: vol. IV, 1947, 806–807.

114. See Memo, Reams to Marshall, 18 June 1948, in *FRUS*: vol. IV, 1948, 1073.

115. On the history of the Soviet-Yugoslav split, see Adam B. Ulam, *Titoism and the Cominform* (Cambridge: Harvard University Press, 1952); and Vladimir Dedijer, *The Battle Stalin Lost: Memoirs of Yugoslavia, 1948–1953* (New York: Viking, 1971).

116. See Miscamble, *George F. Kennan and the Making of American Foreign Policy*, 190.

117. See PPS 35 "The Attitude of This Government towards Events in Yugoslavia," 30 June 1948, in Anna Kasten Nelson, ed., *State Department Policy Planning Staff Papers*, vol. II, 1948, 317–321.

118. Ibid., 318–319.

119. Robert Lee Wolf in *The Balkans in Our Time* (Cambridge: Harvard University Press, 1974) made this description, as quoted in Miscamble, *George F. Kennan and the Making of American Foreign Policy*, 192.

120. This position was strongly supported by the London Meeting of Chiefs of Mission held October 24–26 1949. See "Conclusions and Recommendations of London Conference" in the "Eastern Europe" File, Box 29 RG 59, General Records of the Department of State, Records of the Policy Planning Staff, 1947–1953, Archives II.

121. Miscamble, *George F. Kennan and the Making of American Foreign Policy*, 193.

122. PPS 49 "Economic Relations between the United States and Yugoslavia," 10 February 1949, in Nelson, *State Department Policy Planning Staff Papers*, vol. III, 1949, 14–24.

123. Ibid, 20.

124. See Miscamble, *George F. Kennan and the Making of American Foreign Policy*, 195.

125. Minutes of Meeting, 1 March 1949, "Meetings 1949," Box 32, RG 59, Records of the Department of State, Records of the Policy Planning Staff, 1947–1953, National Archives II.

126. S/P meeting, 10/18/49, in file "Meetings 1949," ibid.

127. S/P meeting, 10/18/49, in file "Meetings 1949," ibid.

128. S/P meeting, 11 January 1950, in file "Meetings 1950," ibid.

129. S/P meeting, 1/11/50, in file "Meetings 1950," ibid.

130. Under Secretary of State meeting, 8/25/49, in file "Meetings 1/49–12/49," RG 59, Records of the Department of State, Records of the Executive Secretariat, Minutes of the Under Secretaries Meetings, 1–287, National Archives II.

131. See Miscamble, *George F. Kennan and the Making of American Foreign Policy*, 205–206.

132. PPS 59 "United States Policy toward the Soviet Satellite States in Eastern Europe," 25 August 1949, in Nelson, *State Department Policy Planning Staff Papers*, vol. III, 1949, 124–138.

133. Ibid., 124.

134. Ibid.

135. We may presume that this was a belated rejoinder to those staff members who felt that U.S. policy should not be seen to condone communist regimes, however nationalist.

136. Under Secretary of State meeting, 8/25/49, file "Meetings 1/49–12/49."

137. S/P meeting 1/18/50, in file "Meetings 1950," in Box 32, RG 59, Records of the Department of State, Records of the Policy Planning Staff, 1947–1953, National Archives II.

138. Ibid.

139. See "Conclusions and Recommendations of the London Conference of October 24–26 of U.S. Chiefs of Mission to the Satellite States," Eastern European File, Box 29, RG 59, General Records of the Department of State, Records of the S/P 1947–1953. Assistant Secretary of State Perkins, Allen Dulles, Charles Bohlen, Robert Joyce, and the U.S. ambassador to the Soviet Union, Alan Kirk, attended the conference.

140. Ibid.

141. S/P meeting, 11 January 1950, in file "Meetings 1950," Box 32, RG 59, Records of the Department of State, Records of the Policy Planning Staff, 1947–1953, National Archives II.

142. Ibid.

143. Memo to NSC from Under Secretary of State James Webb, "Third Progress Report on the Implementation of NSC 58/2," File Folder: NSC Meetings File #93, 6/6/51, PSF-NSC Meetings Series, Box 212, HSTL.

144. See memo, Bohlen to Barbour, 15 May 1952, regarding NSC 58/2, in Eastern Europe File, Box 29 in RG 59, General Records of the Department of State/Records of the Policy Planning Staff 1947–1953, National Archives II.

145. The most comprehensive analysis of U.S.-British covert action in Albania is Nicholas Bethell, *The Great Betrayal: The Untold Story of Kim Philby's Biggest Coup* (London: Hodder and Stoughton, 1984). For his analysis of Western paramilitary training facilities, see 66–73.

146. Dmitri Volkogonov, *Stalin: Triumph & Tragedy* (New York: Grove Weidenfeld, 1988), 531.

147. John Loftus and Mark Aarons, *Unholy Trinity: The Vatican, the Nazis, and Soviet Intelligence* (New York: St. Martin's Press, 1991), 172–206. See Simpson's *Blowback: America's Recruitment of Nazis and Its Effect on the Cold War* (New York: Weidenfeld & Nicholson, 1988). See also Loftus, *The Belarus Secret* (New York: Knopf, 1982).

148. See Harry Rositzke, *The CIA's Secret Operations: Espionage, Counterespionage, and Covert Action* (New York: Reader's Digest Press, 1977), 18–38.

149. See in particular Bethell, *The Great Betrayal*. See also Rositzke, 171–173; Robin Winks, *Cloak and Gown: Scholars in the Secret War, 1939–1961* (New Haven: Yale University Press, 1987), 393–401; and Miscamble, *George F. Kennan and the Making of American Foreign Policy*, 207–209.

150. See Bethell, *The Great Betrayal*, 39.
151. For details of the operations, see Bethell, *The Great Betrayal*.
152. See Bethell, *The Great Betrayal*, 3. On Philby's devastating impact on James Angleton, see David Wise, *Molehunt: The Secret Search for Traitors That Shattered the CIA* (New York: Random House, 1992), 43.
153. We shall see in chapter four that the Eisenhower administration no longer considered Albania a significant target and concentrated its efforts on other satellite states.
154. See Bethell, *The Great Betrayal*, 83.
155. Memo to NSC on "Scope and Pace of Covert Operations," 8 May 1951, File Folder: Legislative Background on 10/5, 091.411, SMOF-PSB, Box 13, HSTL.
156. I thank Dr. Eduard Mark for informing me of this policy change. The State Department also supported this change. See the memorandum entitled "Col. Booth's Paper on Paramilitary Organization," John Sherman to C. Tracy Barnes, 7/22/52, in File Folder 091.411 Miscellaneous Materials Re: NSC 10/5, Box 13, SMOF-PSB. According to this memorandum, the State Department hoped to "divorce" paramilitary planning from other elements of psychological warfare "so that the preoccupation with paramilitary activities in the CIA, and for that matter in Defense, would not prejudice these other CIA operations." Charles Stelle of Nitze's Policy Planning Staff was a leading advocate of this separation.

Chapter Two

1. JIC 502 in file "471.6 USSR (11-8-49) S.1," Box 88, RG 218, Records of the Joint Chiefs of Staff, JCS Geographic File, 1948–1950, 190/1/26/7, National Archives II.
2. Scholars have sharply criticized these estimates and consider them the consequence of Cold War hyperbole. See in particular Samuel Wells, "Sounding the Tocsin: NSC 68 and the Soviet Threat," *International Security* 4 (Fall 1979): 116–148. In his authoritative study of the Soviet nuclear program, David Holloway stresses that even today we do not know the official stockpile figure for Soviet nuclear weapons from 1949 to 1954. He believes, however, that the actual Soviet figure was probably closer to the lower figures in the U.S. estimate range (roughly fifty atomic bombs). See his *Stalin and the Bomb: The Soviet Union and Atomic Energy, 1939–1956* (New Haven: Yale University Press, 1994), 322. While the issue of accuracy is important, it is not germane to this study. What is most crucial is what the American decision-making elites believed and how that influenced their policy decisions.
3. The leader of this viewpoint is John Lewis Gaddis. See *Strategies of Containment* (New York: Oxford University Press, 1982), 89–126.
4. See Robert Bowie and Richard Immerman, *Waging Peace: How Eisenhower Shaped an Enduring Cold War Strategy* (New York: Oxford University Press, 1998), 16–23.
5. See Melvyn P. Leffler, *A Preponderance of Power: National Security, the Truman Administration, and the Cold War* (Stanford: Stanford University Press, 1992), 355–360.
6. By 1956 the Eisenhower administration would conclude that "because of the increasing importance of forces-in-being in an age of nuclear weapons, economic and industrial potential for production after war begins is becoming a less dependable measure of the ability to achieve victory in general nuclear war than in past years." NSC 5602/1 in Marc Trachtenberg, ed., *The Development of American Strategic Thought: Basic Documents from the Eisenhower and Kennedy Periods including Basic National Security Papers from 1953–1959* (New York: Garland Press, 1988), 119–155.
7. See PPS 58 "Political Implications of Detonation of an Atomic Bomb by the USSR," 16 August 1949, in *State Department Policy Planning Staff Papers*, vol. III, 1949, Anna Kasten Nelson, ed., 122–123. This document was a speculative study prepared two weeks prior to the detection of the Soviet atomic blast; therefore it does not represent the official S/P position on this matter.
8. "The Soviet Atomic Explosion," 30 Sept. 1949, in file "Paul Nitze (Atomic Energy 1948–1950)," Box 50, RG 59, Records of the Department of State, Records of the Policy Planning Staff, 1947–1953, Members—Chronological File, National Archives II.

9. Ibid.
10. Ibid.
11. Memo, Kennan to Rusk, 3 Oct. 1949, in ibid.
12. Ibid.
13. S/P meeting, 11/3/49, in file "Meetings 1949," Box 32, RG 59, Records of the Department of State, Records of the Policy Planning Staff, 1947–1953, S/P Meetings 1947–1950, National Archives II.
14. Memo, Kennan to Acheson, in *FRUS*: vol. II, "National Security," 1950, 165.
15. S/P Meeting, 3 November 1949, file "Meetings 1949," Box 32, RG 59, Records of the Department of State, Records of the Policy Planning Staff, 1947–1953, S/P Meetings 1947–1950, National Archives II.
16. See minutes of the 148th meeting of the Policy Planning Staff, Oct. 11, 1949, in *FRUS*: vol. I, 1949, National Security, 399–403.
17. Minutes of the 171st meeting of the Policy Planning Staff, December 16, 1949, in *FRUS*: vol. I, 1949, "National Security," 413–416.
18. Ibid. See also Gaddis, *Strategies of Containment*, 81.
19. JIC 502, in file "471.6 USSR (11-8-49) S.1," Box 88, RG 218, Records of the Joint Chiefs of Staff, JCS Geographic File, 1948–1950, 190/1/26/7, National Archives II.
20. See Memo from the President to the Secretary of State, January 31, 1950, in *FRUS*: vol. I, 1950, "National Security," 141–142.
21. Walter Poole, *History of the Joint Chiefs of Staff: The Joint Chiefs of Staff and National Policy, volume IV, 1950–52* (Wilmington, Del.: Michael Glazier Inc., 1980), 6. Kennan had resigned as director of the S/P but remained counselor to Acheson until July 1951.
22. NSC 68 would lower this threshold to one hundred atomic weapons. See Thomas Etzold and John Lewis Gaddis, *Containment: Documents on American Policy and Strategy, 1945–1950* (New York: Columbia University Press, 1978), 400.
23. Memo, Kennan to Rusk, 3 October 1949, in file "Paul Nitze (Atomic Energy)," Box 50, RG 59, Records of the Department of State, Records of the Policy Planning Staff, 1947–1953, Members Chronological File, Chronological File 48–50, National Archives II.
24. JIC 502 estimated that the United States possessed seventy key military-industrial targets whose destruction would annihilate America's ability to prosecute a global war. In addition, fourteen more targets were identified in Great Britain.
25. Ibid.
26. Ibid.
27. Ibid.
28. Ibid.
29. See Albert Wohlstetter and Fred Hoffman's report "Protecting U.S. Power to Strike Back in the 1950's and 1960's," RAND report R-290, September 1956, in Marc Trachtenberg, ed., *The Development of American Strategic Thought: Writings on Strategy, 1952–1960, Vol. II* (New York: Garland Press, 1988), 127–236, as well as Wohlstetter's "The Delicate Balance of Terror," RAND report P-1472, November 1958, ibid. vol. III, 1–47.
30. Discussion of the impact of JIC 502 comes from a review prepared by Mose Harvey of OIR, who represented the State Department on the Joint Ad Hoc Intelligence Committee. Harvey wrote this review in an effort to explain to George Kennan why he and his staff came to accept the conclusions of JIC 502. See his memo to W. Park Armstrong, 23 June 1950, in file "Atomic Armaments, 1950," Box 7, RG 59, Records of the Department of State, Records of the Policy Planning Staff, 1947–1953, Subject Files, National Archives II.
31. Ibid.
32. Ibid.
33. A revised version of this document was published as ORE 91-49, on 6 April. According to the foreword to ORE 91-49, this report is a slightly revised version of the 10 February report. See ORE 91-49 "Estimate of Effects of the Soviet Possession of the Atomic Bomb upon the Security of the United States and upon the Probabilities of Direct Soviet Military Action," in file CIR-ORE, 1949, 90-100, Box 257, PSF-Intelligence Files, HSTL.
34. Ibid.

35. Air Force dissent, appendix D of ORE 91-49, ibid.
36. Army dissent, appendix B of ibid.
37. Memo, Harvey to Armstrong, 23 June 1950, ibid.
38. OIR dissent to ORE 91-49, in ibid.
39. Ibid.
40. Memo, Harvey to Armstrong, 23 June 1950, ibid. Emphasis in original.
41. ORE 32-50, 9 June 1950, file "CIR-ORE 18-35," Box 257, PSF-Intelligence Files, HSTL.
42. Ibid.
43. See PPS 33 "Factors Affecting the Nature of the U.S. Defense Arrangements in the Light of Soviet Policies." Nelson, *State Department Policy Planning Staff Papers*, vol. II, 1948, 282.
44. "Is War with Russia Inevitable? Five Solid Arguments for Peace," 21 February 1950, in file "Kennan Speeches," Box 48, RG 59, Records of the Department of State, Records of the Policy Planning Staff, 1947–1953, Members Chronological File, National Archives II.
45. Kennan memo to Bohlen, 12 April 1950, in "Chronological File: 1950," Box 34, RG 59, Records of the Department of State, Records of Charles E. Bohlen, National Archives II.
46. As quoted in Harvey memo to Armstrong, 23 June 1950, in ibid.
47. Ibid.
48. Ibid. Harvey provides no dates for these events; however, the meeting with Nitze must have occurred between 20 January and 10 February when the first CIA report examining the conclusions of JIC 502 was distributed.
49. "Minutes of the 171st Meeting of the National Security Council," December 16, 1949, *FRUS*: vol. I, 1949, 413–416. "Study Prepared by the Director of the Policy Planning Staff," February 8, 1950, in *FRUS*: vol. I, 1950, "National Security," 146.
50. Ibid.
51. Memo, Nitze to Executive Secretary McWilliams, 10/1/48, in NSC 20 file, Box 54, RG 59, General Records of the Department of State, Records of the Policy Planning Staff 1947–1953, National Archives II.
52. See memo, Tufts to Nitze "The Revision of National Political-Military Strategy," 7/10/52, File Folder "Review of NSC 68-114, July–August 1952," Box 56, in RG 59, General Records of the Department of State, Records of the Policy Planning Staff, 1947–1953, National Archives II.
53. Robert Bowie and Richard Immerman mistakenly consider Kennan's article "Is War with Russia Inevitable? Five Solid Arguments for Peace" as a response to NSC 68. As it was published in the March 1950 edition of *Reader's Digest* and Nitze's committee began work in early February, the article had to have been written well before President Truman authorized NSC 68. See Bowie and Immerman, *Waging Peace*, 18, fn. 31. Some of the voluminous responses to NSC 68 have been printed in *FRUS*: vol. I, "National Security," 213–314.
54. Bohlen to Nitze, 5 April 1950, in *FRUS*: vol. I, "National Security," 221–225.
55. Leffler, *Preponderance of Power*, 356.
56. See NSC 68/2, in File Folder NSC Meetings #68, in Box 209, 9/29/50, in PSF-NSC Meetings 65-70, HSTL.
57. Ibid., 437–438.
58. NSC 68/1 "United States Objectives and Programs for National Security," 21 September 1950, in File Folder NSC Meetings #68, 9/29/50, in Box 209, PSF NSC Meetings, 65-70, HSTL.
59. See Wilson Miscamble, *George F. Kennan and the Making of American Foreign Policy, 1947–1950*, 199, and Etzold and Gaddis, *Containment*, 203, 383–385. See also the selections in *American Cold War Policy: Interpreting NSC 68*, Ernest R. May, ed. (New York: St. Martin's Press, 1993).
60. Gerald Miller, "Office of Policy Coordination, 1948–1952," http://www.foia.ucia.gov (search FOIA requests: covert operations).
61. Memorandum for the Record by Charles Hulik of OPC, 19 April 1950, in *The CIA under Harry Truman*, ed. Michael Warner (Washington, D.C.: CIA, 1994), 323.
62. Ibid. Joyce added the underlining for emphasis. This phrase came directly from NSC

68; see *Containment: Documents on American Strategy, 1945–1950*, Etzold and Gaddis, eds., 435–436.

63. Hulik memorandum in Warner, *CIA under Harry Truman*.

64. Memo to NSC on "Scope and Pace of Covert Operations," 8 May 1951, File Folder: Legislative Background on 10/5, 091.411, SMOF—PSB, Box 13, HSTL.

65. Miller, "Office of Policy Coordination."

66. Extensive literature exists recounting the uses and misuses of covert activities by the United States throughout the postwar period. Sources, such as Thomas Powers's *The Man Who Kept the Secrets: Richard Helms and the CIA*, John Prados's *Presidents' Secret Wars: CIA and Pentagon Covert Operations since World War II*, and Christopher Simpson's *Blowback: America's Recruitment of Nazis and Its Effect on the Cold War*, provide us with fascinating accounts of worldwide clandestine U.S. operations coordinated by the CIA and the Office of Policy Coordination. This literature, however, has not had the benefit of numerous documents only declassified since 1990, providing a wealth of details about the objectives of covert strategy planned by the Psychological Strategy Board and by the highest levels within the Truman administration.

67. Kennan, NSC 20/1, in Etzold and Gaddis, *Containment*, 183.

68. A number of psychological-warfare specialists did disagree that preponderant military power was a prerequisite for aggressive covert action behind the Iron Curtain. See Wallace Carroll, "The Intermediate Strategy," 1 November 1951, in *Declassified Documents Catalogue* vol. XVII, no. 6, November–December 1991, fiche 314, document 3539.

69. "NSC 68," in Etzold and Gaddis, *Containment*, 435–436.

70. Edward Lilly, "The Development of American Psychological Operations, 1945–1951," in Box 14, Registry Series, WHO-NSC Staff Papers: 1948–1961, Dwight D. Eisenhower Library.

71. Ibid.

72. Ibid.

73. See *FRUS*: vol. I, 1951, "National Security," 58.

74. Lilly, "Development of American Psychological Operations." See also Gordon Gray's views in "Report to the President," President Truman File, in Box 3, PSB Series 1952 (1), Gordon Gray Papers 1946–1976, Dwight D. Eisenhower Library. A further discussion of PSB-State relations can be found in a memo from Joseph Phillips to Under Secretary of State James Webb and Assistant Secretary of State for Public Affairs Edward Barrett, 8/9/51, in File 040 State Department, in Box 3 SMOF-PSB Files 040-063, HSTL.

75. A similar view is expressed in a draft PSB policy paper entitled "The PSB: Functional Relationship to the President and the NSC," in File 334 Staff Coordination and Liaison with the White House, Box 25 SMOF-PSB files 334, HSTL. Two other CIA studies also supported the belief that the scope of the board's responsibilities needed to be very broad to meet the president's directive. According to these studies (one dated 23 July 1951 and the other undated), the president's directive defined psychological operations as "every kind of activity in support of U.S. policies, except global 'hot' warfare and overt economic warfare."

76. See Magruder memo to Walter Bedell Smith, in "PSB staff Coordination and Liaison with the White House," in Box 25 SMOF-PSB files 334, HSTL.

77. See Memorandum of Discussion, ibid.

78. The following discussion comes from a lengthy report prepared by Charles Burton Marshall of the Policy Planning Staff commenting on the various definitions of the PSB's jurisdiction. See Memo from Charles Burton Marshall of the State Department Policy Planning Staff to the PSB, 29 July 1951, in *Declassified Documents Catalogue* vol. XVII, no. 4, July–August 1991, fiche 210, document 2254.

79. Prados, *Presidents' Secret Wars*, 87.

80. Memorandum Nitze to Webb, 3 August 1951, in file "Political and Psychological Warfare," Box 11a, RG 59, Records of Department of State, Records of Policy Planning Staff, 1947–1953, Subject Files, National Archives II. NSC 59/1 "The Foreign Information Program and Psychological Warfare Planning" called for the creation of a single organization to coordinate

the foreign information program and psychological warfare. The document is located in File Folder "NSC Memo Approvals 283," Box 193, PSF: Subject Files, NSC Series, HSTL.

81. Summary of Secretaries Daily Meetings, 8/12/51, in File 1951, Box 2, RG 59, Records of the Department of State, Records of Executive Secretariat, 1949–1952, National Archives II.

82. Wallace Carroll, "The Philosophy of the PSB," 12 September 1951, Memo to Director of PSB Gordon Gray, File Folder 091.411, "Agenda for PSB," Staff Members Office Files (SMOF)—PSB, Box 14, Harry S. Truman Library (HSTL). Carroll had worked with the State Department on U.S. propaganda programs for the Korean War and had been offered directorship of State's National Psychological Strategy Board.

83. Ibid.

84. Carroll, "Philosophy of the PSB." See also PSB D-4 "Role of PSB under 4/4/51 Presidential Directive," 28 September 1951, File Folder-Subject File-NSC Memo Approval 10/2, Papers of Harry Truman, Records of PSB, PSF Subject Files, NSC Box 193, HSTL. This document referred to the PSB as the "nerve center for strategic operations."

85. Consequently, the PSB was forced to grow in accordance with these new responsibilities. Underneath the board were three sections each headed by an assistant director: the Office of Plans and Policies, the Office of Coordination, and the Office of Evaluation and Review. The staff eventually reached seventy-nine members. See "Background Notes on the Psychological Strategy Board," 3 January 1952 (no author), *Declassified Documents Catalogue* vol. XVII, no. 1, January–February 1991, fiche 53, document 542.

86. See Ludwell Lee Montague, *General Walter Bedell Smith As Director of Central Intelligence, October 1950–February 1953, Vol. IV—The War Emergency and Clandestine Services*, 36, in Box 1, RG 263, Records of the Central Intelligence Agency, Office of the Director of Central Intelligence Historical Staff, DCI Historical Series, National Archives II.

87. Memo to NSC on "Scope and Pace of Covert Operations," 8 May 1951, File Folder: Legislative Background on 10/5, 091.411, SMOF—PSB, Box 13, HSTL. See also Miller, "Office of Policy Coordination, 1948–1952," ibid.

88. Ibid.

89. Ibid.

90. Ludwell Lee Montague, *General Walter Bedell Smith As Director of Central Intelligence, Vol. IV*, 39. According to Montague, Smith believed that only one psychological-warfare operation influenced the World War II effort: when a parcel carrying thousands of leaflets failed to open in the air and accidentally sunk a German tugboat.

91. Walter Bedell Smith to James Lay, in ibid.

92. See memo to Lay, 28 March 1951, in File Folder: Subject File—NSC Memo Approvals—10/2, PSF—Subject File: NSC Memo Approval, Box 193, HSTL.

93. See Montague, *General Walter Bedell Smith As Director of Central Intelligence.*

94. See "Study on Scope and Pace of Covert Operations," 27 June 1951, File Folder: Subject File—NSC Memo Approvals—10/2, PSF—Subject File: NSC Memo Approval, Box 193, HSTL.

95. Ibid.

96. Ibid.

97. "Study on Scope and Pace of Covert Operations," 15 August 1951, File Folder: Subject File—NSC Memo Approvals—10/2, PSF—Subject File: NSC Memo Approval, Box 193, HSTL.

98. Ibid.

99. Montague, *General Walter Bedell Smith As Director of Central Intelligence*, 41–42. See also "Implications of JCS Procedure for Supporting Covert Operations," 22 August 1951, in File Folder NSC Memo Approvals—10/2. This decision was made with the concurrence of the JCS representative.

100. Memo, Bradley to Marshall 1/15/51, in Box 55, NSC 68 file, Jan–June 1951 in RG 59, General Records of the Department of State; Records of the Policy Planning Staff, 1947–1953; National Archives II.

101. NSC 10/5 "Scope and Pace of Covert Operations," 23 October 1951, File Folder: NSC Memo Approvals—10/2, PSF—Subject File, NSC Memo Approvals, Box 143, HSTL.

102. See Memo by Col. Paul Davies, 26 July 1951, "List of Psychological Operations Activities Additional to Those Embraced by NSC 10/2 and NSC 59/1," in File Folder 091.411-Agenda for PSB, Box 14 SMOF-PSB, HSTL.

103. "Draft Memorandum for Meeting of the Group With the Director," 11-26-51, in Box 23 "Directors Group File," SMOF-PSB files, 323–334, HSTL.

104. Warner, *CIA under Harry Truman*, xxxviii; *Who's Who in America*, Volume 27, 1952–1953 (The A.N. Marquis Co., 1953), 2323.

105. See in particular Stevens's "A National Strategy for the Soviet Union," 1-25-51, in File 091.411 Drafts of National Psychological Strategy—papers #1, in Box 14 SMOF-PSB files 091.411 to 091.412, HSTL.

106. Memorandum from T. R. Philbin to Gordon Gray, 10-12-51 in Box 23 "Directors Group File," SMOF-PSB files, 323–334, HSTL.

107. For Kennan's role as a consultant see Gordon Gray's statement to the Director's Group in the *Declassified Documents Catalogue* vol. XVII, no. 2, March–April 1992, fiche 87, document 1109. See also Third Meeting of the Director's Group in Box 23 "Director's Group file," SMOF-PSB files, 323–334, HSTL. Burnham was the author of *Containment or Liberation? An Inquiry into the Aims of United States Foreign Policy* (New York: The John Day Co., 1952).

108. Memo for Gordon Gray from Lt. Col. T. R. Philbin "First Meeting of the Director's Board," 6 November 1951, *Declassified Documents Catalogue* vol. XVII, no. 6, November–December 1991, fiche 314, document 3539. The *Declassified Documents Catalogue* presented all of the five strategy papers within this citation.

109. Memo Philbin to Gray, "Third Meeting of the Director's Group," in Box 23 "Director's Group file," SMOF-PSB files, 323–334, HSTL.

110. "Notes on a Strategic Concept," in Box 23 "Director's Group file," SMOF-PSB files, 323–334, HSTL.

111. "Planning Priorities for the PSB," 16 November 1951, *Declassified Documents Catalogue* vol. XVII, no. 4, July–August 1991, fiche 211, document 2269. Some material presented here comes from an earlier draft of this document dated 20 September 1951. See ibid., fiche 143, document 2264.

112. "Planning Priorities for the PSB: Tab D Policy Review Questions," 16 November 1951. In ibid.

113. PSB report "Towards a Psychological Strategy," 12 November 1951, in *Declassified Documents Catalogue* vol. XVII, no. 4, July–August 1991, fiche 212, document 2295.

114. Ibid.

115. Ibid.

116. Marshall to Nitze, 19 November 1951, in file "Political and Psychological and Warfare 1951–1953," in Box 11a, RG 59, Records of Department of State, Records of the Policy Planning Staff, 1947–1953, Subject Files, National Archives II.

117. Ibid.

118. Summaries of Secretary's Daily Meetings, 11/19/51, in File 1951, Box 2, RG 59, Records of the Department of State, Records of Executive Secretariat, Daily Meetings, 1949–1952.

119. Memorandum from the Director's Group to C. Tracy Barnes, 12/14/51 in ibid. Colonel Kilbourne Johnston replaced Wisner as assistant director for policy coordination. See Miller, "Office of Policy Coordination, 1948–1952."

120. "Minutes of the Director's Group Meeting," ibid.

121. Ibid.

122. "Paul Nitze's comments on PSB draft of 11-15-51," 12-7-51, in file "Political and Psychological and Warfare 1951–1953," in Box 11a, RG 59, Records of Department of State, Records of the Policy Planning Staff, 1947–1953, Subject Files, National Archives II.

123. "Accepted Method of Formulating a National Psychological Strategy," in File 091.411 Drafts of National Psychological Strategy #1 [1 of 2], in Box 14 SMOF-PSB files 091.411–091.412, HSTL.

124. Ibid. These four points were included at the urging of Paul Nitze.

125. See for instance Paul Nitze's memo to Gordon Gray's special assistant Lt. Col. Philbin, 8-1-52, in File Folder 091.411, Drafts of National Psychological Strategy, #1 [1 of 2] Box 14, SMOF-PSB files 091.411–091.412.

126. See General Staff Meeting 4/18/52, in File Folder 337 Staff Meetings [3 of 3], Box 27 SMOF-PSB files 337, HSTL.

127. Summaries of Secretary's Daily Meetings, 12/20/51, File 1951, Box 2, RG 59, Records of the Department of State, Record of Executive Secretariat, Meetings 1949–1952, National Archives II.

128. See memo from Under Secretary of State David Bruce, Deputy Secretary of Defense William C. Foster, and Director of Central Intelligence Walter Bedell Smith, "Subject: Interim Approval of the Packet of 12-15-51," 19 May 1952, in File Folder 091.411: Actions Taken on NSC 10/5—All Items Included, SMOF-PSB, Box 13, HSTL.

129. Charles Bohlen, "The Possibilities of External Action Against Soviet-Type States," n.d., in file "General Collection 1952–1955," Box 9, RG 59, Records of the Department of State, Records of Charles E. Bohlen, National Archives II.

130. Bohlen, "The Possibilities of External Action Against Soviet-Type States," ibid.

131. On U.S. psychological-warfare policy toward Germany see PSB D-21 "Operation PLUTONIC" [draft #2], 21 March 1952 in Box 6, SMOF-PSB, Files 091 Germany, HSTL. See also the Wallace Carroll–Hans Speier plan for the unification of Germany entitled "Taking the Offensive," 20 September 1951, in File "091.411, Drafts of National Psychological Strategy papers #1 [1 of 2]," in Box 14, SMOF-PSB 091.411–091.412, HSTL. See also two articles by Christian Ostermann: "The United States, the East German Uprising of 1953, and the Limits of Rollback," Working Paper No. 11, Cold War International History Project, Woodrow Wilson International Center for Scholars, December 1994; and "'Keeping the Pot Simmering': The United States and the East German Uprising of 1953," *German Studies Review* 19 (February 1996): 61–69.

132. Memorandum entitled "Col. Booth's Paper on Paramilitary Organization," John Sherman to C. Tracy Barnes, 7/22/52, in file folder 091.411 Miscellaneous Materials Re: NSC 10/5, Box 13, SMOF-PSB. According to this memorandum, by late 1951 the State Department hoped to "divorce" paramilitary planning from other elements of psychological warfare "so that the preoccupation with paramilitary activities in the CIA, and for that matter in Defense, would not prejudice these other CIA operations." Charles Stelle of Nitze's Policy Planning Staff was a leading advocate for this separation.

133. "Overall Strategic Concept for Our Cold War Operations," by Mallory Browne, director of the Office of Evaluation and Review, in File Folder 091.411, Drafts of National Psychological Strategy Papers [1 of 2], Box 14 SMOF-PSB files, 091.411–091.412, HSTL.

134. On this point see "Notes on Lecture on Possibility for Revolution" by Stefan Possony in *Declassified Documents Catalogue* vol. XVII, no. 4, July–August 1991, fiche 216, document 2330. Notes were taken by Edmund Taylor, director of the Office of Plans and Policy.

135. The four points come from a top-secret report declassified in 1994 called Project TROY. The report was an extensive review of psychological warfare prepared in the fall of 1950 and presented to Secretary of State Acheson on 1 February 1951 by a group of scholars including physicists, historians, and psychologists from Harvard, MIT, and RAND. See Project TROY file, in Box 33, RG 59 General Records of the Department of State, Records of the S/P 1947–1953.

136. In 1953 when Stalin did die such operations were in fact attempted. See chapter four for a complete discussion.

137. Allan A. Needell, "'Truth is Our Weapon': Project TROY, Political Warfare, and Government-Academic Relations in the National Security State," *Diplomatic History* 17, no. 3 (Summer 1993): 399–420.

138. Project TROY file, in Box 33, RG 59 General Records of the Department of State, Records of the S/P 1947–1953.

139. Ibid.

140. Ibid.
141. Ibid.
142. Ibid.
143. Dulles memo 1 June 1951 in *Declassified Documents Catalogue* vol. XVII, no. 4, July–August 1991, fiche 170, document 1809.
144. Sherman memo, 3 July 1952 in File Folder "Responsibilities and Precedents under 10/5," Box 13, SMOF-PSB files 091.411, HSTL.
145. For purposes of clarification Soviet and Eastern European nationals were divided into three classifications: refugees, ordinary people who escaped the East; escapees, high-level officials who left for the West whether induced or not; and defectors, high-level officials who were enticed to defect to the West but remained within the Soviet Union serving as agents.
146. Project TROY, Main Report. The report estimated that some 1,500 Soviet and satellite peoples defected each year.
147. SPONGE Roundup No. 1 in File "Displaced Persons and Refugees," Box 9, RG 59, Records of the Department of State, Records of the Policy Planning Staff, 1947–1953, Subject Files, National Archives II.
148. According to annex 12 of Project TROY several defectors did return to the USSR due to bungled handling by Western relief agencies.
149. See memo, Kennan to Acheson, 12 July 1950, in File "Displaced Persons and Refugees," Box 9, RG 59, Records of the Department of State, Records of the Policy Planning Staff, 1947–1953, Subject Files, National Archives II.
150. 2/21/52, File "383 Psychological Aspects of Phase 'A' Defection Program [1 of 2]," Box 32, SMOF-PSB Files, HSTL.
151. Fourth Meeting of the PSB, in File "383-Psychological Aspects of Phase A Defection Program [2 of 2]," in Box 32, SMOF-PSB files, HSTL.
152. Memo "Terms of Reference for PSB Working Group on Defector-Refugee Problem," 9 November 1951, ibid.
153. PSB D-18a, "Psychological Operations Plan for Soviet Orbit Escapees," 20 December 1951, in file "383.7 Escapee Program, Section one, [5 of 6]," Box 33, SMOF-PSB Files, HSTL.
154. Ibid. Although the document was declassified in October 1994, the section regarding CIA responsibilities in the program remains classified. We may presume, however, that it directs the CIA to utilize escapees in its covert programs.
155. "Terms of Reference for Phase B of Psychological Operations Plan for Soviet Orbit Escapees," 21 February 1952, in File "383 Psychological Aspects of Phase 'A' Defection Program [1 of 2]," in Box 32, SMOF-PSB Files, HSTL.
156. PSB D18a/1 File Folder: PSB D-18, Box 2, PSB Working File: 1951–1951, Executive Secretariat Series, RG 59 Records of the Department of State, National Archives II.
157. Ibid.
158. NSC 143 "A Volunteer Freedom Corps," May 20 1953, in File NSC 143, Box 2, Records of the National Security Council, National Archives II.
159. In the "long telegram" Kennan wrote, "success of the Soviet system is not yet finally proved. It has yet to be demonstrated that it can survive supreme test of successive transfer of power from one individual to another. Lenin's death was the first such transfer, and its effects wracked the Soviet state for 15 years."
160. Project TROY, annex 15. This report was written by John A. Morrison, a professor of geography at the University of Maryland who was deputy chief of the USSR Division Research and Analysis branch of the OSS between 1941 and 1945, and chief of the Eastern European Branch, Division of Research for Europe, Department of State, from 1945 to 1947.
161. Ibid. According to Morrison, during the "Time of Troubles" of the late sixteenth and early seventeenth centuries there was a widely held belief that Czar Alexander I had not died but was living in a monastery.
162. Ibid. The MVD stood for the Ministry of Internal Affairs, brother institution to the MGB, the Ministry of State Security. After Stalin's death these organizations were combined to form the KGB.

163. See PSB D-24 in File Folder PSB D-24, Box 4, PSB Working Files: 1951–1952, Executive Secretariat Series, RG 59, Records of the Department of State, NA II. A memorandum from Joseph Philips to Assistant Secretary of State Edward Barrett explains the relationship between Project TROY and PSB D-24. See Philips to Edward, 29 October 1952, in ibid.

164. Ibid.

165. See memorandum from Francis Stevens, director of the Eastern European desk, October 22, 1952, ibid.

Chapter Three

1. See Robert Bowie and Richard Immerman, *Waging Peace: How Eisenhower Shaped an Enduring Cold War Strategy* (New York: Oxford University Press, 1998), 28–31.

2. My view of Charles Bohlen challenges the conventional view of Bohlen as a timid administration official. See for instance T. Michael Ruddy, *The Cautious Diplomat: Charles E. Bohlen and the Soviet Union, 1929–1969* (Kent, Ohio: Kent State University Press, 1987); and David Callahan, *Dangerous Capabilities: Paul Nitze and the Cold War* (New York: Harper Collins, 1990), especially 135–138.

3. The Senior Staff was composed of Paul Nitze (State Department), Frank Nash (Defense), J. Murray Mitchell (Office of Defense Mobilization), Brigadier General Frank Roberts (Mutual Security Agency), C. D. Olenndening (Treasury Department), Admiral T. E. Wooldridge (JCS), William H. Jackson (CIA), Burton Klein (Council of Economic Advisors), Paul Porter (Economic Cooperation Administration), and Robert Macy (Bureau of the Budget). The list is located in File Folder "Planning Board Organization, 1950–1960," Box 14, WHO-NSC Staff Papers, 1948–1961, Executive Secretary's Subject, Dwight D. Eisenhower Library (DDEL).

4. NSC 114 "Status and Timing of Current U.S. Programs for National Security," 27 July 1951, file folder NSC Meeting #98 8/1/51, PSF NSC Meetings Box 214, Meeting 98-103, HSTL.

5. Ibid. The report offers the date 1950 for the new estimate of Soviet nuclear capabilities, an obvious misprint. I have chosen to use the date 1953 instead since it is the date given in later drafts of the NSC 114 series.

6. This point was argued by the director of central intelligence, Walter Bedell Smith, in a memo to the NSC dated 11 December 1950 and was one reason why Truman declared a state of emergency five days later. See his memo "Probable Soviet Reaction to Full-Scale U.S. Mobilization," *FRUS*: vol. I, 1951, 2–3.

7. On the need for greater efforts to achieve the military buildup see Nitze's memo to Acheson, 31 July 1951, in *FRUS*: vol. I, 1951, 110–112.

8. See memo, Bohlen to Nitze, 28 July 1951, in *FRUS*: vol. I, 1951, 106.

9. See memo, Bohlen to Nitze, 22 August 1951, in *FRUS*: vol. I, 1951, 165.

10. Ibid., 163.

11. Memo, Bohlen to Nitze, 28 July 1951, in *FRUS*: vol. I, 1951, 107.

12. This term comes from a JCS policy paper discussed at the NSC Senior Staff Meeting, 12 July 1952, in File Folder 334, NSC Files, Box 24, SMOF-PSB files 323–334, HSTL. The reports from the NSC Senior Staff meetings come from summaries of discussions by the PSB member on the Senior Staff. On 16 July 1951 President Truman authorized the inclusion of a PSB representative on the Senior Staff with the purpose of keeping the PSB informed of policy formulation and making sure that psychological elements were incorporated into these analyses. These representatives (Robert Cutler from 16 August to 3 December 1951, C. Tracy Barnes from 3 to 28 December, and George Morgan from 28 December until 2 September 1953, when the PSB was transformed into the OCB) wrote memoranda of discussion for the director. These memoranda are the only summaries of discussion of the Senior Staff meetings that I have been able to locate, although minutes of these meetings exist and are located in the NSC files at the National Archives. All the following discussions of NSC Senior Staff meetings are from these PSB sources.

13. Ibid.
14. Ibid.
15. See paragraph one of NSC 114, ibid.
16. Memo, Bohlen to Nitze, 28 July 1951.
17. Memo, Bohlen to Acheson, 25 Sept. 1951, in *FRUS*: vol. I, 1951, 177–178.
18. Ibid., 108.
19. Memo, Koch to Ferguson, 24 August 1951, in *FRUS*: vol. I, 1951, 166–169.
20. Ibid., 167.
21. Ibid. See also a report from Schwartz to Ferguson, "Review of NSC 68," 17 August 1951, File Folder "NSC General File," No. 16, 1 of 2, Box 60, Subject Files relating to National Security Policy: 1950–1957, Miscellaneous Lot Files, RG 59, Records of the Department of State, National Archives II.
22. Memo, Robert Hooker to Paul Nitze, n.d., in NSC 68 file, Box 55, RG 59, General Records of the Department of State, Records of the Policy Planning Staff, 1947–1953, National Archives II.
23. Ibid.
24. Memo of Conversation, by the Executive Secretary of the NSC (Lay), May 12, 1950, "Fourth Meeting of the Ad Hoc Group" in *FRUS*: vol. I, 1950, "National Security," 312–313.
25. NSC 68, in Thomas Etzold and John Lewis Gaddis, eds., *Containment: Documents on American Policy and Strategy, 1945–1950* (New York: Columbia University Press, 1978), 386–387.
26. See in particular Nitze's 31 July memo to Acheson where he spells out his concern that Secretary of Defense Marshall, and his deputy Robert Lovett, placed greater emphasis on the long-term sustenance of the military program than on preparing for a set of circumstances, and ultimately would support the Bureau of the Budget attempt to stretch out the military program rather than intensify it. See ibid., 110–112.
27. On the stretch-out option see Doris Condit, *The Test of War: 1950–1953* (Washington, D.C.: Office of the Secretary of Defense, 1980), 276–280.
28. Memo, Nitze to Acheson, 22 Sept. 1951, in *FRUS*: vol. I, 1951, 172–175.
29. Memo, Bohlen to Acheson, 25 Sept. 1951, in ibid., 177–178. Emphasis in original.
30. Ibid.
31. Bohlen had since replaced Nitze as the State Department representative to the Senior Staff; also Harlan Cleveland replaced Paul Porter as the representative of the Economic Cooperation Administration.
32. 27 September meeting of the NSC Senior Staff, in File Folder 334, NSC Files, Box 24, SMOF-PSB files 323–334, HSTL.
33. NSC Senior Staff Meeting 27 September 1951, ibid. According to Cutler's memoranda, NSC 114/2 was prepared in part by Robert Tufts and Charles Noyes of State and Marion Boggs of the NSC.
34. See memo from Nitze to Acheson, 22 September. For Bohlen's opposition see his memo to Acheson, 21 September, 170–172.
35. Ibid.
36. Ibid.
37. Ibid.
38. 10 October Senior Staff meeting, in File Folder 334, NSC Files, Box 24, SMOF-PSB files 323–334, HSTL.
39. 11 October Senior Staff meeting, ibid.
40. 16 October Senior Staff meeting, ibid.
41. *FRUS*: vol. I, 1951, 234.
42. Ibid., 237.
43. NSC Senior Staff meeting, 24 October 1951, in File Folder 334 NSC Files, Box 24, SMOF-PSB files 323–334, HSTL.
44. During the previous eight months Bohlen wrote a number of drafts and received advice from a number of quarters, including George Kennan. Unfortunately, Kennan's remarks

focused largely on obscure aspects of the Russian revolution. These materials are located in file "Bohlen 1952," Box 9, RG 59, Records of the Department of State, Records of Charles Bohlen, National Archives II. See Kennan's letter of 11 December in same file.

45. Ibid., "Bases of Soviet Action."

46. Ibid.

47. Bohlen further warned that the Soviets could decide to go to war if they were convinced that an attack from the West was imminent, or through miscalculation, or by a crisis escalating out of control.

48. See discussion of Kennan in chapter one.

49. We shall see in the next section how this affected the PSB's strategic concept paper, with which Bohlen was equally involved.

50. Senior Staff meeting, 8 July 1952, in File Folder 334, NSC Files, Box 24 SMOF-PSB files 323–334, HSTL. The conclusion had enormous ramifications for the strategic concept paper, which will be discussed below.

51. This paragraph comes from Bohlen's top-secret address to the National War College, 30 October 1952, entitled "Basis of Soviet External Action and Possible U.S. Countermeasures," in File "Bohlen 1952," Box 9, RG 59, Records of the Department of State, Records of Charles E. Bohlen, National Archives II.

52. NSC Senior Staffmeeting, 8 July, in File Folder 334, NSC Files, Box 24, SMOF-PSB files 323–334, HSTL. Apparently President Truman remarked to a Romanian delegation that their country would be liberated in their lifetime.

53. Ibid.

54. Ibid.

55. Ibid.

56. Ibid.

57. Ibid.

58. Memorandum by Robert Tufts, 21 May 1952, in *FRUS*: vol. II, 1952–1954, 18–20.

59. Ibid.

60. Tufts memo, File "Review of NSC 68-114 July–August 1952," Box 56, RG 59, General Records of the Department of State, Records of the S/P, National Archives II.

61. Ibid. See also John Ferguson's memo to Nitze, 7-22-52, in *FRUS*, ibid.

62. Ibid., 64.

63. Ibid., 59.

64. Ibid.

65. Ibid., 65.

66. Ibid. Joyce added the underlining for emphasis. This phrase came directly from NSC 68. See *Containment*, Etzold and Gaddis, 435–436.

67. Memorandum for the Record by Charles Hulik of OPC, 19 April 1950, in *The CIA under Harry Truman*, ed. Michael Warner (Washington D.C.: CIA, 1994), 323.

68. 24 July NSC Senior Staffmeeting, ibid.

69. *FRUS*: vol. II, 1952–1954, 68–73.

70. Ibid., 69.

71. Ibid., 71. The phrasing "and as practicable intensify" was included at the behest of George Morgan, PSB representative on the NSC Senior Staff. He argued that the new policy statement must include language calling for the United States to continue building its political-warfare capabilities, since "our capabilities behind the Iron Curtain had in the main been decreasing and that we had no clear way to increase them in sight; hence that we should avoid phraseology suggesting mere hopeful continuation along present lines and stress the need to invent and develop new capabilities." See 10 July NSC Senior Staff meeting, ibid.

72. PSB D-31 "A Strategic Concept for a National Psychological Program with Particular Reference to Cold War Operations under NSC 10/5," file PSB D-31, Box 5, PSB Working Files: 1951–1953, Executive Secretariat, RG 59, Records of the Department of State, NA II.

73. NSC 135/3 in FRUS: vol. II, "National Security," 72.

74. NSC 135/1 Annex "Reappraisal of United States Objectives," 22 August 1952; NIE "Estimate of the World Situation through 1954," 21 November 1952, in *FRUS*: vol. II, "National

Security," 1952–1954, 188; NSC 140/1, Report of the Special Evaluation Subcommittee on the NSC "Summary Evaluation of the Net Capability of the USSR to Inflict Direct Injury on the United States up to July 1, 1955," in ibid., vol. II, 333–347; and Melvyn P. Leffler, *A Preponderance of Power: National Security, the Truman Administration, and the Cold War* (Stanford: Stanford University Press, 1992), 487.

75. NSC 140/1.

76. NSC 135/1 Annex "Reappraisal of United States Objectives." The Eisenhower administration would refer to this situation as "enoughness." See the discussion in chapter four.

77. By 1955 the United States would have 2,250 weapons as compared with an estimated 300 for the Soviets.

78. We shall see in chapter four that when the United States did achieve a position of strategic superiority, capable of launching a "decisive nuclear strike" against the Soviet Union, the Eisenhower administration refused to heighten its political-warfare campaign as a number of leading experts urged.

79. NSC 135/1 Annex "Bases of Soviet Actions." This report was prepared by Bohlen himself.

80. See Kennan's NSC 20/1 "U.S. Objectives towards Russia," 18 August 1948, in chapter one; see Palmer Putnam, "Basic Strategic Concepts," 1 November 1951. *Declassified Documents Catalogue*, vol. XVII, November–December 1997, fiche 314.

81. See 25 June draft of "Bases of Soviet Action," in file "Bohlen 1952," Box 9, RG 59, Records of the Department of State, Records of Charles Bohlen, NA II.

82. Most historical accounts do not consider that the policies established in NSC 20/4 and pursued in NSC 68 were superseded, and while NSC 135/1 did not formally supersede either document, unofficially it was recognized that established policy had changed. The retrenchment discussed in this chapter was also recognized by the Eisenhower administration in a review of American national security policy completed on 8 June 1954 and declassified on 18 January 1995. See "Report on U.S. Policy for the Exploitation of Soviet Vulnerabilities," in file "USSR-Report on U.S. Policy for the Exploitation of Soviet Vulnerabilities," Box 18, WHO-OSANSA Records, NSC Series, 1952–1961, Briefing Notes Subseries, DDEL.

83. Memo by Paul Nitze to Dean Acheson, "Re-examination of United States Programs for National Security," 12 January 1953, in *FRUS*: vol. II, 1952–1954, "National Security," 204.

84. On Bohlen and Wisner's friendship see Burton Hersh, *The Old Boys: The American Elite and the Origins of the CIA* (New York: Scribners, 1992), 306. According to Hersh, Bohlen was a frequent guest of Wisner's.

85. Memorandum Stelle to Admiral Stevens, 4 February 1952, in *Declassified Documents Catalogue* vol. XVII, no. 3, May–June 1991, fiche 168, document 1772. A memo from Colonel T. R. Philbin to various members of the PSB points to this specific document as one of the State papers. See Philbin's memo "Status of National Psychological Strategy Paper," 19 March 1952, in file "Drafts of National Psychological Strategy #1 [1 of 2]," Box 14, SMOF-PSB 091.412–091.417, HSTL.

86. Ibid.

87. Ibid.

88. Kennan argued an almost identical position three years earlier. See S/P meeting 18 October 1949, in file "Meetings 1949," in Box 32, RG 59, Records of the Department of State, Records of the Policy Planning Staff, 1947–1953, S/P Meetings, NA II.

89. CIA "Means Paper," 15 May 1952, in file 091.411 Agenda for PSB, Box 14 SMOF-PSB HSTL. This version is the fourth draft of the paper.

90. Mallory Browne, "Overall Strategic Concept for Our Psychological Operations," 7 May 1952, File 091.412 #2 The Field and Role of Psychological Strategy in the Cold War [2 of 2], Box 15 SMOF-PSB 091.412–092.3, HSTL.

91. Ibid.

92. Ibid.

93. See Putnam memo to George Morgan, 21 May 1952, in file 000.1 RAND Corporation Study [International Communication and Political Warfare] Box 1 SMOF-PSB Files, Gordon Gray Chronological File to 014.5, HSTL. Memo from John Sherman, Office of Coordination,

to Mallory Browne, 22 May 1952, *Declassified Documents Catalogue* vol. XVII, no. 2, March–April 1991, fiche 106, document 1126.

94. Sherman to Browne, ibid.

95. Memo, Stevens to Raymond Allen and C. Tracy Barnes, 13 May 1952, file 091.411 Drafts of National Psychological Strategy #1 [1 of 2], Box 14 SMOF-PSB 091.411–091.412, HSTL. The most significant criticism came from Admiral Stevens, who considered the paper to be "over-simplified." He felt that any public discussion of liberation would have such negative worldwide repercussions that he doubted any positive benefit. He strongly disagreed with Browne's characterization that the present strategic concept was nothing more than passive containment.

96. "A Strategic Concept for a National Psychological Program," 30 June 1952, in File 091.411, Drafts of National Psychological Strategy #1 [1 of 2], Box 14, SMOF-PSB files, HSTL.

97. Memorandum from George Morgan to Raymond Allen "Re Meeting on Political Warfare," 12 May 1952, in File 000.1, RAND Corporation Study, Box 1, SMOF-PSB files, HSTL.

98. Allen Dulles was in an especially difficult position, not wanting to openly attack the administration in which he was working, yet not willing to contradict a position held by his brother John Foster Dulles and many in the room with which he would be working in a future Republican administration. On most issues he simply straddled the fence, arguing that the United States was in a "position to take the offensive, at least in some areas" and later exclaiming that the United States should push for a more offensive policy.

99. The guest list and statement of purpose are located in the file "Princeton Statement," in Box 7, RG 59, Records of Department of State, Records of Charles E. Bohlen, Memoranda, 1942–1952, NA II.

100. Morgan, "Re Meeting on Political Warfare," 12 May 1952, in File 000.1, RAND Corporation Study, Box 1, SMOF-PSB files, HSTL. Allen Dulles had in fact become quite concerned about the possible success of RFE broadcasts into Czechoslovakia. He informed the House Committee on Foreign Affairs that "I must admit that there are times when I feel we have almost stirred up Czechoslovakia too much without the military ability to do something." See Vojtech Mastny, *The Cold War and Soviet Insecurity: The Stalin Years* (New York: Oxford University Press, 1996), 120.

101. 12 May 1952, in File 000.1, RAND Corporation Study, Box 1, SMOF-PSB files, HSTL. The quoted material represents a summary of opinions held by Jackson and Galantier, both of whom were closely associated with RFE.

102. Ibid.

103. Ibid. The comparison to John Foster Dulles's argument is not coincidental as Jackson was close friends with both Dulles brothers, and Foster Dulles's article in *Life* magazine was scheduled for release only a week later.

104. Ibid.

105. Princeton Statement in file "Eastern Europe: 1949–1953," in Box 29, RG 59, Records of Department of State, Records of the Policy Planning Staff, 1947–1953, NA II.

106. Memo, Bohlen to David Bruce, 13 May 1952, in file "Memoranda 1952," Box 5, RG 59, Records of Department of State, Records of Charles E. Bohlen, Memoranda, 1942–1952, NA II.

107. Memo, Ferguson to David Bruce, 1 July 1952, in "Eastern Europe: 1949–1953," in Box 29, RG 59, Records of Department of State, Records of the Policy Planning Staff, 1947–1953, NA II.

108. Ibid. Morgan learned that part of Jackson's hubris over the possibility of action in Eastern Europe was due to somebody convincing him that there was a serious chance of revolt in Czechoslovakia.

109. On 26 April 1952 the *Economist* warned that the transmissions from the VOA, RFE, and other "so-called black radio stations" as well as the "alleged activities of the Central Intelligence Agency behind the Iron Curtain" would be seen in Moscow as part of a "systematic and sinister" effort on the part of the West to encourage revolt in Eastern Europe, an effort which would have to have a planned military element as a component. The editorial

feared that the uncertainty of the Kremlin leadership could lead to serious instability in Europe. This editorial was of great concern to both sides of the Princeton meeting. "Containment Plus?" *Economist*, 26 April 1952.

110. Report prepared by Walter W. Rostow in file "Exploitation of Stalin's Death," Box 1, Records of C. D. Jackson, DDEL.

111. John Foster Dulles, "A Policy of Boldness," *Life*, 19 May 1952.

112. Bohlen's remarks are found in a memo to Howland Sargeant, 6 June 1952, in file "Memoranda 1952," Box 5, RG 59, Records of the Department of State, Records of Charles E. Bohlen, Memoranda 1942–1952, NA II.

113. Soon after the North Korean attack, the Truman administration itself began to explore the potential of issuing an ultimatum along Dulles's lines. Several drafts of an NSC Senior Staff statement led nowhere and apparently discussion was dropped. See the final draft "Basic Issue on the Use of U.S. Armed Forces to Counter Further Soviet or Satellite Aggression," 5 April 1951, in *Declassified Documents Catalogue* vol. XVIII, no. 3, May–June 1992, fiche 109, document 1503.

114. Bohlen to Sargeant, 6 June 1952.

115. See PSB D-31 in File Folder PSB D-31, Box 5, PSB Working Files: 1951–1953, Executive Secretariat, RG 59, Records of the Department of State, NA II.

116. PSB D-31, ibid.

117. Ibid.

118. Ibid.

119. Ibid.

120. Memoranda of discussion from George Morgan to PSB staff, 5 August 1952, in file "Drafts of National Psychological Strategy #1 [1 of 2]," Box 14, SMOF-PSB 091.411–091.412.

121. See memo, Nitze to Bruce, 26 August 1952, in file "Political and Psychological Warfare," Box 11a, in RG 59, Records of the Department of State, Records of the Policy Planning Staff, 1947–1953, NA II.

122. Allen memo, 12 August 1952, file 014.3 "Social Science Research Report [1 of 2]," Box 1, SMOF-PSB Files, HSTL.

123. Putnam memo, "Critique of Stevens Paper," 18 August 1952, File 091.411 Drafts of National Strategy Papers #1 [1 of 2], SMOF-PSB 091.411–091.412.

124. Taylor to George Morgan, n.d., in ibid.

125. Letter, Barnes to Gray, 11 January 1952, File "President Truman PSB 1952 (1)," Box 3, Gordon Gray Papers 1946–1976, DDEL.

126. Ibid.

127. Letter, Gray to Barnes, 5 March 1952, in ibid.

128. Letter, Barnes to Gray, 2 September 1952, in ibid.

129. Letter, Barnes to Gray, 15 May 1952, in ibid. See Staff Conference of the Director of Central Intelligence, 27 October 1952, in Warner, *CIA under Harry Truman*, 469.

130. "Report to the President," President Truman File, Box 3, PSB Series 1952 (1), Gordon Gray Papers, 1946–1976, DDEL.

131. Letter, Gray to Wallace Carroll, 16 April 1952, in ibid.

132. Letter, Carroll to Gray, 14 April 1952, in ibid.

133. Ibid.

134. Letter, Gray to Dulles, 16 June 1952, in ibid.

135. Memo by Dr. Raymond Allen for the Psychological Strategy Board, "Procedure for Handling 10/5 Matters in PSB," 14 February 1952, File Folder 091.411 Legislative Background on 10/5, SMOF-PSB, Box 13, HSTL.

136. "Briefing to the Psychological Strategy Board on Some 10/5 Problems by the Chairman of the 10/5 Panel," 7 May 1952, in File Folder 091.411 Responsibilities and Precedents Under 10/5, in SMOF-PSB, Box 13, HSTL.

137. See Barnes's "Aide Memoire for a Critique of the Revision of NSC 68 and NSC 114," delivered to Charles Bohlen on 7 July 1952, in File Folder Central Correspondences, 1952–1955, Box 9, RG 59, Records of the Department of State, Records of Charles Bohlen, NA II.

138. Minutes of the Meeting of the Psychological Strategy Board, 8 May 1952, in *Declassified Documents Catalogue* vol. XVII, no. 4, July–August 1991, fiche 211, document 2271.
139. Ibid.
140. Ibid.
141. Memo to C. Tracy Barnes, author censored, 18 August 1952, in *Declassified Documents Catalogue* vol. XVII, no. 4, fiche 215, document 2321. See also "Draft of Proposed Program and Project Clearance Procedure," n.d., *Declassified Documents Catalogue* vol. XVII, no. 1, January–February 1991, fiche 54, document 543. Gerald Miller, "Office of Policy Coordination, 1948–1952," http://www.foia.ucia.gov (search FOIA requests: covert operations).
142. Memo to Barnes, 18 August 1952. See also Miller, "Office of Policy Coordination, 1948–1952," who points out that the review by the "Murder Board" allowed Smith to reduce the covert operations budget by one-third.
143. See "The Vulnerability of the Soviet Union and Its European Satellites to Political Warfare," in File Russia (2), Box 62, White House Central Files, Confidential File, DDEL.
144. Memorandum from Assistant Secretary of State Edward Barrett to Under Secretary of State James Webb, entitled "PSB Agenda Item No. 4A-Plan Cancellation," 20 December 1951, in file "PSB D-24," Box 4, PSB Working Files 1951–1953, Executive Secretariat, RG 59, Records of the Department of State, NA II.
145. "Vulnerability of the Soviet Union."

Chapter Four

1. See Walter Hixson, *Parting the Curtain: Propaganda, Culture, and the Cold War: 1945–1961* (New York: St. Martin's Press, 1997), 87–119.
2. See "Review of Basic National Security Policy," 6 February 1953, in *FRUS*: vol. II, 1952–1954, 223–231.
3. Ibid., 231.
4. Eisenhower established the Jackson committee on 24 January 1953 to review U.S. information programs. The document is located in *FRUS*: vol. II, part II, 1952–1954, 1795–1876.
5. On Jackson's career see Burton Hersh, *The Old Boys: The American Elite and the Origins of the CIA* (New York: Scribner's, 1992), 189.
6. Jackson committee report in ibid.
7. See chapter three for their views on the outcome of psychological efforts during late 1952.
8. The irony of this criticism, exactly the same as those Charles Bohlen and the Policy Planning Staff leveled at the foreign-policy pronouncements of the Eisenhower campaign, is stunning.
9. Ibid., 1799. Given the large role these gentlemen played in formulating the more aggressive elements of the Truman administration psychological strategy, this indictment is somewhat inexplicable. They were the ones who initially called for such efforts and furthermore were the most resistant to Charles Bohlen's efforts to restrain American activities in this field.
10. "Report to the President," President Truman File, Box 3, PSB Series 1952 (1), Gordon Gray Papers, 1946–1976, Dwight D. Eisenhower Library (DDEL).
11. See Klaus Larres, "Eisenhower and the First Forty Days after Stalin's Death: The Incompatibility of *Détente* and Political Warfare," *Diplomacy and Statecraft* 6, no. 2 (July 1995): 431–469.
12. James David Marchio, "Rhetoric and Reality: The Eisenhower Administration and Unrest in Eastern Europe, 1953–1959" (Ph.D. dissertation, American University, 1990), 91–101.
13. The possibilities of dramatic change in Soviet policy in the post-Stalin period were discussed as early as 1946 in George Kennan's "long telegram." See chapter one for discussion.
14. See PSB D-24 in File Folder PSB D-24, Box 4, PSB Working Files: 1951–1952, Executive Secretariat Series, RG 59, Records of the Department of State, National Archives II.

15. Emmet J. Hughes, *The Ordeal of Power: A Political Memoir of the Eisenhower Years* (New York: Atheneum, 1963), 101.

16. Bohlen memo, 7 March 1953, File "USSR 1953," Box 23 RG 59, Records of Department of State, Records of the Policy Planning Staff 1947–1953.

17. Bohlen memo, 10 March 1953, ibid.

18. Bohlen memo, 7 March 1953, ibid.

19. Nitze to Dulles, 10 March 1953, ibid.

20. Ibid.

21. SE-39 "Probable Consequences of the Death of Stalin and of the Elevation of Malenkov to Leadership in the USSR," 10 March 1953 file "PSB Plans for Psychological Exploitation of Stalin's Death," Box 1, C. D. Jackson Papers, DDEL.

22. Report by Walt Rostow, "Notes on the Origins of the President's Speech of April 16, 1953," in file "PSB Plans for Psychological Exploitation of Stalin's Death," Box 1, C. D. Jackson Records 1953–1954, DDEL.

23. Ibid.

24. PSB D-40 "Psychological Exploitation of Stalin's Death," 23 April 1953, in file PSB 000.1 USSR #2, Box 8, PSB Central Files, WHO-NSC Staff Papers: 1948–1961, DDEL. See also Edmund Guillon, "Principles for Exploitation of the Situation in the Soviet Union and Follow-up of President Eisenhower's April 16 Speech," 31 July 1953, File "Political and Psychological Warfare, 1951–1953," Box 11a, RG 59, Records of the Department of State, Records of the Policy Planning Staff, 1947–1953, National Archives II.

25. "Report on U.S. Policy for the Exploitation of Soviet Vulnerabilities," 8 June 1954, in File "USSR Report on U.S. Policy for Exploiting Soviet Vulnerabilities, Box 18, White House Office—Office of the National Security Council, Records, NSC Series 1952–1961, Briefing Notes Subseries, DDEL.

26. Ibid.

27. File Folder "PSB D-43" Box 6, PSB Working Files 1951–1953, Executive Secretariat, RG 59, Records of the Department of State, NA II.

28. Memo, Philips to Smith, 15 July 1953, in file folder "Luncheon Meetings," Box 8, PSB Working File: 1951–1953, Executive Secretariat, RG 59, Records of the Department of State, NA II.

29. Guillon, "Principles for Exploitation of the Situation in the Soviet Union and Follow-up of President Eisenhower's April 16 Speech."

30. Letter to John Foster Dulles from Jackson, 10 March 1953, File Folder Time Inc. File—Stalin's Death Speeches, Text, Comments, Box 85, C. D. Jackson Papers, 1931–1967.

31. Ibid.

32. "Notes on the Origins of the President's Speech of April 16, 1953," in file "PSB Plans for Psychological Exploitation of Stalin's Death," Box 1, C. D. Jackson Records 1953–1954, DDEL. Max Millikan was a former CIA official who was then a professor of economics at MIT.

33. Ibid. Rostow should not have been too surprised since Kennan had begun to publicly criticize containment. According to John Ferguson, in a presentation given in London Kennan stated that "he did not believe that containment was enough," and was for the first time speaking publicly since "he did not want to land in the campaign." See report to Paul Nitze, file "Europe 1952–1953," Box 29, RG 59, Records of the Department of State, Records of the Policy Planning Staff, 1947–1953, Country and Area Files, National Archives II.

34. "Notes on the Origins of the President's Speech of April 16, 1953," ibid.

35. Ibid.

36. Ibid.

37. Ibid.

38. Ibid.

39. Memo from Smith to acting PSB director George Morgan, 10 March 1953, in *FRUS*: vol. VIII, 1952–1954, 1111–1113.

40. Ibid.

41. Letter from Jackson to Dulles, 10 March 1953, in file "PSB Plans for Psychological Exploitation of Stalin's Death," Box 1, C. D. Jackson Records 1953–1954, DDEL.

42. NSC meeting, 11 March 1953 in Box 4, Eisenhower Papers, Ann Whitman File, 1953–1961, NSC Series, DDEL.

43. Ibid.

44. Ibid.

45. Ibid.

46. Eisenhower argued that Stalin while the leader of the USSR ruled as a member of a committee, not as an undisputed dictator; therefore, the ascension of Malenkov did not represent a sudden shift of power. Ibid.

47. This idea was from a letter Eisenhower received from a friend. Ibid.

48. See "The Chance for Peace" in *FRUS*: vol. VIII, "Eastern Europe and the Soviet Union," 1952–1954, 1147–1155.

49. Ibid.

50. Memo from Carlton Savage to Nitze, 1 April 1953, in ibid., 1138. Many people within the PSB were deeply resentful over the fact that it was Malenkov and not Eisenhower who first called for a four-power meeting, thus making Eisenhower's address a response to Malenkov's gesture and not a grand American initiative. See in particular Charles Norberg's memo to Mallory Browne, "Answering the Malenkov Speech," 16 March 1953, in file PSB 000.1 USSR #2 (4), Box 8, NSC Staff Papers, PSB Central Files, DDEL.

51. Memo, Bohlen to Dulles, 25 April 1953, in *FRUS*: vol. VIII, 1952–1954, 1162–1164.

52. SE-42 "Current Communist Tactics," 24 April 1953, ibid., 1160. See also Allen Dulles's comments at the 139th meeting of the NSC, 8 April 1953, Box 4, Dwight D. Eisenhower Papers, Ann Whitman File, 1953–1961, DDEL.

53. Memo, Bohlen to Dulles, 24 April 1953, ibid., 1156–1159. The PSB concurred with Bohlen's position. See "The Communist Peace Offensive," 25 June 1953, in File "PSB 092 USSR (3), WHO-NSC Staff Papers 1948–1961, PSB Central Files Series, DDEL. See also memorandum of discussion by Arthur Cox to Horace Craig, 3-26-53, in file PSB 000.1 USSR #2 (5), Box 8, NSC Staff Papers, PSB Central Files. Cox describes a conversation he had with Mose Harvey, chief of the Division of Research, USSR and Eastern Europe, who saw no possibility that Malenkov's soft approach signaled a détente with the West.

54. This did not mean that the Eisenhower administration believed Malenkov had successfully ensconced himself as Stalin's successor. Some estimated that Malenkov's tenure as leader of the post-Stalin coalition would last at most three years, a correct estimate. See in particular William Morgan to Horace Craig, "Malenkov as Stalin's Successor," 4 March 1953, in File PSB 000.1 USSR #1 (2), Box 8, NSC Staff Files, PSB Central Files, DDEL.

55. Marchio, "Rhetoric and Reality," 104–105. See also Allen Dulles's report at the 150th Meeting of the NSC, Box 4, Dwight D. Eisenhower Papers, Ann Whitman File, NSC Series, 1953–1961, DDEL.

56. Ibid.

57. 151st Meeting of the NSC, 6/25/53, Box 4, Dwight D. Eisenhower Papers, Ann Whitman File, NSC Series, 1953–1961, DDEL.

58. NSC 158 "United States Objectives and Actions to Exploit the Unrest in the Satellite States," File "President's Papers 1953 (5)," Box 1, WHO-OSANSA Special Assistant Series, Presidential Subseries, DDEL. The document is also located in an article written by Christian Ostermann of the National Security Archive entitled "Implementing 'Roll-Back': NSC 158," *SHAFR Newsletter* 27, no. 3 (September 1996). I would like to thank Christian Ostermann for bringing this article to my attention.

59. Military units composed of Soviet bloc refugees.

60. This position was included at the behest of John Foster Dulles at the 25 June Meeting. See 151st NSC Meeting.

61. Ibid. In the original document "stimulating" was misspelled as "simulating" with a handwritten addendum "(SIC)" attached next to the word.

62. 150th Meeting of the NSC, 6/25/53, Box 4, Dwight D. Eisenhower Papers, Ann Whitman File, NSC Series, 1953–1961, DDEL. See also Christian Ostermann, "The United States,

the East German Uprising of 1953, and the Limits of Rollback," Working Paper No. 11, Cold War International History Project, Woodrow Wilson International Center for Scholars, December 1994.

63. This distinction was made by Robert Cutler in a memo to Under Secretary of State Smith, 24 November 1953, in File: Special Assistant (Cutler) Memoranda 1953 (5), WHO-NSC Staff Papers: 1948–1961, Executive Secretaries Subject file, DDEL.

64. "Terms of Reference for Working Group on USSR and Soviet Satellites in Eastern Europe," File OCB 091.4 Eastern Europe File #(2), WHO-NSC Staff Papers: 1948–1961, OCB Central Files, DDEL.

65. A memorandum for the record by Robert Cutler reads "Upon the President's direction and as a matter of urgency, the alternatives outlined in the attachment will be explored and presented to the National Security Council." This seems to indicate that Eisenhower and his national security advisor arrived at the three alternatives without input, at least initially, from the National Security Council. See *FRUS*: vol. II, "National Security," 1952–1954, 323–326. On this point and the Solarium project as a whole see Richard Immerman's "Confessions of an Eisenhower Revisionist: An Agonizing Reappraisal," *Diplomatic History* 14, no. 3 (Summer 1990): 319–342, especially 337. According to Immerman the participants found these restrictions very frustrating.

66. Memorandum for the Record By Robert Cutler, 15 May 1953, in *FRUS*: vol. II, "National Security," 1952–1954, 327–328.

67. Ibid. Cutler still continued to characterize the Truman policy as "defensive," although his work on the Jackson committee report showed clearly that he knew otherwise.

68. Dulles further argued that the USSR "is already overextended and represents tyrannical rule over unwilling peoples. If we keep our pressures on, psychological and otherwise, we may either force a collapse of the Kremlin regime or else transform the Soviet orbit from a union of satellites dedicated to aggression, into a coalition for defense only." See Memorandum of Discussion at a Special Meeting of the National Security Council, March 31, 1953, in *FRUS*: vol. II, 1952–1954, 267.

69. "Project Solarium: Principal Points Made by JFD," file "Project Solarium (3)," Box 15, WHO-NSC Staff Papers 1948–1961, Executive Secretary's Subject File, DDEL.

70. Ibid.

71. Ibid.

72. Ibid.

73. "Paper Prepared by the Directing Panel of Project Solarium," 1 June 1953, in *FRUS*: vol. II, 1952–1954, 360–366.

74. "Memorandum by the President to the Secretary of State," 20 May 1953, in *FRUS*: vol. II, 349–354. Given the unceremonious nature of his departure from the Foreign Service, and C. D. Jackson's inability to convince Dulles to bring Kennan back into the State Department for fear of a significant congressional backlash, it is surprising that Kennan was chosen to be a task force chairman. One wonders if Jackson may have used his influence with Eisenhower to secure the position.

75. For Kennan's view of the Solarium project see his *Memoirs, 1950–1963* (Boston: Little, Brown & Co., 1972), 181–182. In addition to Kennan, Task Force A included C. Tyler Wood, former associate director of the Mutual Security Agency; Rear Admiral H. Page Smith, former director of the Office of Military Affairs, Department of Defense; Colonel George A. Lincoln; Colonel Charles H. Bonesteel, assistant for National Security Council affairs, Department of Defense, and Defense representative on the NSC Planning Board after June 1953; Captain H. E. Sears, USN; and General John Maury Jr.

76. Robert Bowie and Richard Immerman contend that Task Force A represented containment. See *Waging Peace: How Eisenhower Shaped an Enduring Cold War Strategy* (New York: Oxford University Press, 1998), 128–131. For a contrary position see Marc Trachtenberg, "A 'Wasting Asset': American Strategy and the Shifting Nuclear Balance of Power, 1949–1954," *International Security* 13, no. 3 (Winter 1988/89): 36.

77. See Task Force report A, File Folder Task Force report (3), NSC Series-Subject Subseries, Box 9: Project Solarium, White House Office: Office of the Special Assistant for Na-

tional Security Affairs (hereafter WHO-OSANSA) Records, 1952–1961, DDEL, p. 1. Unless otherwise noted all task force report references will be derived from this task force report.

78. Task Force report A, 2.

79. Task Force report A, 18.

80. Task Force report A, 10. This was also the conclusion of an extensive study prepared by an interdepartmental working group working at the same time as the Solarium project. See "U.S. Prestige Report," 2 September 1953, in File "U.S. Prestige File," Box 8, WHO-NSC Staff Papers: 1948–1961, OCB Secretarial Series, DDEL.

81. Task Force report A, 15.

82. Task Force report A, 13.

83. Task Force report A, 15–16.

84. Ibid.

85. Ibid.

86. Task Force report A, 129.

87. Task Force report A, 130.

88. Task Force report A, 86.

89. The task force believed that once legitimate occupation rights were extinguished in Germany and Austria, the provisions in the Potsdam agreement allowing military forces in neighboring countries (Poland, Hungary, and Romania) in order to maintain lines of communication with the Soviet Union would be annulled, possibly leading to the removal of Soviet forces from these countries.

90. Task Force report A, 130–131.

91. Task Force report A, 131.

92. Task Force report A, 132.

93. Ibid.

94. Task Force C was chaired by Vice Admiral R. L. Conolly and included Lieutenant General Lyman L. Lemnitzer, George F. Reinhardt, who headed the State Department's Eastern Europe desk during the Truman administration, Kilbourne Johnston, Colonel Andrew J. Goodpaster, Leslie Brady, and Colonel Harold K. Johnson.

95. Task Force report of Project Solarium, File Folder Task Force report "C" (1), NSC Series: Subject Subseries, Box 9: Project Solarium, WHO-OSANSA, 1952–1961, DDEL, 1.

96. Ibid. The task force's statement of purpose clearly bears Dulles's imprint.

97. Task Force report C, 3.

98. Task Force report C, 106–111.

99. This was a limitation imposed upon Task Force A by Eisenhower and Cutler.

100. "Synopsis of Project Solarium" prepared by John Campbell of the S/P, 8-11-53, in File "Project Solarium (4)," Box 15, WHO-OSANSA, NSC Staff Reports, 1948–1961, Executive Secretary's Subject File, DDEL.

101. Task Force report C, 4.

102. Task Force report C, 5.

103. Task Force report C, 6.

104. Task Force report C, 8.

105. Ibid.

106. Ibid. Again, the overthrow of the Soviet regime is not evident in the original task force report and comes from the synopsis discussed above.

107. Task Force C chairman Admiral Conolly noted that "the military build-up of the program should be predicated on the assumption that this program can be completed in 10 years but at the end of that time, success can be foreseen in the not too distant future. On the other hand, the time might be less since it is possible that after the first set-backs, Soviet power might become demoralized and rapidly collapse." *FRUS*: vol. II, "National Security," 393.

108. Task Force report A, 28–32.

109. *FRUS*: vol. II, 1952–1954, "National Security," 393.

110. See "Report on U.S. Policy for the Exploitation of Soviet Vulnerabilities, 8 June 1954, in Box 18, Office of the Special Assistant for National Security Affairs, NSC Series, Briefing Notes Subseries, DDEL.

111. Ibid.
112. Ibid.
113. Ibid.
114. Memorandum of Discussion of the 157th Meeting of the National Security Council, 30 July 1953, in *FRUS*: vol. II, 1952–1954, 438. The committee consisted of Everett Gleason (chairman); Robert Bowie, Policy Planning Staff director; Frank Nash, assistant secretary of state for international security affairs; Robert Amory, assistant directory of the Office of Research and Reports, CIA; and Air Force Major General John Gerhart. General Lemnitzer (from Task Force C), Major General McCormack (Task Force B), and Colonel Bonesteel (Task Force A) represented the task forces. See "Overall Comments on Policy Paper Sept. 18/53, of Solarium Special Committee," 20 September 1953, in File "Cutler Memoranda 1953 (7)," Box 17, WHO-OSANSA, Special Assistant Series, NSC Staff Papers 1948–1961, Executive Secretary's Subject File, DDEL.
115. "Points for Consideration in Drafting New Policy," Cutler Memorandum, 31 July 1953, in *FRUS*: vol. II, 1952–1954, 440–441.
116. See Dulles to Cutler, on 1 August 1953, in File "Review of Basic National Security Policy, 1953, June–August," Box 66, RG 59, Records of the Department of State, Records of the Policy Planning Staff, 1947–1953, National Archives II.
117. Ibid.
118. "Report on U.S. Policy for the Exploitation of Soviet Vulnerabilities."
119. "Overall Comments on Policy Paper of Solarium Special Committee," 20 Sept. 1953, ibid. Averell Harriman was a favorite target of criticism for the disgruntled Truman administration PSB officials who opposed the State Department's usurpation of the psychological-warfare program.
120. Ibid.
121. "Report on United States Policy towards the Exploitation of Soviet Vulnerabilities," 8 June 1954, ibid.
122. NSC 162 "Review of Basic National Security Policy," 30 September 1953, in *FRUS*: vol. II, 1952–1954, 491.
123. Ibid., 493.
124. Ibid.
125. Ibid.
126. Ibid., 513. A footnote in the source text indicates that this position represented the views of the State Department and the CIA.
127. Ibid., 513–514. This comment is in reference to discussion within the Solarium review that the United States could use military force to roll back Soviet power in Albania and Chinese power in Hainan.
128. Memorandum of Discussion at the 165th meeting of the National Security Council, 7 October 1953, in *FRUS*: vol. II, 1952–1954, 529.
129. Ibid.
130. Ibid., 514.
131. Memorandum of Discussion at the 165th meeting of the National Security Council, 7 October 1953, in *FRUS*: vol. II, 1952–1954, 529. Robert Bowie claims that these criticisms were a result of Cutler's incorrect presentation of side A. See *Waging Peace*, 162–163.
132. Ibid.
133. Ibid., 529–530.
134. Ibid.
135. Ibid., 531.
136. NSC 162/2 "Basic National Security Policy," 30 October 1953, in *FRUS*: vol. II, 1952–1954, 577–597.
137. Statement made by John Foster Dulles at the special NSC meeting held on 31 March 1953, in *FRUS*: vol. II, 1952–1954, 276–268.
138. Ibid., 595.
139. Ibid.
140. Ibid.

141. Memo, Bohlen to Dulles, 24 April 1953, in *FRUS*: vol. VIII, 1952–1954, 1156–1159.
142. Special Estimate 42: "Special Communist Tactics," 24 April 1953, in ibid., 1160–1162.
143. Ibid.
144. Memo, Beam to Robert Bowie, 23 September 1953, in File "USSR: 1953" Box 23, RG 59, Records of Department of State, Records of Policy Planning Staff, Country Files, National Archives II.
145. "Problem of Soviet-Western Accommodation" no author, no date, in File "USSR 1953" Box 23, RG 59, Records of Department of State, Records of Policy Planning Staff, 1947–1953, Country Files, National Archives II.
146. Owen to Bowie, "Alternative U.S. Policies," 9 Sept. 1953, in File "Review of Basic National Security Policy," NSC 153–162: Sept.–Dec. 1953, Box 65, RG 59, Records of Department of State, Records of Policy Planning Staff, 1947–1953, National Archives II.
147. Ibid.
148. Ibid. It seems that the Eisenhower administration did give serious thought to the use of paramilitary and military force against Albania and Hainan, much as it would do in Guatemala and Iran. Owen mentions SE-34 as intelligence guidance concerning U.S. military occupation of Albania. U.S. intelligence studied the impact of a U.S. attack on Hainan Island as well. See SE-50 "Probable Reactions to a Chinese Nationalist Retaking of Hainan with Direct United States Air and Naval Participation," in File "Project Solarium (3)," WHO-OSANSA, NSC Staff Papers 1948–1961, Executive Secretary's Subject File, DDEL.
149. Ibid. Note the great similarity between Owen's conclusions and Bohlen's "doctrine of rational hope" from 1952.
150. Memorandum by the Secretary of State, 6 September 1953, in *FRUS*: vol. II, 1952–1954, 457–460.
151. Memorandum by the President to the Secretary of State, 8 September 1953, in *FRUS*: vol. II, 1952–1954, 460–464.
152. Ibid.
153. Memo, Louis Fuller to Bowie, "Review of Attached NSC Draft Paper on Satellite Policy," 26 May 1953, in "Eastern Europe File," Box 29, RG 59, Records of Department of State, Records of Policy Planning Staff, 1947–1953, National Archives II. A memo from Bohlen to Walworth Barbour of the Eastern Europe desk dated 7 February 1953 indicates that a revision of NSC 58/2 was under way before Eisenhower's inauguration. See file "Memoranda, 1953," Box 5, RG 59, Records of the Department of State, Records of Charles Bohlen, Memoranda 1942–1952, National Archives II.
154. See the discussion in chapter one.
155. Unfortunately, Bowie discusses neither this study nor the administration's Eastern European policy in *Waging Peace*.
156. Memo, Louis Fuller to Bowie, "Review of Attached NSC Draft Paper on Satellite Policy," 26 May 1953, in "Eastern Europe File," Box 29, RG 59, Records of Department of State, Records of Policy Planning Staff, 1947–1953, National Archives II.
157. Cover memo from Elmer Staats on OCB 16 "National Operations Plan—USSR and Satellites," File Folder "OCB 091.4 Eastern Europe File #(1)," Oct. 1953–Jan. 1954, Box 66, WHO-NSC Staff Papers: 1948–1961, OCB Central Files, DDEL.
158. The Foreign Operations Administration replaced the Mutual Security Administration.
159. "Establishing the Operations Coordinating Board," 3 Sept. 1953, file "OCB [vol. I] (1)," Box 21, WHO-OSS Records, 1952–1961, Subject Series, Alphabetical Subseries, DDEL. While differences in the mandates between the two agencies certainly existed, for most PSB officials the most significant change was remembering to cross out PSB and replace it with OCB when composing an official document. Not only did the OCB use PSB stationery, it also took over the PSB headquarters at 708 Jackson Place.
160. Cutler to Smith, 24 November 1953, in File "Special Assistant (Cutler)—Memoranda 1953 (5)," Box 17, WHO-NSC Staff Papers: 1948–1961, Executive Secretary's Subject file, DDEL.
161. No records of the meeting have been located; however, no further drafts of a document combine an analysis of Eastern Europe and the Soviet Union whereas evidence exists

pointing to an attempt to create a draft paper focusing solely on Soviet vulnerabilities. See memo from Elmer Staats to the Board Assistants, 28 December 1953, in File "OCB 091.4 Eastern Europe file #(2)," Box 66, WHO-NSC Staff Papers: 1948–1961, OCB Central Files, DDEL.

162. NSC 174 "United States Policy toward the Soviet Satellites in Eastern Europe," in *FRUS*: vol. VIII, "Eastern Europe," 1952–1954, 114.

163. Ibid.

164. Ibid., 120. On this problem, see Memorandum from Edward O'Connor of OCB Directorate of Operations to Elmer Staats, 2 June 1954, in *Declassified Documents Catalogue* vol. XX, No. 3, May–June 1994, fiche 149, document 1788.

165. "Suggested Procedures for the Working Group on Coordination of NSC 174 and Related Matters Concerning the Satellites and USSR," 11 February 1954, in File "091.4 Eastern Europe File # (2)," Box 66, WHO-NSC Staff Papers: 1948–1961, OCB Central Files, DDEL.

166. NSC 140/1 "Summary Evaluation of the Net Capability of the USSR to Inflict Direct Injury on the United States up to July 1, 1955—Report of the Special Evaluation Subcommittee," in *FRUS*: vol. II, "National Security," 1952–1954, 328–349. See also Report from the Special Evaluation Committee to the Vice Chief of Naval Operations, 24 March 1953, in File "NSC 140: USSR Net Capability (1)," Box 13, WHO-NSC Staff Papers: 1948–1961, Executive Secretary's Subject File, DDEL.

167. NSC 140/1, ibid.

168. 148th meeting of the NSC, 6/18/95, Box 4, DDE Papers, Ann Whitman File, 1953–1961, NSC Series.

169. See Richard Rhodes, *Dark Sun: The Making of the Hydrogen Bomb* (New York: Simon and Schuster, 1995), 524.

170. 160th Meeting of the NSC, 8/25/53.

171. By way of comparison, the fireball of the ten kiloton atomic bomb that destroyed Nagasaki measured eight hundred yards (roughly the size of midtown Manhattan); the fireball of the 1952 Mike test measured three *miles*—capable of annihilating all five boroughs of New York City; Newark, New Jersey; and devastating much of suburban New York. See "Meeting the Threat of Surprise Attack," Report of the Killian Commission, in *The Development of American Strategic Thought: Basic Documents of the Eisenhower and Kennedy Periods 1953–1959*, Marc Trachtenberg, ed. (New York: Garland Publishing, 1988), overlay p. 338.

172. See Trachtenberg, *A Constructed Peace: The Making of the European Settlement: 1945–1953* (Princeton: Princeton University Press, 1999), particularly chapter five.

173. Robert C. Sprague, Report to the NSC, 16 June 1955, in *Declassified Documents Catalogue* vol. XXIII, no. 2, March–April 1997, fiche 75, document 1052.

174. See for instance, Summary of Meeting of the Ad Hoc Committee on Armaments and American Policy and the Senior Staff of the National Security Council, 16 March 1953, in *FRUS*: vol. II, 1952–1954, 1136–1137. Although these figures came from a source prepared a year after the Soviet "Joe-4" detonation, they correspond with contemporary estimates.

175. 163rd Meeting of the NSC, 24 September 1953, in *Declassified Documents Catalogue* vol. XXIII, no. 2, March–April 1997, fiche 75, document 1049. This portion, section one of the NSC meeting, was declassified in late 1999.

176. See Memo to Dulles, 8 September 1953, in *FRUS*: vol. II, 1952–1954, p. 461. As we shall see later in this section, this was not a momentary consideration, as only a year later Eisenhower would establish a committee to prepare a report on the circumstances that might force such an action.

177. See Memorandum by Cutler to Secretary of State, 3 September 1953, in *FRUS*: vol. II, "National Security," 1952–1954, 455–457. See also Memorandum by President to Secretary of State, 8 September 1953, in ibid., 460–463.

178. Report to the NSC on Continental Defense, 16 June 1955, in *Declassified Documents Catalogue* vol. XXIII, no. 2, March–April 1997, fiche 75, document 1052.

179. Both Albert Wohlstetter's report and the Killian Commission Report can be found in Marc Trachtenberg, ed., *The Development of American Strategic Thought: Writings on Strategy, 1952–1960* (New York: Garland Press, 1988).

180. As Marc Trachtenberg has shown, Eisenhower never did come to have confidence in

deterrence and continued to question whether the United States should launch a preventive war as late as 1960. See his "A 'Wasting Asset'. "

181. Memorandum of Discussion at the 190th Meeting of the National Security Council, 25 March 1954, in *FRUS*: vol. II, 1952–1954, 639.

182. Ibid., 640.

183. Ibid., 641.

184. Ibid.

185. NSC 5422 "Tentative Guidelines under NSC 162/2 for FY 1956," 14 June 1954, in *FRUS*: vol. II, 1952–1954, 655.

186. See NSC 5408 "Continental Defense," 11 February 1954, in *FRUS*: vol. II, 1952–1954, 611–624.

187. Memorandum by the Special Assistant to the Secretary of State for Intelligence to the Acting Secretary of State, 28 April 1954, in *FRUS*: vol. II, 1952–1954, 646–647.

188. Basic National Security Policy (Suggestions of the Secretary of State), 15 November 1954, in *FRUS*: vol. II, 1952–1954, 774–775.

189. Memorandum of Discussion of the 225th Meeting of the National Security Council, 24 November 1954, in *FRUS*: vol. II, 1952–1954, 791.

190. See *FRUS*: vol. XIX, 1955–1957, 1, fn. 1.

191. See Trachtenberg, "A 'Wasting Asset'." For a contrary view see Bowie and Immerman, *Waging Peace*, 205.

192. "Report on U.S. Policy for the Exploitation of Soviet Vulnerabilities," in File: "USSR-Report on U.S. Policy for Exploiting Soviet Vulnerabilities," Box 18, WHO-OSANSA Records, NSC Series 1952–1961, Briefing Notes Subseries, DDEL. These conclusions were supported by a separate study prepared by the NSC 174 Working Group. See "Memorandum for the Operations Coordinating Board List of Agreed Courses of Action for the Period 7/1/54–12/31/54 to Implement NSC 174," 25 August 1954, in *Declassified Documents Catalogue* vol. XIX, no. 1, January–February 1993, fiche 51, document 575.

193. Ibid. PSB D-31 was dropped as effective policy by the OCB and not replaced.

194. Ibid.

195. "The Vulnerabilities of the European Satellites," 21 September 1954, File Folder OCB 091.411: Europe (File #2) (6), WHO-OSANSA, NSC Papers, 1948–1961, DDEL.

196. Ibid.

197. "Estimate of the Situation with Respect to the Major European Satellites," 5 November 1954, in File Folder OCB 091.411: Europe, (File #2) (8), WHO-OSANSA, NSC Papers, 1948–1961, DDEL. Two annexes discussing potential U.S. action in East Germany and Czechoslovakia remain classified.

198. "Analysis of the Situation with Respect to Possible Detachment of a Major European Satellite," 5 January 1955, File Folder: OCB 091.411, Eastern Europe (File #3) (4) December 1954–May 1955, WHO-NSA Staff Files: Papers 1948–1961, OCB Central Files Series, Box 67, DDEL. Although the final draft was completed on 5 January 1955, the NSC had available the first draft dated 10 December 1954.

199. For Allen Dulles's statement see 134th meeting of the NSC 25 February 1953, in *FRUS*: vol. II, "Atomic Energy; Arms Regulation," 1111. Dulles's full quote reads: "This [enoughness] he explained as the problem which would exist when the Soviet Union possessed a stockpile sufficient to deal the United States a damaging blow, regardless of the fact that the United States might itself possess a much larger stockpile of weapons."

200. See NSC 174 Special Study "Estimate of the Situation with Respect to the Major European Satellites," 5 November 1954, in File Folder OCB 091.411: Europe (File #2) (6), WHO-OSANSA, NSC Papers, 1948–1961, DDEL.

201. The following discussion comes from the Memorandum of Discussion at the 229th Meeting of the National Security Council, 21 December 1954, in *FRUS*: vol. II, 1952–1954, 832–844.

202. Ibid., 833.

203. Ibid., 833–834.

204. Ibid., 834–835.
205. Ibid., 836.
206. Ibid., 837.
207. Ibid., 839–840.
208. Memorandum of Discussion at the 230th Meeting of the National Security Council, 5 January 1955, in *FRUS*: vol. XIX, 1955–1957, 9–24. NSC 5501 "Basic National Security Policy" in ibid., 24–38.
209. Once again we see the influence of the Soviet Vulnerabilities Project by Walt Rostow.
210. NSC 20/1 "U.S. Objectives with Respect to Russia" in File Folder NSC Meetings, 8-19-48, Box 204, PSF-NSC Meetings 14–27, HSTL.
211. Or, as Kennan remarked, "If, however, analogous situations could again be created, and the Soviet leaders compelled to recognize their reality . . . then they might have a permanent modifying effect on the outlook and habits of Soviet power." Ibid.
212. NSC 5505/1 "Exploitation of Soviet and European Satellite Vulnerabilities," in *Declassified Documents Catalogue* vol. XVIII, no. 1, January–February 1992, fiche 24, document 311. An editorial note in *Foreign Relations of the United States* states that NSC 5505 was based upon a study chaired by Max Millikan of the Center for International Studies at MIT.
213. Ibid., 5.
214. Minutes of 234th NSC meeting, 27 January 1955, in Box 6, Dwight D. Eisenhower Papers, Ann Whitman File, 1953–1961, DDEL.
215. Ibid.
216. Ibid.
217. Memo from Rockefeller to Chairman of OCB "Review of NSC Policy on Soviet European Satellites (NSC 174 and NSC 5505)," 30 September 1955, in File "NSC 174, #4" Box 1, WHO-NSC Staff Papers 1948–1961, Planning Coordination Group Series, DDEL.
218. NSC 5412/2 "National Security Council Directive on Covert Operations," File Folder 1955 (1), WHO-OSANSA, Records 1952–1961, Special Assistants Series-Presidential Subseries, Box 2, DDEL.
219. NSC 10/5 "Scope and Pace of Covert Operations," File Folder: Subject File-NSC Memo Approvals-10/2, NSC-Memo Approvals, PSF-Subject File, Box 143, HSTL.
220. See NSC 5602/1, the Eisenhower administration's basic national security policy for 1956. The document charged that "The United States is now capable of inflicting massive nuclear damage on the USSR, and will acquire by about mid-1956 the capability to mount a decisive nuclear strike against the USSR. The United States will have a marked net superiority in nuclear striking power from then until some time in 1958. During that year, and thereafter, the USSR will have almost certainly developed and maintained the net capability to strike a crippling blow at the United States, but the United States should still be able to inflict equal or greater damage on the USSR provided that it takes adequate steps to protect and to continue the development of its effective retaliatory power." Annex to NSC 5602/1 in Trachtenberg, ed., *The Development of American Strategic Thought: Basic Documents from the Eisenhower and Kennedy Periods*, 145.
221. "Report of the Quantico Vulnerabilities Panel," in Box 17, WHO-NSC Staff Papers: 1948–1961, NSC Registry Series, 1947–1961, DDEL.
222. Ibid.
223. "Meeting the Threat of Surprise Attack," 14 February 1955, in *FRUS*: Volume XIX, 1955–1957, 41–67, quote p. 43.
224. The report is published in full in Trachtenberg, ed., *The Development of American Strategic Thought: Writings on Strategy 1952–1960*, vol. 1, 163–587.
225. Jackson to Luce, 21 June 1955, Time Inc. File log 1955, Box 56, C. D. Jackson: Papers, 1934–1967, DDEL.
226. Memo "Recollections of the Geneva Summit," July 1955, file Correspondence and Related Material, 1954–1957, Box 2, Livingston T. Merchant Papers, Mudd Library, Princeton University.
227. On the potentially negative impact of the Geneva Summit on U.S. efforts in Eastern

Europe see the OCB report "Psychological Implications of Geneva for U.S. Information Programs," 31 August 1955, in *FRUS*: vol. XXV, 1955–1957, 72.

228. Adam Ulam, *The Communists: The Story of Power and Lost Illusions, 1948–1991* (New York: Charles Scribner's Sons, 1992), 125–128.

229. 280th Meeting of the NSC, 22 March 1956, Box 7, Ann Whitman File, 1953–1961, NSC Series, DDEL.

230. *Declassified Documents Catalogue* vol. XVIII, no. 4, July–August 1992, fiche 188, document 2686.

231. NSC 5608/1 in ibid.

232. 296th Meeting of the NSC, 7 September 1956, Box 8, Ann Whitman File, 1953–1961, NSC Series, DDEL.

233. The following account relies upon Adam Ulam's *The Communists*, 137–157. See "New Evidence on Soviet Decision-Making and the 1956 Polish and Hungarian Crises," in *Cold War International History Project Bulletin*, Issues 8–9, Winter 1996/1997.

234. Ibid., 155.

235. Cord Meyer, *Facing Reality: From World Federalism to the CIA* (New York: Harper & Row, 1980), 122.

236. Telegram from Budapest to Secretary of State, No. 200, 31 October 1956, file, Dulles, John Foster, Oct. 1956 (1), Box 6, Dulles-Herter Series, Dwight D. Eisenhower papers as President, DDEL.

237. Bohlen's remarks are found in a memo to Howland Sargeant, 6 June 1952, in file "Memoranda 1952," Box 5, RG 59, Records of the Department of State, Records of Charles E. Bohlen, Memoranda 1942–1952, NA II.

238. 24 May 1958, File Folder NSC 5811, Box 47, RG 273: Records of the NSC, Policy Papers: 5807–5812, National Archives II.

Conclusion

1. See Eduard Mark, "The War Scare of 1946 and Its Consequences," *Diplomatic History* 21, no. 3 (Summer 1997): 383–414. Mark also informed me of his research regarding the 1948 war scare. For an alternative perspective, see Melvyn Leffler, *A Preponderance of Power: National Security, the Truman Administration, and the Cold War* (Stanford: Stanford University Press, 1992), 110–114. Regarding the Soviets' role in the Korean conflict see Kathryn Weathersby, "To Attack, or Not to Attack? Stalin, Kim Il Sung, and the Prelude to War," *Cold War International History Project Bulletin*, Issue 5, Spring 1995.

2. On Kennan's view of concerns regarding democracy see John Lewis Gaddis, *We Now Know: Rethinking Cold War History* (New York: Oxford University Press, 1997), 288–289.

3. "History of the Central Intelligence Agency," in *The Central Intelligence Agency: History and Documents*, William Leary, ed. (Tuscaloosa, Ala.: University of Alabama Press, 1984), 11–115.

4. See Leffler, *Preponderance of Power*, and Trachtenberg's article "A 'Wasting Asset': American Strategy and the Shifting Nuclear Balance, 1949–1954," *International Security* 13, no. 3 (Winter 1988–89): 5–49. See also Trachtenberg's *A Constructed Peace: The Making of the European Settlement, 1945–1963* (Princeton: Princeton University Press, 1999), especially chapter five.

5. See the excellent review of Cold War historiography by J. Samuel Walker entitled "Historians and Cold War Origins: The New Consensus," in Thomas G. Paterson, ed., *Major Problems in American Foreign Policy, Vol. II: Since 1914* (Lexington, Mass.: D. C. Heath and Co., 1984), 315–335.

6. See Robert Pollard's *Economic Security and the Origins of the Cold War, 1945–1950* (New York: Columbia University Press, 1985).

7. See John Lewis Gaddis, *Strategies of Containment: A Critical Appraisal of Postwar American National Security Policy* (New York: Oxford University Press, 1982), 54–81.

8. Ibid., 48.

9. Leffler, *Preponderance of Power*, 491.

10. See in particular Pollard, *Economic Security and the Origins of the Cold War.*

11. Memorandum, Nitze to Acheson, 12 July 1952, in *FRUS*: vol. II, "National Security," 1952–1954, 64.

12. Leary, ed., *Central Intelligence Agency: History and Documents*, 43–44.

13. Ibid. Joyce added the underscore for emphasis. This phrase came directly from NSC 68; see *Containment*, Etzold and Gaddis, ed., 435–436.

14. Hulik memorandum, ibid.

15. Gerald Miller, "Office of Policy Coordination, 1948–1952," http://www.foia.ucia.gov (search FOIA requests: covert operations).

16. Charles Bohlen, "The Possibilities of External Action Against Soviet-Type States," n.d., in file "General Collection 1952–1955," Box 9, RG 59, Records of the Department of State, Records of Charles E. Bohlen, National Archives II.

17. Bohlen, "Possibilities of External Action Against Soviet-Type States," ibid.

18. The four points come from the Project TROY report. See Project TROY file, in Box 33, RG 59, General Records of the Department of State, Records of the S/P, 1947–1953.

19. In 1953 when Stalin did die such operations were in fact attempted. See chapter four for a complete discussion.

20. See in particular David McCullough's Pulitzer Prize–winning biography *Truman* (New York: Simon & Schuster, 1992).

21. Vojtech Mastny argues to the contrary that U.S. activities did indeed have an impact on communist control in Eastern Europe. See *The Cold War and Soviet Insecurity* (New York: Oxford University Press, 1996), 116–121.

22. The most recent example of this criticism can be found in Walter Hixson's *Parting the Curtain: Propaganda, Culture, and the Cold War, 1945–1961* (New York: St. Martin's Press, 1997).

23. NSC 114 "Status and Timing of Current U.S. Programs for National Security," 27 July 1951, file folder NSC Meeting #98, 8/1/51, PSF NSC Meetings Box 214, Meeting 98-103, HSTL.

24. For Allen Dulles's statement see 134th meeting of the NSC 25 February 1953, in *FRUS*: vol. II, "Atomic Energy; Arms Regulation," 1111. Dulles's full quote reads: "This [enoughness] he explained as the problem which would exist when the Soviet Union possessed a stockpile sufficient to deal the United States a damaging blow, regardless of the fact that the United States might itself possess a much larger stockpile of weapons."

List of Primary Sources

Harry S. Truman Library, Independence, Missouri
- Acheson, Dean: Papers, 1931–1971
- Ayers, Eben: Papers, 1908–1953
- Clifford, Clark: Papers, 1946–1952
- Connelly, Matthew J.: Papers, 1945–1953
- Elsey, George: Papers, 1941–1953
- Gray, Gordon: Papers, 1950–1954
- Gray, Gordon, Oral History
- Henderson, Loy W., Oral History
- Hickerson, John D., Oral History
- Hulten, Charles M.: Papers, 1942–1963
- Lock, Edwin A.: Papers, 1941–1953
- Marshall, Charles Burton, Oral History
- Nitze, Paul H., Oral History
- Ohly, John N.: Papers: 1940–1975
- Sargeant, Howland: Papers, 1940–1983
- Souers, Sidney W.: Papers, 1925–1972
- Stohl, Ralph N.: Papers, 1947–1955
- Symington, Stuart: Papers, 1946–1950
- Thayer, Charles W.: Papers, 1920–1968
- Webb, James E.: Papers, 1928–1980
- Truman, Harry S.: Papers, Presidents Secretary File, National Security Council Meetings, 1947–1953
- Truman, Harry S.: Papers, Psychological Strategy Board Files, 1951–1953
- Truman, Harry S.: Papers, Staff Members Office Files

Dwight D. Eisenhower Library, Abilene, Kansas
- Bowie, Robert, Oral History
- Cutler, Robert: Papers, 1952–1956

Primary Sources

Dulles, John Foster: Papers, 1951–1959
Eisenhower, Dwight D.: Papers As President of the United States, 1953–1961, Ann Whitman File
Eisenhower, Dwight D.: Records As President, White House Central Files, 1953–1961, Confidential File
Gray, Gordon, Oral History
Jackson, C. D.: Papers, 1931–1967
Jackson, C. D.: Records, 1953–1954
Smith, Walter Bedell: Papers, 1942–1961
White House Office, Office of the Special Assistant for National Security Affairs (Robert Cutler, Dillon Anderson, and Gordon Gray): Records, 1952–1961
White House Office, National Security Council Staff: Papers 1948–1961
White House Office, Office of the Staff Secretary: Records of Paul T. Carroll, Andrew J. Goodpaster, L. Arthur Minnich, and Christopher H. Russell, 1952–1961
Seeley G. Mudd Library, Princeton University
Dulles, Allen: Papers
Dulles, John Foster: Papers
Forrestal, James V.: Papers
Kennan, George: Papers
Library of Congress, Washington, D.C.
Bohlen, Charles: Papers
Davies, Joseph: Papers
Harriman, W. Averell: Papers
Henderson, Loy: Papers
National Archives of the United States, College Park, Maryland
Record Group 59, General Records of the Department of State
Decimal Files
Papers of Charles E. Bohlen, 1942–1952
Records of the Office of European Affairs, 1934–1947 (John D. Hickerson and H. Freeman Matthews Papers)
Records of the Office of the Executive Secretariat
Memoranda of Conversation with the President, 1949–1952
Memoranda of Under Secretaries Meetings, 1949–1952
Summaries of Secretaries Daily Meetings, 1949–1952
Records of the Policy Planning Staff, 1947–1962
Records Group 263, Records of the Central Intelligence Agency
Records Group 273, Records of the National Security Council
Records Group 218: Records of the Joint Chiefs of Staff and the Central Decimal File 1948–1950
Lilly, Edward: Papers
Department of State: *Foreign Relations of the United States* (Government Printing Office)
FRUS, 1942–1943, Volume I: General, The British Commonwealth, The Far East
FRUS, 1944–1945, Volume I: General, Postwar Economic Policy
FRUS, 1947–1951, Volume I: National Security
FRUS, 1952–1954, Volume II: National Security
FRUS, 1955–1957, Volume XIX: National Security
FRUS, 1950, Volume VIII: The Korean War, parts I and II
FRUS, 1948, Volume III: Western European Security
FRUS, 1949, Volume IV: Western European Security
FRUS, 1950, Volume III: Western European Security
FRUS, 1951, Volume III: Western European Security

FRUS, 1952–1954, Volume V: Western European Security
FRUS, 1948–1951, Volume IV: The Soviet Union
FRUS, 1952–1954, Volume VIII: Eastern Europe, the Soviet Union and the Mediterranean
FRUS, 1955–1957, Volume XXV: Eastern Europe, the Soviet Union and the Mediterranean
Policy Planning Staff Papers, 1947–1950. Ed. Anna Kasten Nelson. 3 Volumes (New York: Garland, 1983)
The Declassified Documents Catalogue, Woodbridge, Conn. Research Publications Inc. Volumes XIII–XVIII

Index

Cornell Studies in Security Affairs

edited by Robert Jervis, Robert J. Art, *and* Stephen M. Walt

Political Institutions and Military Change: Lessons from Peripheral Wars by Deborah D. Avant
Japan Prepares for Total War: The Search for Economic Security, 1919–1941
by Michael A. Barnhart
Flying Blind: The Politics of the U.S. Strategic Bomber Program by Michael E. Brown
Citizens and Soldiers: The Dilemmas of Military Service by Eliot A. Cohen
Military Organization, Complex Machines: Modernization in the U.S. Armed Forces
by Chris C. Demchak
Innovation and the Arms Race: How the United States and the Soviet Union Develop New Military Technologies, by Matthew Evangelista
Guarding the Guardians: Civilian Control of Nuclear Weapons in the United States
by Peter Douglas Feaver
A Substitute for Victory: The Politics of Peacemaking at the Korean Armistice Talks
by Rosemary Foot
The Wrong War: American Policy and the Dimensions of the Korean Conflict, 1950–1953
by Rosemary Foot
The Best Defense: Policy Alternatives for U.S. Nuclear Security from the 1950s to the 1990s
by David Goldfischer
The Soviet Union and the Politics of Nuclear Weapons in Europe, 1969–1987
by Jonathan Haslam
The Meaning of the Nuclear Revolution: Statecraft and the Prospect of Armageddon
by Robert Jervis
Fast Tanks and Heavy Bombers: Innovation in the U.S. Army, 1917–1945
by David E. Johnson
The Vulnerability of Empire by Charles A. Kupchan
Anatomy of Mistrust: U.S.–Soviet Relations during the Cold War by Deborah Welch Larson
Cooperation under Fire: Anglo-German Restraint during World War II by Jeffrey W. Legro
Conventional Deterrence by John J. Mearsheimer
Liddell Hart and the Weight of History by John J. Mearsheimer
Reputation and International Politics by Jonathan Mercer
The Sacred Cause: Civil-Military Conflict over Soviet National Security, 1917–1992
by Thomas M. Nichols
Liberal Peace, Liberal War: American Politics and International Security by John M. Owen IV
Bombing to Win: Air Power and Coercion in War by Robert A. Pape
A Question of Loyalty: Military Manpower in Multiethnic States by Alon Peled
Inadvertent Escalation: Conventional War and Nuclear Risks by Barry R. Posen

The Sources of Military Doctrine: France, Britain, and Germany between the World Wars by Barry Posen
Dilemmas of Appeasement: British Deterrence and Defense, 1934–1937 by Gaines Post, Jr.
Crucible of Beliefs: Learning, Alliances, and World Wars by Dan Reiter
Eisenhower and the Missile Gap by Peter J. Roman
The Domestic Bases of Grand Strategy edited by Richard Rosecrance and Arthur Stein
Societies and Military Power: India and Its Armies by Stephen Peter Rosen
Winning the Next War: Innovation and the Modern Military by Stephen Peter Rosen
Fighting to a Finish: The Politics of War Termination in the United States and Japan, 1945 by Leon V. Sigal
Alliance Politics by Glenn H. Snyder
The Ideology of the Offensive: Military Decision Making and the Disasters of 1914 by Jack Snyder
Myths of Empire: Domestic Politics and International Ambition by Jack Snyder
The Militarization of Space: U.S. Policy, 1945–1984 by Paul B. Stares
The Nixon Administration and the Making of U.S. Nuclear Strategy by Terry Terriff
Causes of War: Structures of Power and the Roots of International Conflict by Stephen Van Evera
Balancing Acts by Celeste A. Wallander
The Origins of Alliances by Stephen M. Walt
Revolution and War by Stephen M. Walt
The Tet Offensive: Intelligence Failure in War by James J. Wirtz
The Elusive Balance: Power and Perceptions during the Cold War by William Curti Wohlforth
Deterrence and Strategic Culture: Chinese-American Confrontations, 1949–1958 by Shu Guang Zhang